Age of Secession

The International and Domestic Determinants of State Birth

What are the factors that determine how central governments respond to demands for independence? Secessionist movements are numerous and quite varied in form, but the chief obstacle to their ambitions is the state itself, which can deny independence demands, deploy force if need be, and request that the international community respect its territorial integrity by not recognizing the breakaway region. *Age of Secession* focuses on this crucial but neglected moment in the life of a secessionist movement. Griffiths offers a novel theory using original data on secessionist movements between 1816 and 2011. He explains how state response is shaped by international and domestic factors, when conflict is likely, and why states have proliferated since 1945. He mixes quantitative methods with case studies of secessionist movements in the United Kingdom, Russia/Soviet Union, and India. This is an important book for anyone who wants to understand the phenomenon of secession.

RYAN D. GRIFFITHS is a Senior Lecturer in the Department of Government and International Relations at the University of Sydney. His research examines the dynamics of secession, sovereignty, and international order. He is also a lead investigator on the International System(s) Dataset (ISD) Project. He completed his PhD at Columbia University and has held visiting posts at Johns Hopkins University, Yale University, and the Barcelona Institute of International Studies (IBEI).

'Griffiths provides a simple but powerful explanation of why we live in an 'age of secession', characterized by a steep increase in the number of states since 1945, and why some secessions are peaceful while others are violent. Located at the intersection of International Relations and comparative politics, the book is a finely-crafted analysis of the evolution of the modern international system.'

Jason Sharman, Griffith University

'Ryan Griffiths not only greatly advances our understanding of secession but speaks to broader dynamics in international relations – the trends of colonization and decolonization and now, as he calls it, the Age of Secession. By using both compelling case studies and a sharply designed set of quantitative analyses, Griffiths makes a clear and convincing case for his argument that the reactions of the center to a group's separatist aspirations is the key to understanding the dynamics of fragmentation. This book is a major contribution that will be required reading for anyone seeking to understand ethnic conflict, civil war, sovereignty, and the history of international relations.'

Stephen M. Saideman, Carleton University

Age of Secession

The International and Domestic
Determinants of State Birth

RYAN D. GRIFFITHS

CAMBRIDGE
UNIVERSITY PRESS

CAMBRIDGE
UNIVERSITY PRESS

University Printing House, Cambridge CB2 8BS, United Kingdom

One Liberty Plaza, 20th Floor, New York, NY 10006, USA

477 Williamstown Road, Port Melbourne, VIC 3207, Australia

4843/24, 2nd Floor, Ansari Road, Daryaganj, Delhi - 110002, India

79 Anson Road, #06-04/06, Singapore 079906

Cambridge University Press is part of the University of Cambridge.

It furthers the University's mission by disseminating knowledge in the pursuit of education, learning and research at the highest international levels of excellence.

www.cambridge.org
Information on this title: www.cambridge.org/9781107161627

© Ryan Griffiths 2016

First published 2016

A catalog record for this publication is available from the British Library

ISBN 978-1-107-16162-7 Hardback
ISBN 978-1-316-61400-6 Paperback

Cambridge University Press has no responsibility for the persistence or accuracy of URLs for external or third-party internet websites referred to in this publication, and does not guarantee that any content on such websites is, or will remain, accurate or appropriate.

For Alison, Henry, and Beatrice

Contents

Figures

Maps

Tables

Acknowledgments

The foundation for this book was laid during my time as a PhD student at Columbia, and the fine adjustments were made as a faculty member at the University of Sydney. Chief among the intellectual contributors are my PhD advisors. I was extremely fortunate to have had Tanisha Fazal as a mentor. She supported my early ideas regarding state birth and pushed my research in a direction that balanced the type of big-picture theory that I was drawn to with the level of analytical precision that it required. Her mentorship has left an indelible mark on my work. I am also grateful to Jack Snyder for insights on a range of theoretical points and for his unrelenting support and advice. His willingness to take time to entertain my ideas would surprise anyone unfamiliar with his dedication to graduate advising. Alex Cooley read several versions of this manuscript and provided invaluable intellectual and moral support. I benefited greatly from Michael Doyle's close readings of my work, and his influence helped shape the final product. Robert Jervis was an excellent advisor during my time as a graduate student, and I thank him for his ideas and contributions.

I am indebted to a number of other individuals from the political science department at Columbia. Elise Giuliano was kind enough to serve on my defense committee, and she provided a substantial number of comments on matters related to secessionism. Pablo Pinto gave advisory support during my early days as a graduate student. Page Fortna was extremely generous in her advice and assistance. A truly exceptional seminar with Sheri Berman introduced me to the topics of nationalism and state formation – research areas that will sit at the center of my work for some time. I thank Helen Milner, Alfred Stepan, and Kenneth Waltz for their teaching and their useful comments. At various points I also received valuable feedback from Erik Gartzke, Andrew Gelman, Shigeo Hirano, Robert Lieberman, Robert Shapiro, and Michael Ting. My time as a doctoral student would have been less exciting and less productive without the support of my fellow graduate students, among them Kate Baldwin, Bernd Beber, Michael Beckley, Brooke Greene, Guy Grossman, Seva Gunitsky, Dafna Hochman, Reyko Huang, Suzanne Katzenstein, Adriana Lins de Albuquerque, Eric Mvukiyehe, Joseph Parent, Dianne Pfundstein, Stefanie Pleschinger, Stefano Recchia, Allan Roth, Cyrus Samii, Thania Sanchez, Ivan Savic, Alexandra Scacco, Aqil Shah, Neelanjan Sircar, Jessica Stanton, Alex Weisiger, and Matt Winters. Finally, I received outside council from David Carter, Hein Goemans, David Lake, and Jason Sharman. Bridget Coggins and Phil Roeder were particularly helpful in providing both advice and access to their data.

The University of Sydney provided a second intellectual home and sponsored an excellent book workshop that was attended by Steve Saideman (all the way from Ottawa), Peter Radan, Sasa Pavkovic, and a number of committed participants from my department: James Der Derian, Charlotte Epstein, Rich Frank, Graeme Gill, Ben Goldsmith, Diarmuid Maguire, John Mikler, Jamie Reilly, and Frank Smith. At various other points I received valuable assistance from Max Gromping, Justin Hastings, Megan MacKenzie, Ferran Martínez i Coma, Pippa Norris, David Smith, Rodney Smith, Simon Tormey, and Colin Wight.

I would like to acknowledge financial support from the political science departments at Columbia University and the Johns Hopkins University as well as from the Department of Government and International Relations and the Centre for International Security Studies at the University of Sydney.

I would also like to thank my parents for their love and encouragement over the years. Most of all, I would like to thank my wife, Alison, who read more versions of this book than I can count. I dedicate this work to her and our children.

1 | Introduction

Future Historians may call our era "the age of Secession."
— Allen Buchanan, "Self-Determination,
Secession, and the Rule of Law"

The world map changes all the time, and the dominant trend since the mid twentieth century has been one of state proliferation. One hundred thirty-one sovereign states have been born since 1945, a threefold increase in seventy years. Current events in Ukraine, Scotland, Catalonia, and Myanmar illustrate that nationalism and the demand for self-determination remain potent forces in international life. Although some nations aim merely to exit their existing state and join their kin and co-nationals who have been sundered by borders not of their making, most self-determination movements desire to secede and form an independent country. Moreover, there is a recursive nature to this process as new secessionist movements rise up to replace those that are seceding and forming new sovereign states.[1] If the rate of state birth were to continue at its current pace, there would be 260 countries in the world by 2050 and 354 by the end of the twenty-first century.[2] We are truly living in an age of secession.

This was not always the case, and if we widen the historical lens to encompass the past two centuries, the pattern in the international system shows a clear transition from an era of state aggregation to one of fragmentation (see Figure 1.1).[3] One indicator of aggregation was that the number of sovereign states decreased over time as countries engaged in the processes of unification, conquest, and accession. This

---

[1] Fazal and Griffiths 2014; Coggins 2014.
[2] These calculations are based on a growth rate of a little less than two states a year, the rate between 1945 and 2015. However, given the tendency toward recursive secession (that is, fragmentation within new states), the future growth rate could be much higher and is potentially exponential.
[3] Correlates of War Project 2011; Griffiths and Butcher 2013.

1

Figure 1.1 Number of states in the international system. Data are from Griffiths and Butcher (2013).

trend reached its absolute minimum in 1912, when the international system comprised fifty-one states. That low point was nearly reached again in 1943, when the conquests of World War II reduced the number to fifty-three. A second indicator of political aggregation is an increase in the size of states. David Lake and Angela O'Mahony found that the average state size increased steadily throughout the 1800s and reached its zenith at the turn of the century at a little less than 2 million square kilometers. However, it was after 1945 that the trend toward fragmentation truly began. States have proliferated, and by 2004, the average size had fallen to 854 000 square kilometers, an average roughly similar to what it had been in 1815.[4]

One can discern four general periods to the trend illustrated in Figure 1.1. The first existed from 1816 until roughly 1860. After an initial drop from 135 states, the number held at approximately 130 for the next forty years. This period witnessed both state birth, for example, the Spanish secessions in Latin America, and state death, for example, the independent princely states in India. The second period,

---

[4] Lake and O'Mahony do not include colonial possessions in their calculations (for example, Britain's only net change in size between 1815 and 2004 was the loss of Ireland in 1922). This reduces the size of states and locates the peak of average state size too early, because most overseas possessions remained subordinate territories well into the twentieth century (Lake and O'Mahony 2004). Also see Lake and O'Mahony 2006.

which ran from about 1860 until 1914, witnessed a 63 percent reduction in the number of sovereign states. It was during these years that the number of sovereign states was reduced to unprecedented levels. This era was consonant with the so-called new imperialism and scramble for Africa. The third period, which belonged to the interwar years, is when the great historical pattern of political aggregation finally bottomed out. Indeed, there was an initial uptick in the number of states on account of the collapse of the Habsburg and Ottoman empires. This era began with the Wilsonian Moment, and it was characterized by a surge in nationalist and secessionist demands.[5] However, in the end, the small increase in the number of states was nearly undone by the territorial acquisitions during World War II. The fourth and final period began in 1945 and is notable for the dramatic increase in the number of states. This current era of state proliferation stands in sharp contrast to the earlier periods.

Other scholars have noted this transition from a period of state expansion to one of contraction, and it appears to be part of a larger historical pattern that began well before 1816. Victor Lieberman observes that between 1340 and 1820, twenty-three independent Southeast Asian kingdoms collapsed into three.[6] Similarly, Charles Tilly records that between the early sixteenth and early twentieth centuries, 500 Western European political units condensed into twenty-five.[7] This long wave of aggregation ended in the early to mid 1900s and gave way to a new period of fragmentation. This transition constitutes a major historical event, one that challenges theories that emphasize continuity in international relations, and one that has not been adequately explained.[8]

Understanding state proliferation and the dynamics of secession is important because, apart from the many legal and cartographical issues that attend secessionist activity, the potential for conflict is a genuine

---

[5] Manela 2007.   [6] Lieberman 2003.
[7] Tilly 1975. See Greengrass 1991 for a similar estimate.
[8] A number of scholars have developed models for why states expand, overextend, and then contract (see Gilpin 1981; Kennedy 1987; Snyder 1991; Collins 1995). However, these theories typically draw on a number of domestic and international factors to explain the path of a given state, not the entire set of states or all the great powers. They lack a systemic theory for why states would be undergoing the expansion/contraction cycle at roughly the same time. Indeed, for Gilpin and Kennedy, the expansion of one state typically coincides with the contraction of another.

concern. Secessionism in the post-1945 period has quite often generated violence, and the observation of this pattern led Allen Buchanan to modify his prognostication from "the age of secession" to "the age of *wars* of secession."[9] Indeed, it is easy to see why states would deny independence to secessionists and even fight over the issue. Secession requires that the state surrender authority over a portion of its territory and forfeit the associated benefits. In a larger sense, however, permitting secession risks dissolution. Abraham Lincoln put it well when he said that secession forces the sovereign to choose between dissolution and blood. He said that permitting secession would establish "a marked precedent" that no state could survive and that accepting the Confederacy's argument that secession is legal would be a recipe for further secession, because those who argued for the right could not then deny their own secessionists that same right. It was with an eye on the recursive nature of secession that Lincoln claimed, "The principle itself is one of disintegration, and upon which no government can possibly endure."[10] In such circumstances, a state must choose between dissolution and blood.

Scholarly estimates put the share of civil wars driven by secessionism at about 50 percent.[11] James Fearon and David Laitin calculated that roughly 52 percent of the civil wars between 1945 and 1999 involved secessionism.[12] Jason Sorens claims, "Since the 1980s, at least half of all ongoing civil wars in any given year have been secessionist."[13] Barbara Walter argues that secessionism is the chief source of violence in the world today.[14] My own calculations show that since 1945, there has been an average of fifteen secessionist conflicts per year.[15] This is clearly an important topic, and it would be useful to identify the factors that lead states to accept or deny independence demands, and how those responses shape the likelihood of conflict.

Despite the fact that secession has been researched in the various subfields of political science as well as in other social sciences, there has not yet been a systematic study that ties together the varied explanations that purport to explain the phenomena discussed here. What

---

[9] Buchanan 1997, 301.   [10] Lincoln 1953, 426, 435–436.
[11] Secessionism-driven civil wars are usually differentiated from civil wars aimed at taking over the center of power.
[12] Fearon and Laitin 2003.   [13] Sorens 2012, 3.   [14] Walter 2009, 3.
[15] This calculation uses the threshold of twenty-five battle deaths as identified by the UCDP/PRIO Armed Conflict Dataset (Themnér and Wallensteen 2012).

is missing is an explanation that connects the macrohistorical trend to a theory of metropolitan response. Surprisingly, no one has done this in a comprehensive manner. As David Armitage writes, "the story of how the world came to be so thickly populated with states has hardly begun to be told."[16]

The Puzzle

My investigation into these phenomena is organized around a central question: what are the factors that determine how central governments (that is, metropoles) respond to demands for independence? Secessionist movements come in all shapes and sizes, and their motivations are quite varied. But the chief obstacle to their ambitions is the state itself, which can deny independence demands, deploy force if need be, and request that the international community respect its territorial integrity by not recognizing the breakaway region. My analysis centers on this crucial but neglected moment in the life of a secessionist movement and thus begins after secessionist movements have formed. I do not offer an exhaustive study of how these groups come to be, although I do investigate the relationship between secessionism and the anticipation of metropolitan response. This shift in focus from the secessionist movement to the central government is essential to understanding how patterns in metropolitan response have varied over time and space, why states have proliferated since 1945, and when independence demands are likely to produce conflict. States are the gatekeepers where secession is concerned and need to be brought into the center of the analysis.

To conduct this study, I utilize broad definitions of *secessionism* and *secession*. I conceive of secessionism as the formal demand for independence by a nation from its existing sovereign state, and I identify 403 secessionist movements between 1816 and 2011.[17] Many of these movements have failed to achieve independence (for example, the Confederate States of America), and the success cases are quite varied in terms of whether the central government condoned the secession; whether violence was deployed; and whether the resulting state was classified as an instance of decolonization, dissolution, and so on.

[16] Armitage 2007, 20. See Wimmer 2013 for a discussion on this topic.
[17] See Chapter 3 and Appendix A for more detail.

Accommodating this broad conception of secessionism requires an equally broad understanding of secession. I therefore adopt Peter Radan's definition: "the creation of a new state upon existing territory previously forming part of, or being a colonial entity of, an existing state."[18] This definition includes the violent and the illegal instances of state birth, the states born from decolonization, and the many countries that emerged from state dissolution. It excludes the rare instances of forced fragmentation, for example, East Germany and West Germany after World War II. As I discuss in Chapter 2, secession is a contested term, and some readers will take issue with this broad conception. However, I defend it on theoretical and methodological grounds. Labels such as "decolonization" and "dissolution" are primarily legal ones used to sort out which secessionist movements have the right to independence, and identifying these different groups requires an examination of outcomes. I submit that it is better to begin with a set of secessionist movements that all meet the same criteria and then to scrutinize the factors that yielded these different outcomes. In sum, this study focuses on the governments of all sovereign states between 1816 and 2011, and it looks at how they have responded to any nation declaring independence from their sovereign authority.

The Argument

Donald Horowitz argues that "secession lies squarely at the juncture of internal and international politics."[19] Mindful of this claim, I contend that state size and political boundaries are endogenous to international conditions. However, if states are guided by system-level constraints when they respond to secessionist demands, it is their internal structures that determine how they contract. States aim to downsize in a controlled manner, in a way that is mindful of administrative lines and categories.[20]

With respect to the systemic portion of the theory, I argue that the historical trend from state expansion to contraction is primarily the result of changes at the international level.[21] In earlier periods, competitive pressures among states incited them to expand because larger

---

[18] Radan 2008, 18. Also see Pavkovic 2015.   [19] Horowitz 1985, 230.
[20] As with O'Leary et al. (2001), I use the term *downsizing* when referring to a government's attempt to reduce territory.
[21] Griffiths 2014.

territories usually brought military advantages and added economic benefits pertaining to resources and larger, more diversified economies. Although these pressures appear to extend back into history for some time, they were particularly sharp in the late nineteenth century, when the lead states scrambled to gather as much territory as possible. There were clear zero-sum characteristics to this scramble, and indeed, it accelerated with the feeling that unclaimed land – *terra nullius* – was running out as the core countries effectively brought the entire land surface of the Earth outside of Antarctica into one sovereign state system. Thus states were increasing in size because they were conquering and merging with other states and because they were expanding into supposedly unclaimed territory.[22]

The inflection point in this historical pattern came in 1945, when a combination of security, ideological, and economic factors began to change the milieu in which states evaluated the costs and benefits of holding territory. First, the bipolar system (and later the unipolar system) permitted stable collaborations between strong and weak states on an intersovereign basis. Both superpowers preferred informal control over their respective spheres of influence, and this preference removed the zero-sum competition for territory that characterized the earlier multipolar era. It also generated an environment in which the superpowers encouraged decolonization and then competed for informal control over the emerging states. Second, the consolidation of the territorial integrity norm dramatically reduced the rate of conquest; reinforced the structural preference for informal control; and, by making states safer from predation, decreased the need to hold large territories. Third, the advent of the nuclear age changed the security emphasis for lead states from territorial defense to deterrence. Finally, the development of the liberal global economy reduced the need to possess large economic units. In an era of increasing globalization, small states could survive by plugging in to the global economy to secure capital and resources and leverage their comparative advantage. Together these security and economic factors reduced the value of territory, and

---

[22] It was not until the early years of the twentieth century that the international system achieved its maximum size and came to encompass all landmass outside of Antarctica. Most of the last holdouts – various princely states in India, sultanates in the East Indies, and remote island kingdoms in the Pacific – were brought into the system by 1910.

as a result, states have been more amenable to secessionist demands when the costs of these possessions outweigh the benefits.

But while the international system has rendered peaceful secession more likely, it is the internal structure of states that governs how they downsize. Metropoles use administrative lines and categories when determining which groups can secede without fear of setting a precedent and who they must deny (and potentially fight) to maintain a credible reputation.[23] Internal lines and status categories reduce bargaining problems between center and periphery; they create conceptual distinctions that can become salient in the eyes of all relevant parties; and international law emphasizes administrative territories as a guide for recognizing new states via the principle of *uti possidetis* (as you possess). These factors shape the manner in which metropoles respond to secessionist demands. As a result, secessionist movements that do not cohere with any administrative region are the least likely to be granted independence and the most likely to experience conflict. In contrast, those regions that represent a unique administrative type are more likely to be recognized by their metropoles and less likely to resort to arms. Finally, large compound states sometimes downsize by category, and this helps explain why governments will release one set of units without contest while denying (and potentially fighting) another set from doing the same. In sum, the administrative architecture of states provides them with a means to disassemble in a controlled manner, and in fact, the administrative status of breakaway regions (or lack thereof) is a strong predictor of secessionist outcomes.

This theory combines international and domestic factors to explain the proliferation of states in the post-1945 period.[24] I argue that although the invisible hand of the international system has played a key role in driving state expansion and contraction, it is the internal structure of states that governs how they have downsized. These external and internal factors are intimately connected. When states expanded, they organized their political space by creating administrative units. They classified and ranked these units, giving national distinction to some and local autonomy to others. Although these early administrative decisions were often based on the strength of local cultural and institutional conditions, they were just as often the consequence of

[23] Griffiths 2015.   [24] See Roeder 2007, 342–344, for a discussion on this topic.

interstate security concerns and simple fortune. In making these decisions, metropoles created the embryos of future sovereign states both because they built local institutions around which national consciousness would develop and because these administrative boundaries and conceptual distinctions became increasingly salient in the eyes of the relevant parties. It was upon these lines that future governments – and, indeed, international law itself – would discriminate between secessionist groups when recognizing sovereign status.

In making this argument, I draw on and contribute to several different literatures. First, my attention to the effects that changing international conditions have on the supply of and demand for sovereignty borrows ideas from the literature on the size of states.[25] These arguments hold that state size is endogenous to system-level factors such as the global economy and the threat of conquest. Here a trade-off is posed between the benefits of size (for example, economies of scale, national defense) and local autonomy (that is, moving the locus of decision making closer to local preferences). The optimal size of states is thus determined by the frequency of conquest and corresponding emphasis on defensive capabilities, and on the level of global economic interaction. To use a metaphor, flipping these levers in one direction will make small states more viable; flipping them in the other will select for bigger states. Although this approach calls attention to the importance of the international system, the related research has been mostly theoretical, and insufficient attention has been given to the internal composition of states and how these structures interact with pressures from above.

My solution to the preceding problem is to decompose sovereign states and identify the patterns by which they fragment. In this regard, I draw on another approach that focuses on the administrative organization of states.[26] More comparative in orientation, scholars of this stripe argue that it is the imposition of ethnofederal structures that creates the conditions for secessionism. Such units generate new identities and new nations; they are states in the making. This is primarily an explanation for how nationalist ambitions arise. I argue that this approach is correct, but I extend it in two important ways. First, I show how changing international conditions interact with domestic

[25] For an overview, see Alesina and Spolaore 2005.
[26] Treisman 1997; Bunce 1999; Roeder 2007.

structures to explain trends in state birth. Second, I shift the focus from
the region to the central government to argue that administrative lines
and categories are used by metropoles when selecting which regions
can secede. Whereas the first account helps explain where many secessionist movements come from, my theory explains why secessionist
movements, even ones with a well-developed sense of nation, almost
never secede unless they have the appropriate administrative status.

This consideration over metropolitan preferences connects me to a
third literature that focuses on the need for central governments to
demonstrate resolve to internal secessionists.[27] Walter, who has done
some of the best work on this topic, argues that governments will be
more likely to fight secessionists when they need to build a reputation.
In fact, metropoles may do so even when the region in question is not
particularly valuable. The more movements they face, the more likely it
is that they will resist. I maintain that although this approach is insight-
ful, it cannot explain why metropoles will often fight one movement
(or set of movements) while simultaneously permitting the secession
of others. This was the case when France fought to retain Algeria even
while it was permitting the secession of French West Africa. The explanation is that not all movements are the same in the eyes of the relevant
parties. I expand on the states-in-the-making literature to argue that
large compound states often possess different types of administrative
regions. Some are considered more peripheral or more autonomous,
and these distinctions can be quite salient and provide the metropole
with a means to discriminate between groups.

My theory brings the state into the center of the analysis. The states-
in-the-making literature rightly notes the nation-generating effects of
administrative design.[28] But central governments are not passive play-
ers in this process, merely permitting the fittest nations to secede;
rather, they often deny independence to well-developed secessionist
movements that lacked the right administrative status, and they have
often permitted the independence of administrative units that possessed weak national identities. These administrative determinations
are usually made for reasons other than concerns over future secessionism, such as cost, geography, foreign competition, institutional
habit, and simple chance. But whatever the origins, an aspiring nation's

---

[27] Toft 2002; Walter 2006b; 2009.   [28] Bunce 1999; Roeder 2007.

administrative status (or lack thereof) matters greatly when secession-ism is in the air. States are strategic when dealing with secessionists, and they incorporate administrative lines and categories into their strategies.

My argument directly engages the literatures on international norms and international law. Scholars and policy makers have noted the tension between the right of stateless nations to seek self-determination and the right of states to preserve their territorial integrity. An exclusive emphasis on the former would open the door to considerable fragmentation; a strong bias for the latter would condemn minority nations to a subordinate status. The international legal debate on secession attempts to balance these two norms by defining the special conditions in which breakaway regions have the right to secede. One solution is to insist that the borders of new states adhere to previous administrative boundaries. Known as the principle of *uti possidetis*, this once again calls attention to the internal administrative structure of states. Yet another route to legal secession is based on consent; that is, the metropole permits the secession. I argue that governments will use their internal administrative distinctions when permitting secession, thus enabling one people to seek self-determination while simultaneously denying it to another on the principle of territorial integrity.

Relevance

This theory provides a way to predict when governments are likely to deny secessionist demands. On one level, it should not come as a surprise that new states in the post-1945 period were former administrative units organized in earlier times. After all, states have to come from somewhere. However, the deeper implication is that these administrative architectures govern where states can permit secession without setting a precedent and where they must deny it to show their resolve. The theory therefore provides a mechanism for predicting government denial, which, I argue, is a necessary condition for secessionist conflict. Given the persistence of secessionism and secessionist conflict, this is clearly an important topic.

More theoretically, I address a number of topics that deal with political change. My argument helps us to understand better the observed centripetal and centrifugal trends in world politics as well as the ongoing discussion of how (and if) globalization affects the sovereign state.

With respect to international relations theory, I catalog change in the international system and then proceed to explain that change. I challenge the selection mechanism in neorealism and argue that conditions inherent in the international system are far from immutable. I examine normative principles such as the norm of self-determination and the norm of territorial integrity. Finally, I engage the literature on nationalism by highlighting how nationalist projects are shaped by international and domestic factors.

Methodology

This book looks at secessionist outcomes. I have two main dependent variables: (1) the metropolitan response to a declaration of independence; and (2) secessionist conflict. As I state in the chapters to come, these interrelated outcomes are shaped by international and domestic factors. However, I also examine a third dependent variable: the formation of secessionist movements. This important moment occurs prior to my outcomes of interest – metropolitan response and conflict – but I study it to expose potential selection effects and endogeneity.

My analysis uses a standard mixed-methods approach.[29] I first test the relevant hypotheses in a large-N study using two original datasets.[30] In the first dataset I identify 403 secessionist movements between 1816 and 2011. This is the primary unit of analysis. The second dataset captures the administrative architecture of states. Here I constructed a dataset of 638 proto-states between 1816 and 2011, which are political jurisdictions within states that are above a minimum size and either nationally distinct, geographically distant, indirectly ruled, or else recently transferred from another country. The combined value of these two datasets is that I can separate the formation of secessionist movements from the achievement of secession itself. I can examine the factors that make secessionism more or less likely, and I can then investigate the conditions that permit some secessionist movements to become sovereign. Finally, I can look for unexpected relationships and explore them in the qualitative chapters.

I then examine my theory qualitatively with three case studies of particular metropoles over time: the UK, Russia/Soviet Union, and

---

[29] Lieberman 2005.   [30] See appendices for complete lists.

India.[31] I use a structured, focused approach, and my aim is to provide a qualitative complement to the correlations established in the large-N study.[32] Each case study focuses on a metropole and analyzes its relationship with its secessionist movements, and each case includes a number of proto-states that are categorized in different ways. Moreover, the longitudinal nature of the study adds temporal variation. Overall, my approach is to use both within-case and cross-case analysis.[33]

The investigation in each case study is structured by a set of questions that follow from the overall theory or else the alternative explanations. I first examine the extent to which changing international conditions influence the willingness of metropoles to permit secession. I then explore the consequences of domestic structure, asking how administrative lines and categories shape secessionist outcomes. Finally, it is important to be open to unexpected findings that emerge in large-N studies. I therefore finish each chapter with an analysis of two alternative arguments that find statistical support in the quantitative chapter: (1) Secession(ism) occurs in waves; (2) Regime type matters.

I selected the three case studies because they represent variation along a number of dimensions. First, each metropole has possessed a number of proto-states organized into different categories. This administrative articulation enables me to test my hypotheses regarding proto-states. Second, the British and Russian/Soviet cases existed over the entire range of years and can be examined both before and after 1945. Indeed, the historical expansion and contraction of these two states is consonant with the long arc in the international system. In many ways, the early period of British expansion bequeathed to India an administrative inheritance. Finally, the selected cases provide variation in a host of lesser ways, including regime type, the difference between land-based and sea-based administrative designs, as well as the consequences of purely federal structures (India) as opposed to metropolitan systems that have a clearer core (UK and Russia/Soviet Union).

---

[31] I treat the Russian/Soviet case as one metropole divided into three temporal periods: the Russian Empire, the Soviet Union, and the Russian Federation.

[32] George and Bennett 2005.

[33] George and Bennett 2005, 18, "define case-study methods to include both within-case analysis of single cases and comparisons of a small number of cases."

Plan of the Book

The book proceeds as follows. Chapter 2 is the primary theoretical portion of the book. After highlighting an important gap in the literature, I present a detailed explication of my theory, outlining how changing international conditions combined with the internal structure of states can explain the phenomena of interest. I then anticipate and address several theoretical issues related to the argument.

Chapter 3 provides the quantitative analysis. I begin with preliminary observations about state birth and secession. I next describe the key datasets and develop the relationship between the different secessionist outcomes – my dependent variables. I then specify how I operationalize my core and alternative independent variables, and test my hypotheses in a series of regressions. The primary purpose in this chapter is to detect patterns in the data and (dis)confirm the various hypotheses.

Chapters 4, 5, and 6 provide qualitative case studies on the UK, Russia/Soviet Union, and India. Each chapter centers on a metropole and analyzes its relationship with its secessionist movements. These relationships are the class of events, and it permits me to examine metropolitan responses to secessionism in the context of external and internal constraints. In each case study I include a vignette that illustrates the downstream consequences of administrative design and structure.[34] Overall, the three cases complete the study by adding a deeper level of contextual analysis. They are particularly useful for examining several hypotheses that are more difficult to assess quantitatively, such as the effects that changing perceptions regarding conquest have on the need for metropoles to retain territory.

Chapter 7 provides a summary of these findings, discusses the implications, and highlights several directions for further research. Overall, there are two broad implications to this book. First, the character of the international system changes over time. A competitive system where conquest is common will compel states to expand; a more economically integrated system in which conquest is rare will permit states to contract. Although 1945 appears to have been a historical pivot, what the future holds is far from clear. Fragmentation could continue,

---

[34] The effects of these structures resemble natural experiments (Diamond and Robinson 2010).

or the competitive pressures of earlier times could return and incite states to expand once again. Second, the administrative organization of states has important downstream consequences. Proto-states help to generate new nations, and they can place those nations in a favorable position to be let go later on. Administrative distinctions provide metropoles with a means to navigate calls for independence and avoid uncontrolled fragmentation, and these distinctions are further backed by international law, regardless of their provenance. Thus, the fate of secessionists is to some extent controlled by these earlier administrative decisions.

2 | *Theory of Metropolitan Response*

If every ethnic, religious or linguistic group claimed statehood, there would be no limit to fragmentation, and peace, security and economic well-being for all would become ever more difficult to achieve.

– Boutros Boutros-Ghali[1]

The boundaries that exist at any moment in time are likely to be arbitrary, poorly drawn, the products of ancient wars. The mapmakers are likely to have been ignorant, drunken, or corrupt. Nevertheless, these lines establish a habitable world.

– Michael Walzer[2]

What are the factors that determine how central governments respond to demands for independence? The full answer to that question should explain why states have proliferated and not dwindled over the past seventy years, why states permit secession in some cases and not others, and when conflict is likely to result. Fears over political fragmentation have been a notable feature of the post-1945 international system. In expressing his concerns on this matter, UN Secretary-General Boutros Boutros-Ghali highlights the need to manage fragmentary pressures and prevent conflict. What has been lacking in the literature to date is a theory for how states respond to secessionist demands.

I advance a two-part theory for the general transition toward fragmentation in the post-1945 period and the reasons why metropoles will permit secession in some cases but fight to prevent it in others. I contend that the international environment in the postwar period has made it easier, and sometimes desirable, for metropoles to permit secession. This is because changing perceptions regarding the threat of conquest and the value of large economic units have affected the costs and

---

[1] Boutros-Ghali 1992, 9.   [2] Walzer 1977, 57.

16

benefits of retaining territory. Just as competitive pressures in the nine-teenth and early twentieth centuries compelled states to expand and secure territory and economic resources, changing conditions in the post-1945 period have led to an unwinding of that process as numer-ous states have chosen to contract and permit the secession of periph-eral regions. However, whereas the international system has rendered secession more likely, it is the internal characteristics of states that gov-ern how they downsize. Although states are quite often amenable to secession – and have been more so in the post-1945 period – they can-not always downsize to their optimally preferred point. Indeed, states have to beware lest the release of one unit sets a precedent for others and risks a cascade of further secessionism. I argue that metropoles rely on administrative lines and categories when determining which groups can secede without fear of setting a precedent, and who they must deny and potentially fight to maintain a credible reputation.

This theory suggests a degree of path dependence over the past 200 years. When states expanded in the nineteenth and early twentieth cen-turies, they organized their territories in a variety of ways. They clas-sified and ranked their administrative units, they gave some national distinction, and they determined that others were politically external. These architectures have had lasting consequences since the ability of metropoles to release units in the post-1945 era is connected with the ways in which they were originally organized on an administrative basis.

The remainder of this chapter is given to developing the argument in full. I begin by framing the puzzle within the broader literature, and I show that the metropolitan response to independence demands is a crucial but neglected stage of secession. I next provide a complete treat-ment of the theory. This is the backbone of the chapter, consisting of two sections that explain how the response of states to secessionism is shaped by both the invisible hand of the international system and their own domestic administrative structures. It is in the subsequent section on theoretical considerations that I defend my argument and method-ological approach against a set of potential objections. These include my mixing of decolonization with other forms of secession and state birth, the instrumentalist approach of my argument, the potential for endogeneity where administrative units are concerned, and the dan-ger that I have neglected other causal factors such as the advent of

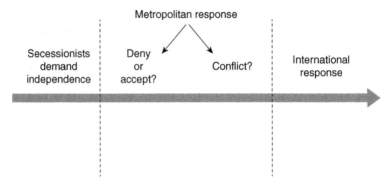

Figure 2.1 Stages of secession.

nationalism across the international realm as well as the complex local conditions that animate any given secessionist movement.

Framing the Puzzle

I use two main dependent variables in this study.[3] The first is the metropolitan response to a secessionist movement's declaration of independence. This is a binary result: denial or acceptance. The second dependent variable is whether the declaration results in conflict between the secessionist group and the metropole. These outcomes have a close relationship given that the likelihood of conflict is increased when the metropole denies independence to the aspiring nation. Indeed, I conjecture that metropolitan denial is a necessary but not sufficient condition for secessionist conflict. Together I use these variables to decompose the response of states to secessionism. However, I also examine a corollary dependent variable: the formation of secessionist movements. I identify this important stage in the life of a secessionist group as the point in time where independence is declared (see Figure 2.1). This crucial decision actually occurs prior to the response of the metropole and the potential initiation of conflict – my main dependent variables – but there are likely selection effects insofar as secessionists attempt to anticipate the outcome of their declaration. I include this corollary dependent variable in my study because

---

[3] See Chapter 4 for a discussion of variables.

it enables me to examine the degree to which secessionism is endogenous to metropolitan response.

My theory and research design targets a gap in the existing literature on secession. Most of the work on this topic examines the factors that drive groups to seek independence. This is the first stage in Figure 2.1. Explanations here focus on economic concerns and ethnonational differences,[4] how elites manipulate these issues,[5] how potential secessionists evaluate the costs and benefits of seeking independence,[6] the bargaining environment between center and periphery,[7] the role of diaspora communities,[8] the degree to which secessionist groups learn from one another,[9] and how the construction of internal administrative units can create the building blocks for future states.[10] Although this research centers on different elements of secessionism, the common theme is a focus on the aspiring nation.

A second body of study investigates the response of the international community.[11] This research has been heavily influenced by international law,[12] but recent work has examined how state's strategic calculations – especially great powers – influence recognition,[13] and how international norms regarding recognition have changed over the past 200 years.[14] This is depicted as the third stage in Figure 2.1, and it occurs for the most part after the response of the metropole from which the aspiring nation is attempting to secede. This stage is, of course, causally connected to that response given that the state in question can influence the reaction of other states. Crucially, however, it is precisely when the metropole contests the secessionist movement that the response of the international community rises in importance. That is because metropolitan acceptance is almost always honored by other

---

[4] Heraclides 1991; Laitin 1998; Horowitz 1985; Hechter 2000; Walter 2006a; Aspinall 2007; Jenne et al. 2007; Hale 2008; Sambanis and Milanovic 2011; Wimmer 2013.

[5] Collier and Hoeffler 2002.

[6] Bartkus 1999; Sorens 2012; Cunningham 2013; Fazal and Griffiths 2014.

[7] Cunningham 2011.

[8] Heraclides 1990; Saideman 2001.   [9] Saideman 1998; Beissinger 2002.

[10] Slezkine 1992, 1994; Breuilly 1994; Treisman 1997, 1999, 2007; Bunce 1999; Cornell 2001; Roeder 2007; King 2012; Smith 2013.

[11] Osterud 1997; Saideman 2002; Fearon 2004.

[12] Ratner 1996; Shaw 1996, 1997; Grant 1999; Crawford 2006; Radan 2012.

[13] Paquin 2010; Coggins 2011; Sterio 2012.

[14] Jackson 1990; Herbst 2000; Fabry 2010.

states;[15] denial, on the other hand, can elicit an international response that supports the secessionists. Ultimately, the chief obstacle to independence is the governing state.

The gap in this literature is how the state responds to secessionist demands.[16] "Despite the centrality of the state, a good portion of the literature depicts secession in a seemingly stateless political space."[17] One of the reasons the state remains underexamined in the extant literature is a long-running belief that it is always averse to secession and that it will always seek to prevent the loss of territory. Michael Hechter supports this view when he says "if there is one constant in history apart from the universality of death and taxes, it is the reluctance of states to part with territory."[18] This perception that state preferences are static has been challenged recently by a number of political scientists who point out that system-level conditions can change the costs and benefits of possessing large territories,[19] and that it is not simply the innate value of territory that drives metropolitan response.[20] Indeed, as Barbara Walter argues, the value that states place on territory is quite variable.

Although the primary aim in this book is to advance a theory of metropolitan response, I recognize that there are feedback effects here insofar as that response is influenced by international law, and the behavior of secessionists (potential and actual) is influenced by the anticipated response of both the state and the international community. The response of the state is highly connected to these other moments. To that end, my theory examines the relationship between these moments and the related potential for endogeneity and selection effects.

Metropolitan Response

The international environment has driven the expansion and contraction of states, but it is the domestic administrative structure of states that determines how they contract. This theory combines

---

[15] The South African Bantustans are some of the few counterexamples. South Africa determined that they were independent, but the international community refused recognition on the grounds that they would be legitimating apartheid.
[16] Ker-Lindsay 2012.   [17] Siroky 2011, 54.   [18] Hechter 1992, 277.
[19] Spruyt 2005; Gartzke and Rohner 2011; Griffiths 2014.
[20] Walter 2006b, 2009.

systemic considerations with unit-level factors. Alexander Wendt argues (echoing Kenneth Waltz) that a theory is systemic "when it emphasizes the causal powers of the international system in explaining state behavior."[21] Most of the arguments on secession point to domestic factors. Such explanations are intuitively appealing, and I test them as alternative hypotheses in my analysis. However, none of these unit-level theories can account for the historical transition from state aggregation to fragmentation. What is needed is a system-level theory, one that draws on insights from other "outside-in" accounts and explains how metropolitan responses to secessionism are shaped by the invisible hand of the international system.[22]

Yet the causal influence of the international system on any one state is also shaped by domestic realities. After all, metropoles have an interest in self-preservation and are therefore keen to manage the process of fragmentation. I contend that the metropolitan response to secessionist demands is structured by their own administrative organization. I further argue that this administrative focus is a common mechanism in political life, one that is frequently observed across time and space.[23] Finally, these administrative designs often have a long-run character to them. Indeed, as I show in later chapters, many of them were created in earlier periods when the international system incited states to expand.

The Invisible Hand of the International System

The international system has over the long run shaped the size of states. I contend that state size is endogenous to system-level factors such as the threat of conquest and the robustness of the global economy. Alberto Alesina and Enrico Spoloare provided a useful model for this relationship when they identified the trade-off between the benefits of size (for example, economies of scale, national defense) and local autonomy (that is, moving the locus of decision making closer to local

---

[21] Wendt 1999, 11. According to Wendt, systemic theories are those that make the international system the independent variable and/or the dependent variable. My theory is mostly of the first type.

[22] I appropriated this phase from Roeder (2007, 344), who appropriated it from Downing (1992, 14). For similar outside-in (second image reversed) explanations, see Gourevitch 1978; Hironaka 2005; Kalyvas and Balcells 2010.

[23] On mechanisms, see Elster 1989, viii; Pierson 2004, 6.

preferences).[24] They pointed out that the optimal size of states is determined by the threat of conquest and related emphasis on defensive capabilities, and on the level of global economic interaction. Essentially, benign international systems make small states viable; perilous systems select for bigger states. I adopt this approach in my analysis of state proliferation and I further specify the relevant actors: the central governments of sovereign states (metropoles) and the potential secessionist regions inside those states.[25] To gain independence, an aspiring nation must either get the consent of its metropole or else take it by force. Meanwhile, metropoles undergo cost-benefit calculations when they decide how to respond to secessionist demands. They estimate the determination of the secessionist movement, the value of the region and people to which the movement makes claim, and the potential loss in revenue and reputation in letting that region secede. These estimates are shaped by international conditions.

I conceptualize the chief causal variable explaining the post-1945 proliferation of states as a more benign international system. Changing security and economic conditions alter the milieu in which metropoles evaluate the costs and benefits of holding territory. Although it is impossible to point to one single factor from which all of the observed changes are derived – the milieu is the product of interacting variables – I identify four key factors: the shift to bipolarity, the consolidation of the territorial integrity norm, the development of nuclear weaponry, and growth of the global economy.

The first of these factors is polarity, which affects how states choose to control territory, a choice that has consequences for secession and the number of sovereign states. In his work on empires, Michael Doyle noted that "multipolar systems tended to require formal institutions of imperial rule; bipolar and unipolar systems, to permit informal arrangements."[26] The multipolar period of the late nineteenth century was one of intense interstate rivalry in which states scrambled to seize formal control over territory.[27] Since a peripheral state "could improve its bargaining position by playing metropole against metropole.... Each metropole consequently had an incentive to establish more formal, more direct, and closer supervision over the periphery." For states

---

[24] Alesina and Spolaore 2005.   [25] Bartkus 1999; Toft 2002; Walter 2009.
[26] Doyle 1986, 343–344. See Waltz 1979, 190–191, for a similar argument.
[27] Doyle contends that the transition to formal colonial control began in the 1870 on account of competitive pressures by great powers (Doyle 1986).

such as the UK, the best response in this zero-sum game was to engage in increasingly formalized types of accession.

As the 1880s proceeded, export outlets were further reduced as her [UK] protectionist rivals began to stake out stretches of the world, occupy them, and then declare them exclusively reserved for their own traders and investors.... [British businessmen]... began urging a policy of annexation on the government to prevent existing or potential markets from being lost to competitors.... Other countries were establishing their own, jealously guarded spheres of influence across the world, and in many instances taking control of so-called "empty" areas in Africa and the Pacific.[28]

Such examples abound in the literature, and they help explain the reduction in the number of states leading into the twentieth century.

In contrast, bipolarity and unipolarity permit informal relationships in which the weaker party remains a sovereign state.[29] During the Cold War, the allegiance of weaker states to each superpower was more stable given that a switch tended to require a domestic revolution. The dominant factions in Soviet satellites could not easily switch allegiance to the West, nor shop around for a different patron.[30] When attempts at regime change did occur, as they did in Hungary in 1956 and Czechoslovakia in 1968, the Soviets stepped in to quell dissent. It is telling that the Soviet invasion of Afghanistan in 1979 was considered an intervention, much as Vietnam had been for the USA. The emphasis was not on annexation or the taking of sovereignty, but rather on the maintenance of a communist Afghanistan. Instead of acquiring territory in a formal manner, both the USA and the Soviet Union sought instead to create spheres of influence and relationships of informal rule.[31] The USA "followed a complex policy intended to court pro-Western independence movements, prevent the rise of anti-Western movements for national liberation, and to facilitate, in some regions,

---

[28] James 1994, 202–203.
[29] The difference between formal and informal relations turns on whether the subordinate party remains sovereign.
[30] On the logic of Soviet informal empire, see Bunce 1985; Liberman 1996.
[31] Nexon and Wright argue that since 1945, the USA has generally preferred informal arrangements to formal rule (Nexon and Wright 2007). For other arguments that American power reduced the relative benefits of empire, see Ruggie 1983; Maier 1987; Ikenberry 2001; Lake 1999, 2003.

the transformation of West European formal empires into informal empires."[32]

The US-Soviet preference over the form of rule affected other states in two important ways. First, it removed the zero-sum competition over formal territorial control. States no longer had to possess territory to prevent a competitor from seizing it, and all else equal, this reduced the benefits of holding territory. Second, the anticolonial rhetoric of the superpowers put pressure on states to grant independence to colonies and internal nations. There was, of course, a strategy behind that pressure, and both powers attempted to draw emerging states into their respective spheres of influence. The result was state proliferation.

The unipolar world after 1991 has had similar, albeit less complicated, effects.[33] For the USA, informal relations with other sovereign states have been the preferred form of control. As with the Cold War, this preference affects the overall milieu in which states evaluate the costs and benefits of holding territory. This, of course, raises the question of what happens when the system once again becomes multipolar, which it appears to be doing (if it has not already). I return to this issue in the conclusion to the book. Overall, periods of bipolarity and unipolarity will be more likely to permit peaceful secession.

The second factor pertains to the post-1945 norm emphasizing territorial integrity. Scholars usually trace the origins of the norm to US President Woodrow Wilson and the League of Nations, but many believe it was not until 1945 that it truly gained adherence. Mark Zacher argues that the norm effectively delegitimized territorial conquest and resulted in a clear reduction in wars over territory.[34] Tanisha Fazal makes a similar claim as part of her explanation for the virtual disappearance of violent state death after 1945.[35] According to Boaz Atzili, changing attitudes regarding conquest and annexation, especially among the elites, combined with other material forces to help consolidate the norm.[36] Here, Atzili highlights many of the same system-level changes that I do – the rising global economy, nuclear

---

[32] Parrott 1997, 16.

[33] Whether unipolarity should generate more or less secession than bipolarity is difficult to say. On one hand, the USA has less incentive to see the emergence of states that are pro-Western. On the other hand, it has less incentive to prevent or delay the emergence of states that are not.

[34] Zacher 2001.

[35] Fazal defines state death as the loss of sovereignty (Fazal 2007).

[36] Atzili 2012, 22.

weapons – which acted like "distinct vectors pointing in the same direction," affecting the milieu in which states evaluate the costs and benefits of holding territory.

Importantly, I contend that the US-Soviet preference for informal rule helped to consolidate the norm. Since neither side was compelled to take formal control over their satellites, both were keen to prevent their opponent from doing so. The USA may well have been the entrepreneur and chief exponent of the norm, but other states also supported it.[37] Chief among them was the Soviet Union that included a clause on the integrity of borders in the 1975 Helsinki Final Act. The result was a bipolar system premised on "the territorial integrity of states" in which "each political champion led a 'family,' that is, a network of dependents and allies."[38]

The post-1945 emphasis on territorial integrity has had a curious effect on secession. On one hand, the community of states has worked to maintain political borders, which by implication, presents an obstacle to secessionists who wish to change them. As Jeffrey Herbst claims, "state boundaries have been singularly successful in their primary function: preserving the territorial integrity of the state by preventing significant territorial competition and delegitimizing the norm of self-determination."[39] On the other hand, the attention to political borders has made states safer from territorial predation since sovereign recognition more or less functions like an insurance policy,[40] and the territorial integrity norm like an arms control agreement.[41] This added security has reduced the need to possess large territories and has made it easier for governments to permit secession where they deem it beneficial. Mikulas Fabry writes that one of the best ways for secessionists to gain international support is through consent from their metropole.[42] Governments may still deny independence for a number of reasons, but all else equal, they are more likely to give consent in a nonmultipolar system that privileges the territorial integrity of states. This factor combines with polarity to render peaceful secession more likely in the post-1945 period. In more precise terms, metropoles ought to be more willing to accept independence demands and less likely to fight a conflict over them.

---

[37] Fazal 2007.   [38] Bates 2001, 75.   [39] Herbst 2000, 253.
[40] Jackson 1992.   [41] Fearon 2004.   [42] Fabry 2010.

A third factor is the development of nuclear weapons. Scholars have noted that nuclear weapons alter the traditional calculus of defense.[43] As a result, the perceived value of large territories and large armies declined as both the superpowers and the states within their nuclear umbrellas began to focus less on territorial possession and more on deterrence. Although Operation Barbarossa had reinforced the value that Moscow placed on territorial depth, Soviet leadership in the postwar period gradually came to appreciate the "efficacy of nuclear deterrence, which reduces the importance of territory and economic size to security." Indeed, Peter Liberman argues that the peaceful secession of the union republics in 1991 was made possible by a belief of Soviet leader Mikhail Gorbachev and others that "nuclear deterrence was enough."[44] For colonial powers such as the British, it became clear early in the Cold War that the British grand strategy – as formalized in the Global Strategy of 1950 – was shifting from a reliance on territorial possession and manpower to one that emphasized nuclear deterrence and the American nuclear umbrella.[45]

Two claims can be made with respect to nuclear weapons and secession. The first, more narrow, claim is that states that possess a nuclear deterrent will be more inclined to give up territory, all else equal. This argument may seem counterintuitive given the presumption that it is weak states that give up territory, and nuclear weapons are usually a sign of strength. But a core theme in this book is that states do not always want to hold territory and that metropoles will often permit secession when they can. A nuclear deterrent increases their ability to do so. The second, broader claim is that the possession of these weapons by only a small set of states ought to affect how nonnuclear states value territory. That is, if the most powerful states are less inclined to seek and/or hold territory, the competitive pressures among states will be reduced and other nonnuclear states will tend to follow suit.[46]

[43] Herz 1976; Deudney 1995.   [44] Liberman 1996, 123–125.
[45] Clayton 1998, 294.
[46] In the quantitative analysis, I directly model the narrower claim for the purpose of precision; I can code the response of every state (nuclear or nonnuclear) to an attempt at secession. However, I also model post-1945 period effects, and I argue that these are the result of several factors including the spread of nuclear weapons.

The fourth factor is that the development of the global economic order has further reduced the importance of large territorial units. In earlier times states had good reason to acquire territory for the material benefits it brought. Beggar-thy-neighbor policies, preferential trading systems, along with higher levels of conquest elevated the perils of autarky. In contrast, the post-1945 multilateral trading system has lowered the risk of conducting relations with other polities on the basis of sovereign equality.[47] Meanwhile, higher levels of foreign direct investment and dispersed production have gradually internationalized economic enterprise.[48] States can now connect with the global apparatus to secure capital, leverage comparative advantage, and profit in economies of scale. This development leads to three related outcomes. First, smaller, economically open states are more viable. Second, the economic value of holding territory is reduced if the relevant goods and services can be obtained on the international market. Thus, "as barriers to international trade declined, the need for large internal (imperial) markets declined as well."[49] Third, this "decoupling of territorial control and national prosperity" should reinforce (and be reinforced by) the changing security factors mentioned earlier.[50] The consequence where secessionism is concerned is that economically integrated states are more likely to permit independence and less likely to fight over the issue.

Collectively, these factors set the background conditions in which metropoles have responded to secessionist demands since 1945. They are additive in the sense that each contributes to the overall milieu, but they are not co-equal. Polarity was arguably the most important variable, and the fact that the Cold War began at a time when states were relatively large on average, and possessed of numerous internal nations, set the stage for a process of state fragmentation in which the superpowers competed for influence. The development of nuclear weapons reinforced this process partly by helping to keep the Cold War from getting hot. Combined with a postwar emphasis on territorial integrity that the superpowers bolstered, there was a subsequent decline in major interstate war, particularly wars of conquest.[51] Commensurate with this decline in major war was the development of the

---

[47] Keohane and Nye 1977; Lake 1999; Gartzke and Rohner 2011.
[48] Brooks 1999.   [49] Kahler 1997, 288. Also see Kahler 1984.
[50] Jervis 2002, 8.
[51] Holsti 1991; Kaysen 1990; Zacher 2001; Mueller 1988, 2009.

global economy, a factor that further encouraged peaceful secession, but one that on its own could not have yielded a period of state prolif- eration. If the late-nineteenth-century era of globalization is any indica- tion, high trade levels alone do not encourage states to permit secession when conquest remains common. How further change in these factors will affect secession in the future is an issue I return to at the end of the book.

This theory helps explain the centrifugal and centripetal patterns to international relations that other scholars have noted.[52] Within states we see patterns of fragmentation as regions acquire greater auton- omy or outright sovereign independence. Among states, we see inte- gration as political and economic blocs are formed, but, curiously, full sovereign integration is rarely the outcome.[53] There is perhaps no bet- ter example of these dual patterns than in the European Union, where terms such as "Independence in Europe" resonate.[54] Regions such as Scotland simultaneously push for decentralization on one level (UK) and centralization on another (Europe). Moreover, such a movement is being negotiated with London in a remarkably nonviolent manner that would have been hard to imagine in earlier times. A 2007 article from *The Economist* describes this pattern as follows:

Here is that most complacent and Euroskeptical of political unions, Britain, facing dissolution partly because Scottish voters are reassured by the exis- tence of a much bigger union embracing 27 countries. As citizens of the EU, citizens of a newly independent Scotland could continue to live and work wherever they wanted in the European Union. Nor would indepen- dent Scots face the prospect of barbed wire, border posts and watchtow- ers sprouting along some latter-day Hadrian's Wall. Travelers in the EU are used to frontier-hopping marked by no more than a change of speed limit and a faint nostalgia for the days when crossing a border earned an exotic stamp in your passport. In short, many things need not change were Scotland to split off from Britain – if it retained uninterrupted membership of the EU.[55]

---

[52] Rosenau refers to this pattern as fragmegration: fragmentation + integration (Rosenau 2000, 223). See also Spruyt 2002; Creveld 2003.

[53] There have been only four nonviolent unifications in the post-1945 period: Egypt and Syria in 1958, Tanganyika and Zanzibar in 1964, East and West Germany in 1990, and North and South Yemen in 1990. In all four cases the unifying dyads were culturally and linguistically similar (Griffiths 2010).

[54] Griffiths and Savic 2009.   [55] *The Economist* 2007.

Although European integration and other similar efforts may one day result in complete unification – and therefore produce fewer states – the pattern so far points to intersovereign relations. I argue that that pattern is made possible by the systemic changes noted earlier.

The Logic of Downsizing

If the hand of the international system makes metropoles more amenable to internal secession, it is their administrative architectures that determine where they will permit it. The importance of administrative organization plays out in three mutually reinforcing ways.[56] First, laying claim to a specific territory with an identified boundary helps the relevant parties – typically the sovereign and the breakaway region – to overcome the basic problem of where to place borders. As David Carter and Hein Goemans point out, administrative boundaries provide clear bargaining solutions and reduce the possibility of conflict.[57] They fit Thomas Schelling's definition of focal points in that they coordinate the participants' expectations as to where borders should be drawn.[58] This is important given that nations are typically fuzzy, overlapping groups rather than discrete, easily delineated units.

Second, administrative organization creates categories. Not all administrative units are the same in the eyes of the central government. Each metropole possesses a unique taxonomy that has an impact on how it downsizes. Just as the Soviets had the so-called nationalities ladder of ordered types, the USA has its incorporated territories (core fifty states), Native American reservations, and unincorporated territories (for example, Puerto Rico). Consider the cases of Hawaii and Puerto Rico, both island units that were acquired by the USA during an expansionary period in 1898. Although both became administrative regions and eventually generated a secessionist movement, their difference in type has profound consequences for their chances of secession. Puerto Rico was admitted as an unincorporated territory, a category that constitutes the outer belt of the various American units. Like other units in that category, Puerto Rico has been given the right to secede. Hawaii, on the other hand, was inducted as an incorporated territory. As a type of unit that is politically internal and subject to the full weight of the US Constitution, Hawaii's chances for eventual secession were

[56] Griffiths 2015.   [57] Carter and Goemans 2011.   [58] Schelling 1960, 70.

dramatically reduced more than 100 years ago when the relevant actors decided to incorporate it. Whereas its secession would set a precedent for the other forty-nine states, the secession of Puerto Rico would not.

Finally, both of the preceding points are reinforced by international law that, since at least the dissolution of the Spanish Empire in the Americas, has emphasized internal administrative territories as a guide for recognizing new states. Based on the principle of *uti possidetis*, international law holds that emerging states should inherit their administrative boundaries at the time of independence.[59] Malcom Shaw writes that "the primary justification of *uti possidetis* ... has been to seek to minimize threats to peace and security, whether they be internal, regional, or international. This is achieved by entrenching territorial stability at the critical moment of transition."[60] Although the application of the principle has received criticism, legal theorists typically defend it as a least-bad solution. As Steven Ratner argues, *uti possidetis* is an example of an idiot rule – a simple, clear norm that offers an acceptable outcome in most situations, "especially in the absence of any other solution."[61]

In practice, the application of *uti possidetis* has changed subtly over time.[62] For the states emerging from the Spanish Empire in the early 1800s, its use was meant to forestall potential disagreements over territory between states.[63] But for the countries that sprang from

---

[59] Ratner 1996; Bartos 1997; Lalonde 2002; Radan 2012; Crawford 2006; Fabry 2010. The principle of *uti possidetis* has two modern variants: (1) *Uti possidetis juris* references legal administrative possession and (2) *Uti possidetis de facto* relates to actual territorial possession. Although *uti possidetis juris* has generally and increasingly been emphasized by the international community, *uti possidetis de facto* did play a partial role in the delineation of states in South America (Radan 2002).

[60] Shaw 1997, 503.   [61] Ratner 1996, 617.

[62] Although *uti possidetis* had been used as a legal principle prior to the Latin American secessions, its main application was to resolve territorial disputes between sovereign states. For example, at the Karlowitz Conference in 1699, the Russians and Ottomans divided the frontier regions on the northern Black Sea coast based on existing informal possession (Boeck 2009, 137–138).

[63] With a few exceptions, all of the modern Spanish American states were once an imperial *audiencia*. There was, however, a second reason behind the application of *uti possidetis* in Latin America: it made a legal argument for formal possession over the entire continent, thus preventing foreign powers from claiming ownership over unoccupied areas of the hinterland under the principle of *terra nullius* (Bartos 1997, 44).

decolonization, the principle was used less to delineate territory between states than to disqualify secessionist claims within them. With the wave of secessionism that attended the Yugoslav and Soviet collapse, international law pushed the principle one more step to accept only first-order administrative units and exclude lower-order units regardless of their provenance.

The weight of the presumption of *uti possidetis* is variable. It can indeed only operate where there is an internal border or administrative line. The more unitary the state, the weaker the presumption. On the other hand, the more entrenched a particular administrative line may be, the stronger the presumption. In the case of federal states where the component units have meaningful jurisdictional powers and indeed may even have the right of secession domestically proclaimed (as in the former Yugoslavia and the former USSR), the presumption would be at its least assailable.[64]

The track record and protean nature of the principle highlights the interaction between metropolitan response and legal theory.[65] It demonstrates the iterative manner in which international law both reacts to events on the ground, and, at least until the next big event, defines the legal environment for aspiring nations. Administrative lines and categories present states with a natural blueprint for how to disassemble. That this mechanism should become codified in international law is unsurprising given the practical aims of legal theory and the fact that states are the primary authors of that law.

My theory synthesizes several directions in the existing literature. First, I emphasize administrative units, much like Valerie Bunce and Philip Roeder.[66] However, their work focuses on the generative capacity of administrative units that, they argue, provide an institutional apparatus around which national identities can coalesce. Such units generate new identities and new nations; they are states in the making. This is primarily an explanation for how nationalist ambitions arise. In

---

[64] Shaw 1997, 504. One criticism of the expanding application of *uti possidetis* is that it unfairly creates barriers to groups in unitary states (Radan 2002, 5).

[65] The changing application of *uti possidetis* is controversial. Bartos argues that the principle has not only been applied incorrectly, it has failed in its aim of preventing boundary disputes (Bartos 1997, 45).

[66] Treisman 1997; Bunce 1999; Roeder 2007. See Mampilly 2011 on the relationship between rebel groups and administrative organization.

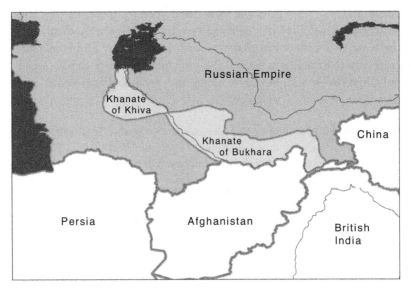

Map 2.1 Bukhara and Khiva.[67]

contrast, I shift the focus from the region to the central government to argue that administrative lines and categories are used by states when selecting which regions can secede. Whereas the first account helps explain where many secessionist movements come from, my theory explains why secessionist movements, even ones with a well-developed sense of nation, almost never secede unless they have the appropriate administrative status.

This generative/selective distinction can be illustrated with examples from the Russian/Soviet metropole. When the Tsar's forces expanded into Central Asia, a number of local sovereign states came under the Russian flag.[68] Two of them, the Emirate of Bukhara and the Khanate of Khiva, continued as informally ruled, external protectorates for nearly sixty years until, in 1924, the Soviet government decided to dissolve these units and reorganize the larger region into the republics of Uzbekistan and Tajikistan (see Map 2.1).[69] It did so in an attempt to reshape local identities and make them more loyal to the Soviet state. Judging from the sovereign states that emerged nearly seventy

[67] Bregel 2003; Lehner and Döll 2004; GADM 2012.
[68] Griffiths and Butcher 2013.   [69] Becker 1968.

years later, the project was at least partly successful in generating new nations.[70]

When the Russian/Soviet metropole finally downsized in 1991, it selected to release its first-order units (union republics) and keep its second-, third-, and fourth-order units (autonomous republics, autonomous *oblasts*, and autonomous *okrugs*), even though these latter categories were organized on an ethnonational basis and many of them had secessionist movements.[71] Although a unit's rank often changed over the decades as Moscow periodically upgraded and downgraded units – sometimes as a punishment and sometimes for efficiency – what mattered most was the rank when the state did finally downsize. Unlike the lower-ranked units, the first-order republics had been guaranteed the right to secession under the Soviet constitution, and this was the legal and historical distinction on which Moscow and the emerging central governments of the former republics could erect a barrier to further secession.[72] Moscow could not release any lower-order units because doing so would set a precedent, and thus it denied independence to Chechnya even as it permitted the secession of the union republics. Large, multinational states cannot always downsize to their optimally preferred point. I argue that the attempt is usually done in a justifiable and symmetrical manner that leaves less risk of uncontrolled rollback.

My theory brings the state into the center of the analysis. States are strategic when dealing with secessionists and they incorporate administrative lines and categories into their strategies. To model the strategic behavior of states I draw on Walter's logic of entry deterrence, but I develop it further by highlighting the importance of administrative organization. Walter draws on the chain store model in the economics literature to build her argument regarding metropolitan deterrence.[73] Just as a chain store will engage in a costly price war with an entrant to establish a reputation that deters other potential entrants, metropoles

---

[70] Smith 2013 contends that many nationalist aspirations endured in the absence of ethnofederal status.

[71] In keeping with the state list maintained by the Correlates of War project, Russia is treated as one continuous state between 1816 and 2011. Thus, Russia is the rump state and successor of the Soviet Union.

[72] Toft 2002.

[73] Walter 2006b, 2009. For similar work, see Toft 2002. For the original chain store model, see Selten 1978.

will fight secessionists as a way to deter others from attempting to secede in the future. This is a useful analogy and several key dynamics can be identified. First, the number of potential secessionist movements matters. If there is only one, then there is no risk of setting a precedent by letting the region secede and therefore no reason to fight to demonstrate resolve. As Walter argues, peaceful secession is more likely under these conditions. The Czechoslovakian "Velvet Divorce" was an example, as was the secession of Norway from Sweden in 1905. Second, secessionist commitment can vary. One could imagine a continuum of interest with rather decided regions such as Somaliland on one end and largely uninterested regions such as Vermont or Texas on the other. Located at points along the middle of the spectrum would be Catalonia, Quebec, or the French islands of New Caledonia in the southwest Pacific – regions that continuously reevaluate the costs and benefits of seeking and potentially obtaining independence. That regional preferences are variable is not a problem for the model because part of the reason the metropole needs to demonstrate its resolve is to deter potential secessionists, who adjust their estimates of success with signals coming from the metropole.[74] Third, some territories are less valuable than others and the cost of administering a unit can outweigh the benefits.[75] However, metropoles cannot always pick and choose which units they want to keep. Releasing a low-value territory that is actually not worth keeping can start a cascade effect that would eventually reach a high-value territory.

However, the analogy falls short in one critical way: the assumption that the regions (or entrants) are like types and that the metropole cannot discriminate between them. This is where the model fails to accurately portray the dynamics of secessionism, and where administrative lines and categories matter. The relevant economics literature recognizes that entry deterrence only works if entrants perceive that each market is sufficiently similar; the more variegated the market types, the less deterrence will have an effect.[76] Similarly, Monica Toft notes that whereas precedent setting is an issue when there is a perceived equality of status among secessionist groups, it becomes less of an issue as perceived differences become more salient.[77] In the context of the

[74] Fazal and Griffiths 2014.   [75] Sharman 2013.
[76] Milgrom and Roberts 1982, 303; Scherer 1980, 338–339.
[77] Toft 2002, 94–95.

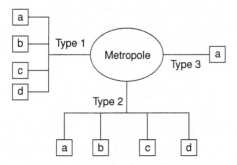

Figure 2.2 Schemata of administrative types.

chain store analogy, I argue that metropoles are typically facing different types of secessionist movements (see Figure 2.2).

Variations in administrative design effectively compartmentalize
secessionism in such a way that cascades often do not travel across
type. There are two general reasons why. First, the conceptual distinction between types can become quite salient in the eyes of the relevant
parties. For example, the USA could permit the secession of Puerto
Rico without fear of inspiring a movement in one of its states. That it
could not so easily permit Hawaii to secede without setting a precedent
for Alaska or Texas demonstrates the cognitive salience on the issue.
This explanation maps onto Ian Lustick's theory regarding the importance of thresholds in state contraction.[78] Despite its distance from
the mainland, Hawaii's attachment to the core is such that no serious contender for political power would currently suggest otherwise.
Meanwhile, Puerto Rican secession is openly discussed and considered
nonthreatening to the core.[79] Lustick is right that these thresholds of
attachment to territory govern how states downsize, but I go further to
argue that there is a tight correspondence between these thresholds and
administrative organization. Therefore, my theory lays out predictions
as to where these thresholds will be located.

Second, it is on these distinctions that metropoles typically draw a
line between those they will permit to secede and those they will deny,

---

[78] Lustick identifies two thresholds (Regime, Ideological Hegemony) that divide,
respectively, an Incumbency stage from a Regime stage from an Ideological
Hegemony stage (Lustick 1993; O'Leary et al. 2001).
[79] Using Lustick's typology, Hawaii is beyond the Ideological Hegemony
threshold and Puerto Rico is below the Regime threshold.

as the UK did when it discriminated between colonial units such as Burma and Uganda, and other colonized nations such as the Karens and the Baganda. Such distinctions are focal in nature, and they clearly sort out the respective groups. Moreover, these distinctions are usually backed by the principle of *uti possidetis*, which shapes the legal and strategic environment for aspiring nations. Naturally, these two explanations interact. Metropoles will defend a line partly because cognitive salience on the issue makes it easier to justify. It is when these distinctions are particularly salient that the metropole will have an easier time and potential secessionists will be dissuaded; conversely, the weaker the salience, the more likely the metropole will actually have to demonstrate its resolve.

This theory can be examined using my data on secessionist movements and internal administrative units (proto-states). As I stated in Chapter 1 and develop further in both Chapter 3 and Appendix B, proto-states are administrative units that are above a minimum size and either nationally distinct, geographically distant, indirectly ruled, or else recently transferred from another country. Using the proto-state data I can produce an administrative grid that can be overlaid on the set of secessionist movements, and a set of hypotheses can be tested.

First, secessionist movements that lack a proto-state stand a poorer chance of being recognized by their metropole and, as a result, a higher chance of experiencing conflict. In my dataset, some 38 percent of the secessionist movements lack a proto-state and I argue that these are the least blessed. Examples include the Circassians, Lakotah, Murrawarri, Thai Malays, and South Kasaians. Most of these groups claim (or claimed) a historical homeland and may once have been a sovereign state, but the territory in question is incongruent with any existing administrative boundaries. Whatever the merits of their claim, their secession presents a problem for the metropoles as to where boundaries should be drawn and how the nation should be delineated, and their lack of status makes the precedent-setting problem more acute since their secession would send a signal to all potential takers.

Other movements cohere with a lower-lever administrative unit but are not proto-states as I have defined them. The organization of political systems is complex, nested, and the number of administrative units is vast. For example, the city of Venice, within the County of Sarasota, within the State of Florida, within the sovereign USA, is an administrative unit, to be sure. However, its nested, third-order status makes it an unlikely case for peaceful secession. After all, how does its candidacy take priority over the county and state of which it is a part, and via what logic could the USA permit its independence while denying it to other towns, cities, counties, and states? It is the higher-level units that stand the best chances of winning independence, especially when the metropole can justify their independence while denying others.

Second, proto-states that are unique in type are more likely to receive metropolitan recognition and less likely to experience conflict. Drawing on the chain store analogy, metropoles are often playing on multiple boards. They may choose to permit the secession of one type of unit – see for example the Type 3 unit in Figure 2.2 – but fight to ward off any other type of challenger. This is particularly so when the unit in question is the sole member of its type, as Norway was for Sweden, Syria during its brief federation with Egypt, and as Bougainville currently is for Papua New Guinea.

Importantly, these cases are not exclusive to so-called binary states. What matters is that there is an administrative unit that is considered unique in type. There are plenty of administrative regions in Papua New Guinea, but Bougainville's special status after 2001 made it unique. Similarly, Hungary had a special status after 1867 that raised it above the many other Habsburg territories. In truth, binary states actually have more than two administrative units. The Czechs regarded Slovakia not as the only other administrative unit, but rather as the only other first-order unit that was organized around a national group. There were other second-order units, *kraje*, that were subordinate to either the Czech or Slovakian units, but these were of lesser rank and they did not qualify as proto-states. In the eyes of the Prague government and the other relevant parties, the Slovakian Republic was different in type from the South Bohemian *Kraj*. Secession for the former did not constitute a precedent for the secession of the latter.

Third, higher-level proto-states are more likely to be permitted independence and less likely to experience conflict. States organize their space in a variety of ways. For example, India used to have three types of units: its core states, its union territories, and its protectorates (until 1975). I contend that it was much easier for India to permit the independence of its protectorates, as it did with Bhutan, because these were regarded as outer-belt territories, different in status from neighboring states such as Assam. In contrast, Assamese independence was denied because it was a core state, because its secession would set a dangerous precedent, and because opening the door to this sort of fragmentation risks the dissolution of India itself. My proto-state dataset identifies these political architectures for all countries between 1816 and 2011 and sorts the constituent proto-states for each country by type. I then developed a ranking system that captures the distinctiveness of these types.

The unifying logic behind these hypotheses is that the administrative architecture of states actually structures how they respond to secessionist demands. These architectures may have been created for other reasons. They may be arbitrary, poorly drawn, or the product of geopolitical calculations or simple institutional habit,[80] but they nevertheless present a blueprint for how states can downsize. They provide states with clear lines and status categories, and the strategic use of these distinctions is backed by the international legal emphasis on *uti possidetis*. I argue that this administrative focus is a common mechanism in political life. The mechanism was evident during decolonization, when the colonial powers relied on an administrative snapshot to recognize some fifty administrative units in Africa and simultaneously deny or dissuade perhaps some 500 nations.[81] It was used by a beleaguered Boris Yeltsin to erect a bulwark to state dissolution.[82] And administrative distinctions continue to feature in both the legal arguments of aspiring nations and in the responses of states and international organizations who decide their fate.

Theoretical Considerations

There are several potential objections to this theory and research design. The first is that I combine decolonization with other forms of secession and state birth. I maintain that this is an appropriate

---

[80] Francophone countries possess comparatively fewer proto-states than their British counterparts. This is evidently a legacy of the French Revolution, which "eliminated the provinces of the *ancien regime*" and created a more centralized system (Ratner 1996, 603). That organizational approach persists in France today and in its descendent states.

[81] Jackson estimates that the application of *uti possidetis* reduced the number of acceptable independence claims in Africa from 400–500 to 40–50 (Jackson 1993, 122).

[82] After the failed August coup of 1991, Yeltsin was in a position to accept emerging independence declarations from the Union Republics and deny or discourage all other claims.

move and I defend it on methodological and conceptual grounds. I define secession as "the creation of a new state upon existing territory previously forming part of, or being a colonial entity of, an existing state."[83] This broad definition is consistent with much recent research,[84] but secession is a contested term and my usage does differ from other views that restrict the term to violent, illegal, and/or noncolonial cases.[85] Methodologically, my definition is appropriate because it provides a base category of aspiring nations before they are awarded independence or denied it.[86] Since the mid twentieth century, international law has attempted to limit sovereign recognition to cases of consent, decolonization, and dissolution, but such designations are often political, *ex post*, and difficult to incorporate into a systematic analysis.[87] For example, despite the fact that Buganda had been an independent kingdom in the nineteenth century, it was denied independence by the British in 1960, two years before the larger territory of Uganda became sovereign.[88] As Robert Jackson states, the international community limited sovereignty to colonial units rather than accommodate all colonized nations. In doing so, it consigned the Karens, Sikhs, and Baganda – and many others – "to the ranks of the abandoned peoples by the transformation of colonial frontiers – which never recognized them – into international boundaries."[89] Rather than treat Buganda and Uganda as completely different phenomena that need to be studied separately, I begin with a set of secessionist movements that all meet the same criteria.

A similar logic applies when considering the independence of the Soviet and Yugoslav Republics. The move to classify these cases as instances of dissolution and not secession is, in part, a legal solution that is meant to justify the former and not the latter. According to Tomas Bartos, "the [Badinter] Commission preferred to view the Yugoslavian situation as one of dissolution, refusing to set a precedent

---

[83] Radan 2008, 18. Also see Pavkovic and Radan 2011, 3.

[84] Pavkovic and Radan 2007; Radan 2008; Goldsmith and He 2008; Armitage 2010; Coggins 2011; Pavkovic and Radan 2011; Pavkovic 2015.

[85] A good example is Crawford 2006, who narrows the concept down to those cases that are not classified as decolonization, that are opposed by the state, and that either use force or threat to use force to achieve their aims (see Radan 2008, 21).

[86] For a legal defense of this definition, see Radan 2008, 18–32.

[87] Fabry 2010, 13.   [88] Minahan 1996, 88–89.   [89] Jackson 1993, 122.

for the secession of national groups within existing States."[90] Some
may regard Estonian independence in 1991 as a case of dissolution,
but many secessionist movements such as Chechnya and South Ossetia were denied independence by Moscow at the same time. The
distinction between secession and dissolution is at best a matter of
degree, and the ethical merits of the distinction are debated in the legal
discourse.[91]

My approach provides a more rigorous analysis by not selecting on
the outcome. I argue, as Ben Goldsmith and Baogang He do, that "one
person's colony is another person's national territory."[92] I have chosen
to identify a group of independence movements – all meeting the same
criteria – prior to these outcomes and accompanying designations. I
therefore include the violent failures (the Confederate States of America), the peaceful failures (Quebec), and the peaceful but contiguous
successes (Norway) alongside the failures and successes of distant colonized peoples (Buganda and Uganda).

Although some argue that empires are qualitatively different from
nonimperial metropoles that have acquired territory, it is not clear
where that line of difference should be drawn.[93] This is the conceptual
problem when upholding the distinction between decolonization and
secession. All of the polities under investigation have been recognized
as sovereign states and all of them are treated as like types in most
of the international relations literature, not to mention the existing
datasets that code for these things.[94] Does the possession of geographically distant, noncontiguous territories denote an imperial state? If so,
then Russia would not have counted after the sale of Alaska in 1867,
though the USA would have after the purchase. Indeed, Pakistan would
have counted as an empire prior to the secession of Bangladesh. Perhaps it is the possession of units that are politically external or assigned
to a specific minority nation. If so, then the existence of Bougainville

---

[90] Bartos 1997, 75.   [91] See Bartos 1997 and Radan 2002 for a critique.
[92] Goldsmith and He 2008, 593. Jackson makes a similar argument when he
points out that the "Russian domination of the Islamic countries of the Soviet
Union or Chinese domination of Tibet" did not count under the practices of
decolonization (Jackson 1993, 122).
[93] See Lake 1997, 32–33, and Motyl 1997, 2001 for a discussion of the varying
conceptions of empire.
[94] Gleditsch and Ward 1999; Fazal 2007; Correlates of War Project 2011;
Griffiths and Butcher 2013.

would be sufficient to make Papua New Guinea an empire, as the Bantustans would have for South Africa. Whether contemporary China, Indonesia, and the USA are empires depends on your terms. There is no perfect indicator. As Hendrik Spruyt says, "one person's Empire is another's multinational state."[95]

A second objection is that my argument is too instrumental and that it stresses the cost-benefit calculi of states when it was really ideological change that led to state proliferation. There is no doubt that the ideas behind self-determination and decolonization assisted numerous nations in winning their independence. However, I submit that the process of decolonization was made possible by changes in the value of holding territory. Some scholars argue against instrumental explanations for decolonization by pointing out that the colonial powers were not so exhausted that they could not retain colonies, nor suddenly disinterested in the economics of territory. If the costs of colonialism had not increased, Neta Crawford argues, then why did states not acquire the "territories of which other powers were prepared to divest themselves?"[96] I agree with these claims, but disagree with the conclusion that if we cannot point to any change in the "balance of material costs and benefits, it seems as though we must resort to normative ideas to explain the change."[97] My theory identifies these cost-benefit changes, explains why state such as the UK would give up territory, and specifies why the superpowers would support decolonization and then compete for informal influence over the emerging states.

The theory also helps explain the transition from an international recognition regime emphasizing *de facto* statehood to one that accorded sovereignty on a constitutive basis. As Mikulas Fabry recounts, that development tracked a transition in the interpretation of self-determination from a negative to a positive right.[98] During much of the nineteenth century, lead states such as the UK and the USA generally took the view that minority nations had the right to win their independence free of outside intervention; it was a domestic affair unless such nations could prevail over their sovereign and thereby demonstrate their self-determination. In contrast, the constitutive regime of the latter twentieth century is based on the premise that the

---

[95] Spruyt 2005, 2–3.   [96] Crawford 2002, 350; Jackson 1993, 131.
[97] Jackson 1993, 130.   [98] Fabry 2010. See Jackson 1990 for related arguments.

international community has an obligation to assist in these efforts and award independence based on "agreed-on" criteria for what groups qualify, regardless of their ability to prevail over their sovereign. I contend that the constitutive regime is made possible by the systemic changes I have noted; promoting the self-determination and assisting in the birth of weakly viable states against the will of the sovereign would be a strange practice in a time where conquest was common. Ultimately, the solution to one of the chief problems with constitutive recognition – deciding who counts – is to focus on administrative lines and categories.[99]

A third objection is that the theory suffers from endogeneity because administrative distinctions are given to already-existing, robust nations, and such distinctions only foment further nationalism. Thus, proto-states are permitted to secede not for strategic reasons on the part of the metropole, but rather because they are the best-organized, most-deserving, and most-persuasive claimants. I concede that these dynamics do operate, and I model them as alternative hypotheses in the analysis, but I contend that the picture is incomplete unless we include the strategic realities of the metropole. Catalonia is a hard case for my theory because it was once a sovereign state, and because its current autonomous status is both the consequence and cause of nationalist ambition. Yet even in this case we can see the strategic realities of the metropole. Madrid cannot recognize Catalan independence without setting a precedent for other *autonomias* such as Galicia and the Basque Country. The Spanish administrative architecture shapes Catalonia's possibilities.

As I discuss in the chapters to come, there are three types of endogeneity where administrative units are concerned. The first is where administrative status is assigned purely as a function of the preexisting level of nationalism. Administrative status is thus rather epiphenomenal, and even if metropoles rely on the resulting internal lines and status categories, it is ultimately the prior coherence of the nations in question that determines these outcomes. Such a view belies the realities of administrative creation because cases such as Catalonia are hardly the standard. Many higher-level administrative units were the product of top-down decisions that had little regard for the contours of local nations. This is a common critique of decolonization and the

---

[99] Fabry 2010.

application of *uti possidetis*,[100] which awarded sovereignty to territories that were the artifacts of European diplomacy rather than regions such as Buganda, a sovereign state in the nineteenth century that was stripped of first-order status and folded into Uganda. Indeed, administrative status was often denied key nations *precisely* because they were robust, well organized, and formerly sovereign. The periphery of Russia is littered with groups such as the Circassians, nations that were refused any status and deliberately divided over several administrative regions in an effort to suppress nationalist ambition.

More threatening to my theory is the second type of endogeneity where administrative categories, regardless of their origins, end up creating and/or strengthening national projects that eventually push for independence. This is what I call the generative aspect of administrative design and the argument is made forcefully in the states-in-the-making literature.[101] This argument is correct, it is just not the full story because metropoles do not simply grant sovereignty to the fittest nations. In fact, many territories with weak national identities but appropriate administrative status suddenly find independence more or less handed to them, as Bhutan, Tajikistan, and many of Britain's former colonies did. Conversely, many historic nations bereft of the right status, such as the Assamese and the Chechens, find that independence is denied them. This strategic aspect of metropolitan response is a major determinant of secessionist outcomes. In all, this administrative focus is a least-bad solution that often yields odd, unfair, and near-miss outcomes. For example, Eastern Karelia was a union republic until 1956, when it was downgraded to the level of autonomous republic. Had it kept its status for the remainder of the Soviet era, there is every reason to expect that it would have seceded peacefully along with the other union republics and would now be a sovereign state.

The final type of endogeneity has to do with the anticipatory effects of administrative design. For some groups – for example, the Central Asian Union Republics, and a number of colonies in Africa – independence was declared rather late when it was clear that other parallel units of the same type were going to secede. In many of these cases the demand for independence and corresponding national identity was relatively weak. But as I recount in the chapters to come, there were many dogs that chose not to bark – for example, the Kachins, the

---

[100] Jackson 1993.   [101] Treisman 1997; Bunce 1999; Roeder 2007.

Gagauz – because they lacked the correct status and knew that secession was unlikely to be permitted. I argue that for many of these cases the choice over secessionism was partly endogenous to the expected response of the metropole, which in turn was shaped by administrative organization. However, I see this potentiality as consistent with my theory: administrative organization shapes the decision to declare independence by encouraging groups who possess the right status and discouraging those who do not.

A related objection to my theory points to nationalism. It is said that the dawn of the age of nationalism in the late eighteenth century transformed the international system by subverting older forms of legitimate rule.[102] I acknowledge the role of nationalism but emphasize that potential nationalists do not mobilize in a vacuum. Their actions are influenced by instrumental considerations and expectations of success.[103] It is telling that secessionism was relatively rare before 1918 and especially before 1945 (see Figure 3.2), more than a century after the French Revolution. I submit that the character of the pre-1945 international system was a partial cause of this scarcity. Metropoles were less keen to give up territory and therefore more likely to fight over it. Of course, prevailing over the sovereign and achieving independence was no guarantee of longevity. Miles Kahler put it well when he said that "before World War II, one deterrent to colonial nationalism was recognition that the alternative to one imperial master was likely to be another and possibly harsher master."[104] This feedback between nationalist mobilization and expectations of success has continued in the post-1945 era, but in a transformed manner. The contemporary international recognition regime emphasizes administrative lines and categories, an emphasis that shapes the strategies and aspirations of potential and actual secessionists.[105]

A final objection is that I do not focus enough on local conditions. As with civil war, many explanations for secessionism point to problems on the ground such as ethnic cleavages, wealth disparities, or grievances over past events.[106] These explanations are important. I

---

[102] Wimmer 2013.   [103] Fazal and Griffiths 2014.   [104] Kahler 1997, 288.
[105] Fazal and Griffiths 2014.
[106] Heraclides 1991; Laitin 1998; Horowitz 1985; Hechter 2000; Collier and Hoeffler 2002; Walter 2006a; Aspinall 2007; Jenne et al. 2007; Hale 2008; Sambanis and Milanovic 2011; Sorens 2012; Cunningham 2011, 2013; Fazal and Griffiths 2014.

believe that they help explain the desire for sovereign independence, and, where possible, I model them in the quantitative chapter. However, they are insufficient on their own. The larger trend in secession and state birth requires a theory of metropolitan response since secessionist behavior is partly endogenous to that response.

All told, these are important theoretical considerations. Rather than dispense with them here, I keep them close throughout the remainder of the book. Some of them are modeled in the quantitative chapter, along with other alternative explanations such as the belief that metropolitan response is determined primarily by economic and strategic factors – that is, how valuable is the seceding region to the state? These considerations are also discussed at length in the case studies and revisited once again in the conclusion.

3 | A Quantitative Analysis of Secessionist Outcomes

The people of Texas do now constitute a free, sovereign, and independent republic, and are fully invested with all the rights and attributes which properly belong to independent nations.

– Texan Declaration of Independence, March 2, 1836[1]

The findings in this chapter indicate that international and domestic factors shape secessionist outcomes. Secession has been more likely in the post-1945 period than in the preceding era, and it has also been more peaceful. Nuclear-armed states are more likely to permit independence and less likely to fight secessionist conflicts. Similarly, trading states are also more amenable to secession. In addition, the administrative status of secessionist groups has a strong effect on the likelihood that they will secede.

The results also point to a number of interesting discoveries. First, the economic and strategic value of breakaway regions matters little. Despite conventional wisdom, these issues influence metropolitan response less than we might think. Second, the fact that a secessionist movement was once sovereign, or has a long history of secessionism, is not a factor that increases its chance of acquiring independence. This finding casts some doubt on the endogeneity-related argument that metropoles simply permit independence to the fittest nations. Third, geographic distance does matter. Secessionist movements that are separated from the larger state by more than 100 miles are more likely to receive a favorable response from their metropole, even after controlling for other variables such as administrative status. Fourth, regime type matters, especially in the conflict stage where democracy seems to render nonviolent outcomes more likely.

Finally, the standard deterrence argument does not hold up under scrutiny.[2] Secessionist groups in a secessionist-prone country are not

---

[1] Armitage 2007, 216.   [2] Walter 2009.

less likely to get a favorable response from their metropole, nor more likely to fight a conflict over the issue. On the contrary, secessionist groups in these circumstances are more likely to get the permission of their metropole. Indeed, they are more likely to declare independence when secessionism is in the air. The results indicate that the best predictor of the choice to declare independence is the number of other secessionist movements inside the state, suggesting that there is a tidal character to secessionism.[3] How much any one group's attempt at secession is influenced by the behavior of other groups, versus some local factor that may actually have catalyzed the wave of secessionism, is an open question. I return to this issue at the end of the chapter and in the case studies.

This chapter takes on the topic of secession at a high level of generality. The large-N approach is useful for discerning broad relationships between the independent and dependent variables, showing some to be unviable and others to be significant.[4] It helps organize the analysis in the subsequent chapters where I zoom in to study secessionist outcomes in the UK, Russia/Soviet Union, and India. The remainder of this chapter proceeds as follows. I begin by examining the historical pattern in peaceful and violent state birth. I then lay the groundwork for the large-N study by describing the data, discussing the different secessionist outcomes – my dependent variables – and highlighting the relationship between them, and specifying the independent variables. I next use these data and variables in a statistical analysis divided into three stages: (1) the decision to form a secessionist movement; (2) the response of the metropole; and (3) secessionist conflict.

An Increase in State Birth and Peaceful Secession

I began Chapter 1 by noting a nearly 200-year pattern in the international system whereby there is a concave trend in the number of states over time (see Figure 1.1). States have proliferated since 1945 and that development contrasts with the gradual reduction in the number of states in previous periods. However, this is a general observation and the character of that trend needs to be decomposed. In this section I turn to two related questions: (1) Has there been an increase in the

---

[3] Beissinger 2002.   [4] Lieberman 2005.

rate of state birth? (2) Has there been an increase in the rate of peaceful secession?

The first question seems obvious at first glance but it is actually somewhat deceptive. This is because the uptick in the number of states after 1945 is a function of both the rate of state death and state birth. Since we know that the rate of state death has declined in that time,[5] it is quite possible that the entry rate of states has actually held constant or even declined and that it is the exit rate that accounts entirely for the trend. What is needed is a calculation of the rate of state birth over time.

That rate can be calculated using the Correlates of War (COW) State Membership List.[6] COW identifies seventy-nine state births between 1816 and 1945, an average of .6 births a year. Meanwhile, there were 141 births between 1946 and 2011, an average of 2.1 births a year. A difference of means test confirms that these averages are statistically different at the 99 percent confidence level. Note that this calculation is similarly robust if one uses the International System(s) Dataset (ISD);[7] the averages are statistically different at the same level of confidence. Overall, the rate of state birth increased after 1945.

The second question listed earlier takes the analysis further by looking at the ratio of violent to peaceful state births. An examination of the data reveals that secession was not only significantly more common after 1945, it was also more peaceful.[8] Overall, there were 186 cases of secession between 1816 and 2005, and fifty-six (30 percent) resulted in conflict. Of the fifty-two cases that occurred in the pre-1945 era, thirty-eight (73 percent) were violent. Meanwhile, of the 134 cases in the post-1945 period, only eighteen (13 percent) were violent. Thus in stark contrast to the years before, peaceful secession has been more common in the post-1945 period. Figure 3.1 provides a graphical illustration of this trend.

Of course, there were peaceful secessions in the pre-1945 era just as there were violent secessions afterward. One of the most

---

[5] Fazal 2007.   [6] Correlates of War Project 2011.

[7] Griffiths and Butcher 2013. The ISD dataset yields the same average of 2.1 in the post-1945 period. However, the average is slightly higher in the pre-1945 years; there were eighty-seven births over a 130-year period, yielding an average of 0.67. The increased rate of birth in the ISD follows from the coding criteria, which identify numerous states (mostly non-Western) that were excluded by COW.

[8] See the section on dependent variables for the coding of secessionist conflict.

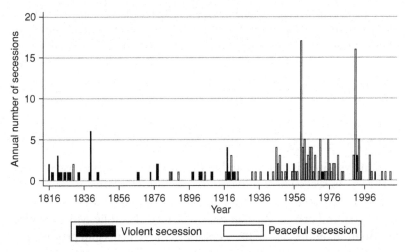

Figure 3.1 Violent versus peaceful secession.

amiable of these breakups was Norway from Sweden in 1905. Others occurred against the background of a weakened country. These include Venezuela and Ecuador from Gran Colombia in 1830, and Finland from Russia in 1917. Other secessions occurred in a more gradual process. Luxembourg's 1890 secession from the Netherlands is an example, but perhaps the best cases are the British dominions of South Africa, Canada, Australia, and New Zealand, which obtained sovereignty as defined in this book between 1885 and 1920. Both the Dominican Republic and Haiti seceded (again) from the USA in 1924 and 1934, respectively. Finally, there were the secessions of Iraq in 1932 and Egypt in 1937, two territories that had fought for independence in the 1920s and gradually wrestled a level of consent from London prior to World War II. Similarly, there were eighteen violent secessions after 1945 and a significant number of attempted secessions that the central government denied. This, however, is understandable even in an era when governments are more amenable to secession. Secessionist groups may lay claim to territory considered too valuable, they may espouse an ideology that is hostile to the parent state, and metropoles may simply be trying to manage multiple secessions in a way that avoids uncontrolled fragmentation.

These findings provide initial support for the argument that metropoles have been more amenable to secession in the post-1945 period – that is, more willing to accept independence demands and less likely to experience secessionist conflict. However, any conclusions are tempered by the fact that all of the failed secessionist movements have not yet been taken into account. Figure 3.1 shows only the successful movements, and a different picture may result from the inclusion of the failed cases.

Data

The analysis in this chapter and in the case studies makes use of original data on secessionist movements and administrative units (proto-states). In this section I describe these data, state how they are operationalized, and present them in several historical graphs. More detailed information on the coding for secessionist movements and proto-states is available in the appendices.

Secessionist Movements

I define secession as "the creation of a new state upon existing territory previously forming part of, or being a colonial entity of, an existing state."[9] This is Peter Radan's definition, and by "new state" he means a sovereign state recognized by the international community.[10] The unit of analysis in this research is the secessionist movement, which I define as a nation that actively seeks to obtain independence from its sovereign. Thus, a secessionist movement is an instance of secessionism, where a nation inside a sovereign state seeks to break away and become a new sovereign state.

I identify secessionist movements using the following criteria:

1. At a minimum, the movement must last at least one week, it must involve at least 1000 people, and it must lay claim to at least 100 square kilometers.
2. The group must have a flag.
3. The group must make a claim to both a territory and a population.
4. The group must formally declare independence from its home state.

[9] Radan 2008, 18. Also see Pavkovic and Radan 2011, 3.
[10] The definition therefore excludes unrecognized *de facto* or quasi-states. See Pegg 1998; Kolsto 2006. It also excludes instances of forced separation (for example, East Germany and West Germany).

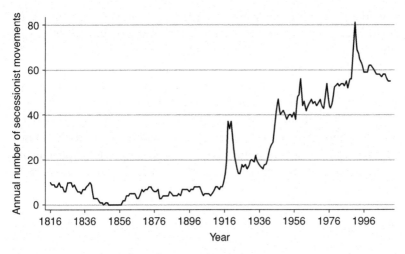

Figure 3.2 Annual number of secessionist movements.

All told there were 403 distinct secessionist movements and 4576 secessionist movement years between 1816 and 2011. The average movement lasted a little more than eleven years. Of the 403 movements, eighty-five began and ended in one calendar year and were thus coded as one observation (the data is annualized). In comparison, seventy secessionist movements lasted more than twenty years. Finally, some secessionist movements were repeat efforts. For example, there were three Lithuanian movements: in 1918, from 1945 to 1952, and in 1991.

Figure 3.2 illustrates the annual number of secessionist movements between 1816 and 2011. Aside from a burst of secessionism in the early nineteenth century – mostly in Latin America – secessionism was a relatively rare event until after World War I when the number of movements spiked at thirty-seven in 1918 and 1920. This dramatic increase provides evidence for what Erez Manela has called the "Wilsonian Moment," a brief surge in nationalist ambitions that were fired by Woodrow Wilson's proclamations on self-determination.[11] However, as Manela writes, these aspirations were short-lived for most of these groups once they realized that the international community was unwilling to honor self-determination in full. Indeed, the vast majority of these nations were denied independence, often violently. As a result,

---

[11] Manela 2007.

more than half of the movements of 1918 died out, and this, along with the low replacement rate, explains the interwar trough that the graph illustrates.

Overall, secessionism has been much more common in the post-1945 era. On average, there have been fifty-two secessionist movements per year since 1945, and there were fifty-five active movements as of 2011. That the number of movements has generally increased over the post-1945 period, even as the number of sovereign states has increased, speaks to a high rate of secessionism: new movements are springing up to replace those that succeeded in gaining their independence.

Proto-states

The second dataset consists of administrative units inside sovereign states. Some of the cases will exhibit secessionism, some will not, and some will eventually become sovereign states and exit the dataset. Others will be reorganized or dissolved over time and cease to be proto-states. Some will endure over the entire range of years.

I define proto-states as identifiable administrative jurisdictions with the following traits:

1. They have a minimum population of 1000 people and a minimum size of 100 square kilometers and,
2. They either possess complete internal independence (indirect rule),
   a. or they are granted specific rights in accordance with a unit-wide ethnic group or nation,
   b. or they are the result of a territorial transfer,
   c. or they are separated from the metropole by at least 100 miles.

As I discuss in Appendix B, this set does not include all administrative units in all countries. That list would be quite vast given the nested nature of administrative organization. Instead, this set captures what I argue are the most relevant units where secessionism is concerned, ones that are above a certain size (the same size threshold as with secessionist movements), and either internally independent, nationally distinct, the result of a territorial transfer, or geographically distant.

An essential feature of this dataset is the mapping of each state's administrative architecture. Given the core theory of the book it is important to know how each proto-state is classified in relation to other proto-states and to the metropole. To that end I developed a system for sorting proto-states into four different levels:

- Level 0. These are proto-states that were recently transferred from another state, but lack any special autonomous or national status. Moreover, they are less than first-order units – that is, they are second order, third order, and so on. An example is Tacna from 1929 to 1948.
- Level 1. These are core-level proto-states. In many cases they are federal units (for example, Hawaii), but oftentimes they are departments, prefectures, and so on, that count as proto-states because of distance (for example, Algeria from 1848 to 1962). Importantly, they are first-order units.
- Level 2. These are intermediate-level proto-states that possess local autonomy or national distinction. They are not politically external units. Examples include Poland (within the Russian Empire) from 1816 to 1864, modern Jersey, the first-order Yugoslav republics, and Aruba since 1986.
- Level 3. These are outer-level units that that are first-order and politically external. A classic example would be India when it was connected to the UK.

Further elaboration on these distinctions is provided in Appendix B, but suffice it to say that the sorting system captures levels of organization while being sensitive to the specific architecture of each metropole. The resulting dataset identifies 638 proto-states between 1816 and 2005 and further records whether secessionist movements between 2006 and 2011 corresponded with a proto-state.[12] In the data these proto-states lasted an average of sixty years.

What is the relationship between proto-states and secessionist movements? Empirically, 62 percent of secessionist movements possessed a proto-state, meaning that the group in question declared the independence of the entire administrative region. Figure 3.3 shows a graphical representation of this relationship. The remaining 38 percent of the movements claimed territories that did not conform to these

---

[12] The mapping of each state's administrative architecture does not extend beyond 2005. I do record whether each secessionist movement possessed a proto-state from 2006 to 2011.

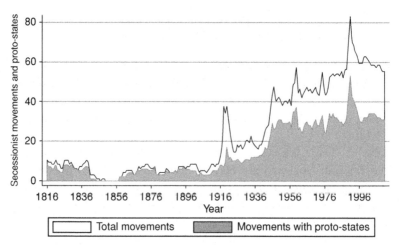

Figure 3.3 Secessionist movements and proto-states.

administrative lines and categories. Conversely, the great majority
(93 percent) of proto-states did not form secessionist movements.

Dependent Variables (Secessionist Outcomes)

The analysis in this chapter examines the effects of the independent
variables on several secessionist outcomes (the dependent variables).
In this section I decompose secessionism into three temporal stages:
(1) the decision to form a secessionist movement; (2) the response of
the central government; and (3) whether or not violence results. These
are stages in the life of a secessionist movement that, for the most part,
occur chronologically.[13] I have argued that the strategic realities of the
state are underexamined and I therefore focus my analysis squarely
on the state itself. As such, I am primarily interested in the latter two
stages depicted in Figure 3.4, but I also examine the first stage to detect
potential selection effects.

Most of the work on secession examines how nationalist groups
form and the factors that drive them to seek independence. This is a
clear moment, illustrated in Figure 3.4 as the formation of a secessionist movement by a proto-state. Note that here I use proto-states as

---

[13] See Figure 2.1 for an illustration.

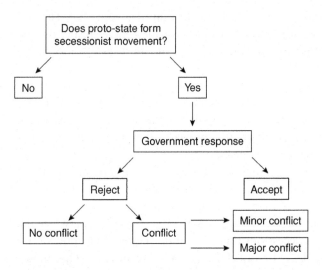

Figure 3.4 Diagram of secessionist outcomes.

a base category of potential secessionist movements.[14] Operationally, I identify the moment where a secessionist movement forms as the year when it declares independence. This is a binary variable: $0 =$ no secessionist movement; $1 =$ secessionist movement formed. There are a number of reasons why the issuance of a declaration of independence is the best moment to identify the activation of a secessionist movement. First, a declaration is a signifier of intent, and it is the most important criterion in my dataset that separates secessionist movements from other forms of mobilization aiming for more modest and nonsovereign forms of local autonomy. Second, declarations of independence are a distinguishable genre of political writing that typically include a statement that nation X is now independent and sovereign, a declaration of rights, and a manifesto detailing grievances of that nation against the current sovereign.[15] In all, the issuance of a declaration is the best signifier for determining (systematically) when a movement begins.

---

[14] Not all proto-states form secessionist movements (only about 7 percent have), and not all secessionist movements were proto-states (about 62 percent were). As such, I do not capture all instances where secessionist movements form. It is quite difficult, however, and perhaps impossible, to identify a base unit from which all secessionist movements originate, and the proto-state dataset captures nearly two-thirds of the cases.

[15] Armitage 2007, 14.

The next two stages directly involve the central government. The first of these addresses how the government (or metropole) responds to a movement's declaration of independence, the most visible and public indication of intent. I coded two outcomes: (0) if the metropole denied the group independence; (1) if the metropole publicly accepted the declaration. Declarations are a trigger event that not only articulate the nation's aspirations, but they also elicit a response. If the metropole chooses to deny independence to a movement, it almost always issues a rejection for the reason Ker-Lindsay stated: "any silence about an act of secession may possibly be read as *de facto* acceptance."[16] If the metropole chooses to accept, it is keen to show that acceptance and demonstrate its role in the birth of the new state.

The third outcome is whether there was a conflict between the metropole and the secessionist movement during the year of the declaration of independence or any of the two subsequent years. This important outcome is similar in form to metropolitan response, but not the same thing. The primary difference stems from those cases where the government denies the region independence, but conflict does not occur (for example, Hawaii, Brittany, and Southern Cameroon). These "middle" cases receive a negative outcome (rejection) in the second stage but a positive outcome (no violence) in the third. There is a correlation between the two outcomes given that metropolitan denial increases the likelihood of conflict. But of course, that same denial is not a sufficient condition for conflict. I explore this close relationship in the analysis that follows.

To code for conflict I used the criteria put forth by the Uppsala Conflict Data Program: a conflict is "a contested incompatibility that concerns government and/or territory where the use of armed force between two parties, of which at least one is the government of a state, results in at least 25 battle-related deaths."[17] I coded this outcome first as a binary variable: (0) no conflict; and (1) conflict. For additional robustness checks I coded it as trinary variable: (0) no conflict;

---

[16] Ker-Lindsay 2012, 77. In a few cases the metropole ignored the declaration, and I treated these as instances of denial.

[17] Themnér and Wallensteen 2012. Although this dataset only begins in 1946, I applied the criteria to all secessionist movements stretching back to 1816. My research in these cases benefited from the following sources: Clodfelter 2002; Sarkees and Wayman 2010; and Fazal and Fortna 2014.

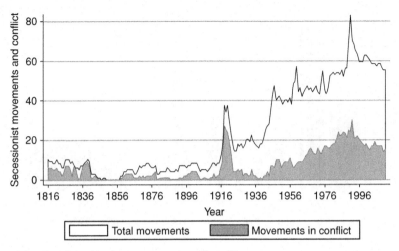

Figure 3.5 Secessionist movements and conflict.

(1) between 25 and 1000 deaths; and (2) more than 1000 deaths.[18] These efforts resulted in 1431 conflict years, a little more than 31 percent of the 4579 secessionist movement years.

Figure 3.5 is a stacked line graph illustrating the trend in secessionist conflict between 1816 and 2011. Noticeable spikes occurred at various points over the range of years, but of these the most startling is the wave of secessionist violence that attended the end of World War I. There were twenty-seven secessionist conflicts in 1918, a high point that would only be reached again in 1992 when there were thirty conflicts. However, whereas the first wave constituted a rather dramatic peak, the early 1990s were the crest of what is essentially a post-1945 period of frequent secessionism. Indeed, there was an average of more than fifteen secessionist conflicts a year between 1945 and 2011. In contrast, before 1945 that average was slightly more than three.

---

[18] Although the threshold criterion of twenty-five battle-related deaths per year is relatively low, it was appropriate for my purposes. Had I selected a higher threshold, such as the standard 1000 deaths that COW uses, I would have elided a number of secessionist-related conflicts that were violent and indicative of metropolitan denial, but yet insufficiently violent to make the cut. However, one could argue that there is a qualitative difference between a civil war where twenty-five people die and larger conflicts that claim thousands. Fortunately, the UCDP data does record whether the conflict also exceeded a threshold of 1000 battle deaths (Themnér and Wallensteen, 2012).

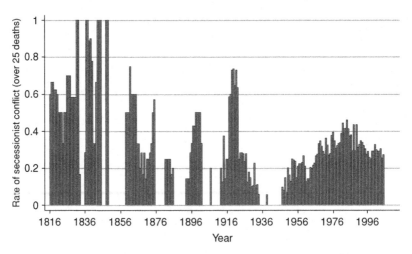

Figure 3.6 Rate of secessionist conflict (more than twenty-five deaths).

Over the long term, it seems that secessionist movements were fighting with their metropole nearly a third of the time. However, this pattern varied by time period. Figure 3.6 depicts the annual rate of secessionist conflict (number of conflicts/number of secessionist movements). Note that this graph uses the lower threshold of twenty-five battle deaths. The average rate of conflict in the post-1945 period is a bit lower at 29 percent versus an average rate of 38 percent in the years before. Yet there is greater variation in the pre-1945 era, partially on account of the fewer cases.

However, this difference between the pre-1945 and post-1945 rate of conflict is more noticeable when only major conflicts involving more than 1000 annual battles are used (see Figure 3.7).[19] The average of major conflict in the earlier period is nearly 21 percent. Meanwhile, in the latter era that rate drops to less than 9 percent. In sum, these data suggest that although secessionist conflict is more likely in contemporary times, the actual rate of conflict is declining once we control for the number of secessionist movements. Secessionism remains an important feature of international life, but an increasing number of nations are choosing not to take up arms over the issue.

To conclude, each of these outcomes is an important stage in the life of a secessionist movement. Each of the outcomes is modeled as a dependent variable in the following analysis. Although I am primarily

[19] For a discussion on this topic, see Fazal and Griffiths 2014.

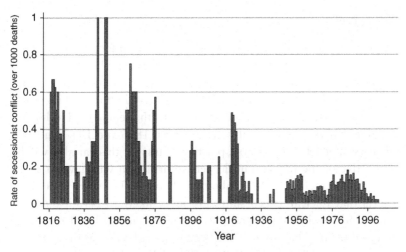

Figure 3.7 Rate of secessionist conflict (more than 1000 deaths).

interested in the second and third stages, which directly involve the reaction of the sovereign, I also study the choice to form a secessionist movement for two reasons: the choices of secessionists are shaped by the regime in which they exist, and those choices ought to anticipate (to some degree) the response of the state.

Independent Variables

There are a number of potential explanations for these secessionist outcomes. In Chapter 2 I developed my theory of metropolitan response and the resulting hypotheses. In this section I state the hypotheses in formal terms and I detail the manner in which they are operationalized. In addition, I discuss several prominent competing hypotheses and explain how they are tested in the statistical analysis. Importantly, each hypothesis is framed as a matched pair specifying the purported relationship between the independent variable and the two primary dependent variables (Stages 2 and 3): the response of the metropole and whether conflict is likely to result. I do not stipulate the relationship between these variables and the decision to form a secessionist movement (Stage 1) in the same way because my theory targets the latter stages. Having said that, many of the same independent variables are used in the first stage as part of the investigation into potential selection effects.

Core Hypotheses

There are three core hypotheses that focus on the international system. The first holds that metropoles will be more amenable to secession in the post-1945 period – they are more likely to permit independence and less likely to experience conflict. This is a period effect and therefore it can be measured with a time variable. To that end I used a dummy variable that assigned 0 to all years between 1816 and 1945, and 1 to all years after 1945. Of course, positive results for this variable will be supportive of the theory, but deeper confirmation will have to await the process tracing in the qualitative chapters. The next hypothesis asserts that nuclear-armed states are more likely to permit independence and less likely to fight a secessionist conflict. I coded nuclear weapons using a dummy variable beginning with the year the state first tested a bomb (US = 1945; USSR = 1949; UK = 1952; France = 1960; China = 1964; India = 1974; Pakistan 1998).[20] For the trade variable I calculated each state's trade openness as a ratio of trade (imports plus exports) to gross domestic product (GDP) using trade data from the COW Project Trade Data Set and GDP data published by Angus Maddison.[21] Unfortunately, these trade data only go back to 1870 and there were a number of missing values.

Formally, these international-level hypotheses can be stated as follows:

H1a: *Metropoles are more likely to permit secession in the post-1945 period.*

H1b: *Secessionist conflict is less likely in the post-1945 period.*

H2a: *Metropoles are more likely to permit secession when they possess nuclear weapons.*

H2b: *Secessionist conflict is less likely when the metropoles possess nuclear weapons.*

H3a: *The likelihood of metropolitan permission increases as the metropole becomes more integrated with the global economy.*

H3b: *The likelihood of secessionist conflict is inversely related to the metropole's level of economic integration in the global economy.*

---

[20] There were no secessionist events in Israel or North Korea after their supposed first nuclear detonations.

[21] Barbieri et al. 2008; Maddison 2008. I adjusted the Maddison figures to current dollars using an inflation calculator put out by the US Department of Labor.

The next three core hypotheses focus on the consequences of administrative design. Stated simply, administrative lines and categories shape the response of metropoles to secessionist demands. In formal terms, these hypotheses can be specified in this manner:

> *H4a: Secessionist movements that lack a proto-state are less likely to be recognized by their metropole.*
>
> *H4b: Secessionist movements that lack a proto-state are more likely to have a conflict with their metropole.*
>
> *H5a: Metropolitan recognition is more likely when the proto-state is the sole member of its type.*
>
> *H5b: Secessionist conflict is less likely when the proto-state is the sole member of its type.*
>
> *H6a: Metropolitan recognition is more likely for higher-level units.*
>
> *H6b: Secessionist conflict is less likely for higher-level units.*

These hypotheses were coded by combining my data on secessionist movements and proto-states. The variable "proto-state" indicates whether the secessionist movement laid claim to a proto-state. I modeled this as a binary variable where "no" = 0 and "yes" = 1. I then tested whether the secessionist movement is a unique unit, the sole member of its administrative type. This is also modeled as binary variable where "no" = 0 and "yes" = 1. Finally, I tested the impact of administrative level based on the respective metropole's administrative architecture, sorted into four levels as stated earlier. This system captures the varied ways in which states are organized. It is sensitive to how units are nested (first order, second order, etc.), and whether they are regarded as politically external, national distinct, and/or autonomous. Each state has its own architecture but higher-level units represent types that are more distant (administratively) from the central government.

Alternative Hypotheses

Various alternative explanations come to mind for the phenomena of interest. One rather commonsensical view suggests that states should devote more blood and treasure to keeping territory that is economically and/or strategically valuable.[22] All else equal, states will

---

[22] Bartkus 1999; Collier and Hoeffler 2002; Fearon and Laitin 2003; Toft 2003; Lujala 2009; Sorens 2011.

be less willing to permit the secession of valuable territory and more willing to fight for it. Secessionist movements claiming valuable territory are therefore more likely to be denied by their metropole, and that denial increases the likelihood of conflict. This logic yields the following hypotheses that focus on the economic and strategic value of territory:

> *H7a: The probability of metropolitan acceptance is inversely related to the economic value of the secessionist territory.*
>
> *H7b: The probability of secessionist conflict increases in proportion to the economic value of the secessionist territory.*
>
> *H8a: The probability of metropolitan acceptance is inversely related to the strategic value of the secessionist territory.*
>
> *H8b: The probability of secessionist conflict increases in proportion to the strategic value of the secessionist territory.*

I quantified the economic value of the secessionist region on a 31-point scale. Higher values indicate high values of marketable resources in the breakaway region.[23] In addition, I summed the number of strategic factors (sea outlet, shipping lane, military base, international border, attack route, mountain range) in the region on a scale from 0 to 6.

In Chapter 2 I discussed the potential for different types of endogeneity in my theory. Although these possibilities are explored primarily in the case studies, I model one form of endogeneity in this chapter: the argument that administrative status is assigned as a function of the underlying level of national cohesiveness. If robust nations tend to negotiate special status from their metropoles, then their eventual secession may have nothing to do with strategic behavior on the part of the metropole. Administrative status categories may be quite epiphenomenal, and it is the underlying strength of each nation that determines metropolitan response. This type of endogeneity can be modeled by looking at the history of proto-states. Is there a record of sovereignty or secessionism prior to becoming a proto-state? If so, these nations are more likely to receive a positive outcome with respect to sovereign recognition and the avoidance of conflict.

> *H9a: Proto-states that were previously sovereign states or secessionist movements are more likely than other proto-states to be recognized by their metropole.*

---

[23] The variables measuring economic and strategic value are taken from Walter's work on government response (Walter 2006b).

> *H9b: Proto-states that were previously sovereign states or secession-*
> *ist movements are less likely than other proto-states to experience*
> *secessionist conflict.*

Operationally, the variable "prior nation" codes for whether the proto-state was previously a sovereign state or a secessionist movement ("no" = 0; "yes" = 1).[24]

A different argument focusing on decolonization holds that it was the postwar drive to liberate colonized peoples that determines whether states will permit secession and whether they will not. This study uses a broad definition of secession, one that encompasses territorially contiguous groups and geographically distant nations. One explanation for the variation in outcomes is to assert that the norms surrounding self-determination and decolonization influenced metropolitan behavior with respect to independence demands.[25] The discrediting of imperial relations over distant nations essentially made metropoles more amenable to secessionism. Thus, colonized nations are more likely to be recognized by their metropoles and less likely to experience conflict. Note that this hypothesis differs from my theory in at least one critical way: it emphasizes distant peoples caught in imperial relations. It does not emphasize administrative distinctions, but rather hews closely to the spirit of decolonization: to liberate colonized nations.

> *H10a: Colonized nations are more likely to be recognized by their*
> *metropoles.*
> *H10b: Colonized nations are less likely to experience secessionist*
> *conflict.*

I model this argument with a variable that indicates whether the secessionist region is separated from the rest of the state by at least 100 miles of water or foreign territory ("no" = 0; "yes" = 1). As I discussed in Chapter 2, it is quite difficult and perhaps impossible to clearly differentiate imperial from nonimperial relationships. One person's colony is another's national territory. I have chosen a distance threshold because it has been used formerly in this way,[26] and it because it is consistent

---

[24] Prior sovereign status was determined using the ISD (Griffiths and Butcher 2013).

[25] Jackson 1993; Crawford 2002; Manela 2007.

[26] Coggins 2011 also uses a 100-mile threshold in her coding. Note that 100 is a median value for the COW dataset on colonial possessions, which uses thresholds of 12, 24, 150, and 400.

with the so-called saltwater test, a rule of thumb used to differentiate maritime empires, for which decolonization would count, from land-based empires, for which it would not.

An important alternative explanation is Walter's deterrence argument that states will attempt to build a reputation to deter potential secessionists.[27] The primary difference between this argument and mine is that it does not differentiate between different types of movements. I model the argument using a variable that sums up the number of parallel secessionist movements inside the same state; values ranged from 0 to 19. The logic for this variable is simple: metropolitan acceptance is inversely related to the number of other movements and conflict is, of course, positively related.

> H11a: *The probability of metropolitan acceptance is inversely related to the number of movements the metropole faces.*
>
> H11b: *Secessionist conflict increases in proportion to the number of movements the metropole faces.*

Finally, I included some additional control variables. I added a democracy measure that uses the Polity2 variable from the Polity IV dataset to identify the regime type of the larger state on a 21-point scale.[28] I also controlled for fixed country effects in the second and third stages of the analysis.

Analysis

I now examine the impact of the core and alternative hypotheses on the three secessionist outcomes. Stage 1 investigates the choice to form a secessionist movement. Stage 2 studies the response of the government to the formation of a secessionist movement. Stage 3 examines whether conflict results from these choices.

Stage 1: The Decision to Form a Secessionist Movement

This section has two purposes: (1) to model the effects of key independent variables on the formation of secessionist movements; and (2) to

---

[27] Walter 2006b, 2009. Also see Toft 2002 for a similar argument.
[28] Marshall and Jaggers 2011.

examine whether there are selection effects with respect to metropolitan response. In other words, it may be that key variables of interest increase the chance of conflict only because they actually increase the chance of forming a secessionist movement.

Table 3.1 shows the results for logistic regressions where the dependent variable is the formation of a secessionist movement.[29] The post-1945 and trade variables are initially excluded in Model 1 and then reintroduced in Models 2 and 3.[30] I sequence them in this manner because post-1945 is a general time variable that should theoretically capture some of the effects of nuclear weapons diffusion and free trade, and because the trade variable has limited data.

The most statistically significant variable is the number of other secessionist movements, implying that proto-states are more likely to declare independence when there are other secessionist movements inside the state. Indeed, the likelihood of declaring independence increases in proportion to the number of other movements. Nevertheless, the marginal effects are still quite small for the variable – potential secessionists are only slightly more likely (1.7 percent) to declare independence when there many other parallel movements as opposed to none. However, these weak effects could be a consequence of the fact that the choice to secede is a rare event in the dataset.[31]

Many of the other variables show significant results. The decision to form a secessionist movement is positively correlated with both the post-1945 period and high trade levels. The remaining core hypotheses vary in their significance depending on the model. Two other variables of interest pertain to prior nations and regime type. Groups that were formerly a sovereign state or possessed a secessionist movement are more likely to declare independence, and secessionism is negatively correlated with democracy. Overall, however, the marginal effects are relatively weak.

The second purpose at this stage was to look for selection effects. To that end I used a Heckman selection model where the second outcome

---

[29] I use time variables to model temporal dependence (Carter and Signorino 2010).

[30] At this stage I exclude the variables measuring economic and strategic value because of limited data. I also exclude the proto-state variable because at this stage all units are proto-states.

[31] Running these regressions using ReLogit produced similar results (see Tomz et al. 1999).

Table 3.1 *Formation of secessionist movements*

	Model 1	Model 2	Model 3
Nuclear weapons	0.23 (0.18)		0.51** (0.19)
% Change			0.2%
Post-1945		0.66*** (0.19)	
% Change		0.2%	
Trade			3.26*** (0.60)
% Change			0.1%
Unique unit	0.88*** (0.29)	0.84*** (0.29)	0.36 (0.40)
% Change	0.4%	0.4%	
Administrative level	−0.28** (.11)	−0.19* (0.12)	0.02 (0.15)
% Change	0.2%	0.2%	
Geographic distance	−0.06 (0.19)	−0.01 (0.19)	0.12 (0.24)
% Change			
Prior nation	0.48** (0.17)	0.49** (0.17)	0.46** (0.21)
% Change	0.1%	0.1%	0.2%
# Other movements	0.41*** (0.02)	0.38*** (0.02)	0.38*** (0.02)
% Change	1.7%	1.7%	1.5%
Democracy	−0.02** (0.01)	−0.03*** (0.01)	−0.06*** (0.02)
% Change	0%	0.2%	0%
Time	−3.03** (1.23)	−3.52*** (1.21)	−4.32** (1.43)
% Change			
Time^2	3.74* (2.0)	4.44** (2.0)	4.8** (2.2)
% Change			
Time^3	−1.22* (0.87)	−1.52* (0.87)	−1.57* (0.93)
% Change			
Constant	−4.48*** (0.28)	−4.75*** (0.30)	−4.82*** (0.37)
N	37 229	37 229	21 162
Wald χ^2	(10) 725.13	(10) 736.11	(11) 627.73
Probability $> \chi^2$	0	0	0
Pseudo-R^2	0.26	0.26	0.3
Log-likelihood	−1052	−1046	−723

Note. Marginal change calculated by moving the variable from low to high while holding the other variables at their mean. The Trade and # Other Movements variables are calculated by increasing the value from 1 SD below the mean to 1 SD above.

*$p < 0.10$. **$p < 0.05$. ***$p < 0.01$.

was the response of the state.[32] That is, I included both the decision to declare independence and the response of the metropole in one regression. Interestingly, there was no evidence of selection bias using this method.[33] Thus, given the current data structure and variables, there is no reason to include both outcomes in the same regression.

Overall, how should these results be interpreted? First, none of the variables are strong predictors of secessionism, at least not given the current data structure. There may well be other, perhaps more local factors that do anticipate secessionism much of the time. However, several of the variables were highly significant. There is some indication that secessionism is more likely among nations that were previously sovereign or secessionist, and that it is more probable in autocracies and in trading states. These implications align generally with common wisdom.

Second, the variable that counts the number of other secessionist movements showed the strongest effects but they are, in some ways, the opposite of what deterrence theory predicts. The results indicate that nations are actually more likely to declare independence when there are other secessionist movements in the same state. One interpretation is that there are clustering or tidal effects to secessionism. Perhaps secessionist movements tend to occur in waves because groups often respond to common triggers and/or adjust their estimates of success based on what internal nations are doing.[34] I explore this conjecture in the pages that follow.

Stage 2: The Response of the Metropole

This part of the analysis uses logistic regressions to study the response of the metropole to a given movement's declaration of independence: rejection or acceptance. It is at this point that the examination shifts focus from the secessionist movement to the central government. Does the metropole exercise its home state veto? Or does it accept the demand for independence? For a secessionist movement this decision is second to none in importance.

The first three models test the core variables in various combinations, and the results are displayed in Table 3.2. These models include

---

[32] Heckman 1976.   [33] Rho was insignificant.
[34] See Beissinger 2002 for a related argument.

Table 3.2 *Response of the metropole*

	Model 1	Model 2	Model 3	Model 4	Model 5	Model 6	Model 7
Nuclear weapons	0.78** (0.39)		0.67* (0.42)	−2.95 (3.80)	1.07** (0.50)	−1.58 (1.19)	1.57*** (0.47)
% Change	9%		13.8%		22.5%		37.4%
Post-1945		1.13** (0.41)					
% Change		9.4%					
Trade			2.84** (1.36)				
% Change			22.6%				
Proto-state	3.72*** (0.67)	3.94*** (0.67)	3.50*** (0.69)	Dropped	4.75*** (0.88)	Dropped	
% Change	35.7%	35.5%	49.2%		60.6%		
Unique unit							4.21*** (0.99)
% Change							58.7%
Administrative level							1.39** (0.32)
% Change							65.2%
Economic value				0.25** (0.12)			
% Change				1%			
Strategic value				−0.92 (1.13)			
% Change							
Prior nation							−0.65 (0.46)
% Change							
Geographic distance	1.33*** (0.35)	1.59*** (0.37)	1.53*** (0.43)	Dropped	2.01** (0.96)		
% Change	15.2%	17.2%	29.4%		37%		

# Other movements	0.13*** (0.03)	0.14*** (0.03)	0.14*** (0.04)	0.36* (0.26)	0.19*** (0.05)	0.31*** (0.09)	0.13*** (0.04)
% Change	8.3%	8.3%	18.5%	2.9%	20.2%	33.8%	7.7%
Democracy	0.08** (0.03)	0.06** (0.03)	0.03 (0.03)	0.41* (0.23)	0.01 (0.06)	0.04 (0.05)	0.04 (0.03)
% Change	13.9%	10%		29.8%			
Belgium (5 obs)					4.51** (1.73)		
% Change					69.8%		
France (36 obs)					−1.86* (1.04)		
% Change					27.2%		
England (73 obs)					−0.63 (0.93)		
% Change							
Russia (52 obs)					−0.71 (1.60)		
% Change							
Colombia (4 obs)					4.41* (2.44)		
% Change					69.2%		
Constant	−6.60*** (0.83)	−7.30*** (0.86)	−6.28*** (0.95)	−14.71** (6.22)	−6.96*** (2.04)	−0.255*** (0.65)	−5.37*** (0.93)
N	393	393	260	54	252	98	233
Wald χ^2	(5) 238.18	(5) 424.11	(6) 166.49	(5) 42.12	(20) 171.80	(3) 33.36	(6) 144.47
Probability $> \chi^2$	0	0	0	0	0	0	0
Pseudo-R^2	0.49	0.5	0.47	0.74	0.5	0.29	0.45
Log-likelihood	−123	−121	−95	−8	−88	−40	−89

Note. Marginal change calculated by moving the variable from low to high while holding the other variables at their mean. The Trade, # Other Movements, and Economic Value variables are calculated by increasing the value from 1 SD below the mean to 1 SD above.

*$p < 0.10$; **$p < 0.05$; ***$p < 0.01$.

all secessionist movements whether or not they corresponded with a proto-state. As such, the variables capturing unique administrative type, administrative level, and prior nations are excluded because they are suitable for comparisons between proto-states. Moreover, the variables measuring economic and strategic value are also excluded because of limited data.

The first model tests the hypotheses regarding nuclear weapons and proto-states. Note that the trade variable is initially excluded on account of limited data, and the post-1945 control variable is removed because its theoretical purpose is to pick up system-level effects that include more precise factors such as nuclear weapons and trade. Overall, the effects of having a proto-state are quite strong, increasing the predicted probability of metropolitan acceptance by 36 percent. The nuclear weapons variable is also significant though the marginal effects are weaker.

In addition, several of the remaining variables are highly significant, though the marginal effects are weaker than with the proto-state variable. Notably, there is a positive relationship between metropolitan acceptance and the number of secessionist movements; this is the opposite of what the deterrence hypothesis predicts.

Model 2 includes a time variable for the post-1945 period. This variable is meant to capture the combined effects of polarity, the territorial integrity norm, the diffusion of nuclear weapons, and the increased trade levels. As such, I exclude the nuclear weapons and trade variables at this stage. The results show that metropolitan acceptance is more likely after 1945, all else equal. Of course, a time variable is a blunt measure and deeper conclusions will have to await the case study chapters. The other results in Model 2 are roughly the same as in Model 1.

The trade variable is introduced in Model 3. The results show that the core variables are all statistically significant. Aside from regime type, the findings are quite similar to the earlier models. In Model 3, metropolitan acceptance is positively correlated with trade volume, offering support for the hypothesis that trading states are more likely to permit secession.

Model 4 includes the variables that quantify the economic and strategic value of the secessionist region. It appears, as Walter argues, that these factors matter less than what is commonly perceived.[35] The

[35] Walter 2009.

variable measuring strategic value is statistically insignificant. Meanwhile, the economic value variable is significant but the sign is in the opposite direction, implying that metropoles are more likely to permit the independence of high-value territories. However, there are limited data for these variables and the model suffers from fewer cases (108 observations). In this reduced set, the proto-state variable now perfectly predicts metropolitan acceptance,[36] but the nuclear weapons variable is rendered insignificant.

I conducted a number of tests to gauge the robustness of my results. Model 5 shows fixed country effects, picking up the potential variation caused by factors unique to individual countries.[37] The marginal effects of proto-states are the strongest here at nearly 61 percent, and the effects of having nuclear weapons increase to 23 percent. Model 6 includes only the secessionist movements that claim territory that is contiguous with the metropole (or within 100 miles). Thus, all geographically distant nations are excluded. In this model, proto-state perfectly predicts metropolitan acceptance. There were twenty-six instances where a metropole permitted the independence of a contiguous group, and in each case the group claimed a proto-state (for example, Norway, Venezuela, and Finland). These results suggest that proto-state status matters greatly for contiguous units.

A closer look at the data helps illuminate the relationship between proto-states and metropolitan acceptance. Although there were numerous cases of proto-states that were denied independence (for example, the Basque Country), there have been only three instances since 1816 where secessionist movements not claiming a proto-state were accepted. Pakistan consisted of a number of proto-states, but it was not one itself. Its rupture with India was extremely violent, but with respect to the UK I coded it as a case of metropolitan acceptance. Rwanda and Burundi constituted a joint administrative unit under Belgium, but they were not individual proto-states when they seceded peacefully in

[36] Since the proto-state variable perfectly predicts acceptance – that is, all accepted cases were proto-states – STATA drops the variable and fifty-two observations in the analysis. The geographic distance variable is dropped for the same reason and two observations are removed.

[37] In this regression, 141 cases were dropped because there was no variation in the outcome. However, most of the dropped states only possessed one movement. Of the dropped states, the outliers were China with sixteen movements and Turkey with ten. Table 3.2 shows the results for five states that are either statistically significant or associated with more than fifty observations.

1962. They were, however, separate kingdoms in the nineteenth century. This small number of cases demonstrates that metropolitan consent for groups that lack a proto-state is a rare occurrence.

The final model includes only those secessionist movements that claim proto-states. Consequently, the variables indicating unique type, administrative level, and prior nations can be tested.[38] The results show that the core variables have a significant impact. Proto-states that are unique in type are significantly more likely to be permitted independence. For these units the probability of acceptance increases by nearly 58 percent. In some of these cases the breakaway region was splitting from a classic binary state: for example, Norway from Sweden, Syria from the United Arab Republic. In others the secessionist territory was an imperial legacy in a class of its own: for example, Papua New Guinea from Australia, Luxembourg from the Netherlands. In only two of these cases have the central government denied secessionist demands: Flanders by Belgium and Republika Sprska by Bosnia and Herzegovina.

The results for the "administrative level" variable indicate that the predicted probability of acceptance for outer units is 55 percent more likely than it is core units. Only 11 percent of the core units were recognized by their metropole. Whereas some forty-two core units were denied independence by their metropole, only five received consent. These five exceptions included Venezuela and Ecuador from Colombia, Singapore from Malaysia, and two core territories that were splitting from binary states: Syria and Slovakia. In contrast, the acceptance rate for outer-level units was 69 percent. Although forty of these territories were denied by the government, eighty-eight were given permission to form their own sovereign state. This is further evidence that administrative status shapes the manner in which states respond.

Overall, the results listed in Table 3.2 are quite supportive of my core theory, but the outcomes for the alternative hypotheses are mixed. The "prior nation" variable shows weak effects and in the wrong direction, implying that prior statehood or secessionism does not increase a proto-state's chance of acceptance. Meanwhile, geographic distance

---

[38] The proto-state variable was excluded since it is now the base category. The variable measuring geographic distance is no longer useful because geographically distant units lacking a proto-state are excluded from the analysis. The economic and strategic value variables are excluded due to limited data, but their results are insignificant when run in separate regressions.

matters greatly, though less than proto-state status. Movements that are geographically distant from the rest of the country have a greater chance of getting their government's acceptance, all else equal. Interestingly, the likelihood of metropolitan permission increases as the number of parallel movements increases. This indicates that states are more inclined to release units in waves, casting some doubt on the standard deterrence hypothesis. Of the remaining hypotheses, only the democracy variable has much support, but the strength of the variable is weak in some of the models.

Stage 3: Secessionist Conflict

The third part of the analysis examines the impact of the independent variables on the likelihood of secessionist conflict. Was there a conflict between the metropole and the secessionist movement the year of the declaration of independence, or either of the two subsequent years? Table 3.3 shows the results from a series of logistic regressions that introduce and utilize variables in the same sequence as in Stage 2.

The first three models test different combinations of the core hypotheses pertaining to the international system. All of the variables are highly significant and show strong marginal effects. The possession of nuclear weapons is inversely (and significantly) related to secessionist conflict, decreasing the predicted probability of conflict by 41 percent in Model 1, and by 18 percent when the trade variable is included and the overall of cases is reduced. The results for the post-1945 variable indicate that secessionist conflict is significantly less likely after World War II. Finally, the results for the trade variable indicate that economically integrated states are less likely to fight secessionist conflicts.

The results for the other variables in Models 1, 2, and 3 are quite interesting. Most importantly, the proto-state variable is now mostly insignificant, implying that administrative status matters less in the conflict stage. Similarly, the variable that counts the number of other secessionist movements is also rendered insignificant; there is no positive or negative correlation between secessionist conflict and the number of secessionist movements subject to the same metropole. Meanwhile, geographic distance remains highly significant, supplying evidence for the hypothesis that colonized nations are less likely to experience secessionist conflict. Finally, the democracy variable shows

Table 3.3 *Secessionist conflict*

	Model 1	Model 2	Model 3	Model 4	Model 5	Model 6	Model 7
Nuclear weapons	−2.25*** (0.45)		−1.24** (0.48)	−1.23* (0.70)	−2.60*** (0.57)	−2.51*** (0.63)	−1.89*** (0.51)
% Change	41.2%		17.8%	29.2%	44.5%	52.5%	30.6%
Post-1945		−0.45*** (0.06)					
% Change		44.5%					
Trade			−2.59** (1.31)				
% Change			13.1%				
Proto-state	−0.21 (0.27)	−0.08* (0.05)	0.15 (0.36)	0.54 (0.49)	−0.90** (0.40)	−0.42 (0.3)	
% Change		10.6%			20%		
Unique unit							−2.74** (1.10)
% Change							24%
Administrative level							−0.58** (0.22)
% Change							36.5%
Economic value				−0.03 (0.03)			
% Change				13.1%			
Strategic value				0.05 (0.05)			
% Change				30.1%			
Prior nation							0.62 (0.39)
% Change							
Geographic distance	−0.99*** (0.30)	−0.22*** (0.05)	−0.67* (0.41)	−0.33 (1.34)	0.84 (0.60)		
% Change	22%	28.4%	10.3%				

# Other movements	0.04 (0.02)	−0.00 (0.00)	−0.06 (0.04)	−0.01 (0.06)	−0.09** (0.04)	0.08** (0.03)	−0.06 (0.05)
% Change					14.5%	12.9%	
Democracy	−0.07*** (0.02)	−0.01** (0.00)	−0.04 (0.03)	−0.05 (0.03)	−0.02 (0.04)	−0.06** (0.02)	−0.05* (0.03)
% Change	33.2%	23.4%				22.3%	19.4%
Turkey (10 obs)					3.43* (1.76)		
% Change					63.7%		
Russia (52 obs)					3.99** (1.48)		
% Change					73.5%		
India (13 obs)					4.14** (1.55)		
% Change					67.2%		
Myanmar (9 obs)					3.07** (1.53)		
% Change					60.5%		
UK (73 obs)					0.32 (1.26)		
% Change							
Constant	1.28*** (0.28)	2.31*** (0.32)	0.75* (0.39)	0.93 (0.65)	−0.48 (1.44)	1.03*** (0.32)	1.93*** (0.57)
N	391	391	260	108	318	234	233
Wald χ^2	(5) 124.09	(5) 148.30	(6) 56.42	(7) 16.97	(34) 148.66	(4) 39.48	(6) 88.28
Probability > χ^2	0	0	0	0	0	0	0
Pseudo-R^2	0.23	0.28	0.19	0.11	0.35	0.12	0.3
Log-likelihood	−205	−192	−118	−66	−140	−140	−102

Note. Marginal change calculated by moving the variable from low to high while holding the other variables at their mean. The Trade, # Other Movements, and EconVal variables are calculated by increasing the value from 1 SD below the mean to 1 SD above.

$*p < 0.10; **p < 0.05; ***p < 0.01.$

strong effects at this stage: secessionist conflict is inversely related to democracy.

Model 4 includes the variables that quantify the economic and strategic value of the secessionist region. Neither variable is statistically significant. Contrary to common wisdom, metropoles do not seem more inclined to fight secessionists in economically or strategically valuable regions. However, there are limited data for these variables and the results may be biased in unforeseen ways.

I tested for robustness in several ways.[39] Model 5 shows fixed country effects, and here nuclear weapons and proto-state are more significant with stronger marginal effects. Meanwhile, the geographic distance variable is now positively correlated with conflict. Model 6 excludes all geographically distant secessionist groups (separated by at least 100 miles of water or foreign territory). In this reduced set the variables regarding nuclear weapons, the number of movements, and democracy remain highly significant. As an additional test (not displayed in the table), I trichotomized the dependent variable into 0 (fewer than 25 deaths), 1 (between 25 and 999 deaths), and 2 (1000 or more deaths). A multivariate regression produced similar effects.

Model 7 conducts comparisons between proto-states and includes the variables that test for administrative uniqueness, administrative level, and prior nationalism. The results provide further confirmation that administrative organization matters. Proto-states that are unique in type are 24 percent less likely to have a secessionist conflict directly after a declaration of independence. Meanwhile, higher-level units are 22 percent less likely than core units to resort to arms. As before, the variable testing for endogeneity, "prior nation," is statistically insignificant. In this model the democracy variable is significantly and inversely related to conflict.

What then is the relationship between the two main dependent variables? I have argued that a necessary condition for secessionist conflict is that a nation demands independence and their metropole denies it. There are no cases in the dataset that falsify this claim – that is, all conflict cases were denied independence. However, denial is not a sufficient condition for conflict. There were 108 cases of metropolitan denial that did not yield conflict. Of these, forty-five were proto-states (for example, Scotland, Faeroe Islands), and sixty-three were not (for

---

[39] A probit model reveals similarly significant results.

example, the Lozi, Maori). It is possible that some of these groups failed to anticipate how their government would respond to a declaration of independence, and, once denied, lacked the will to fight. Of course, many of these groups may have been aiming for other goals, be they symbolic or political.

I checked for potential selection effects in two ways. First, there might be some unmeasured characteristic, such as war propensity, of each dyad (metropole and secessionist movement) that informs the metropole's response to the movement's declaration and, subsequently, affects the likelihood of conflict. I tested for this possibility using a Heckman selection model and found no evidence of selection bias.[40] Second, I excluded all cases of metropolitan acceptance and reran Models 1 and 7. In this reduced set, all of the administrative organization variables are insignificant, implying that these variables do not have an impact on the chance of conflict when we compare between denied cases. In other words, administrative status matters for metropolitan response, but it does not shape the subsequent likelihood of conflict for the nations that received a negative response.

There were 120 cases in the dataset where a secessionist movement was permitted independence and conflict did not occur. Only three of these cases – Pakistan, Rwanda, and Burundi – were not proto-states. Of course, there were seventy-two cases where a proto-state had a conflict with its metropole, ranging from the numerous engagements between Myanmar and its nation-based proto-states, to India's clash with its internal nations, to the many occasions where an empire fought an antisecessionist war with a colonial unit. All of these independence claims had been denied by their sovereigns. It seems that proto-state status is not always a ticket to independence – even when the territory is an outer-level unit – and many nations have attempted to seize their sovereignty.

Importantly, the nuclear weapons, post-1945, and trade variables were consistently significant in Table 3.3. This provides support for the international system hypotheses, and it suggests that these factors

---

[40] I first used Sartori's (2003) method that does not require an exclusion restriction and found similar results, although the estimates failed robustness checks. I then used a Heckman Probit model using the number of other movements as the exclusion restriction, but rho was insignificant and I concluded that there was no evidence of selection bias.

matter at both Stage 2 (metropolitan response) and Stage 3 (secessionist conflict). Relative to the domestic administrative variables, these
variables appear to shape metropolitan behavior even after they have
responded to a declaration of independence. The hand of the international system shapes both the response of metropoles to these declarations and the chances that they will fight over them.

Conclusion

The preceding analysis tested a number of different variables across a
set of secessionist outcomes. The purpose was to study secessionist patterns in the aggregate, build support for (or eliminate) hypotheses, and
identify unexpected patterns in the data.[41] This advances the overall
study and prepares the way for the qualitative research in the subsequent chapters.

The results supported the core theory of the book. The rate of
state birth increased dramatically after 1945 along with a commensurate and statistically significant increase in the rate of peaceful secession. Moreover, the findings supported the core hypotheses regarding nuclear weapons, trade levels, and the administrative structure of
states. Metropoles that possess nuclear weapons are more likely to permit secession and less likely to fight a conflict over the issue. Similarly,
states that are highly integrated into the global economy are also more
likely to permit independence and less likely to fight. However, the
overall effects of the domestic administration variables were slightly
different insofar as these mattered greatly where metropolitan response
is concerned but less with respect to the likelihood of conflict – that is,
matter at Stage 2 but not Stage 3. In sum, all of the core variables
are important when states respond to a declaration, but, once denial is
chosen, the importance of administrative architecture recedes.

The analysis yielded interesting results regarding the choice of secessionism – that is, the decision by a stateless nation to declare independence. As depicted in Figure 3.4, this moment occurs prior to the
response of the metropole and the initiation of conflict. Notably, the
factor that appears to have the biggest impact on the choice of secession is the sum of the number of other movements subject to the same

---

[41] See Lieberman 2005 for a discussion of mixed (or nested) approaches.

metropole. This finding supports those claims in the literature regarding the tidal effects of secessionism.[42] One interpretation is that this variable picks up local factors that incite groups to make a bid for independence, and such bids are clustered. Indeed, the results in Stage 2 imply that metropoles tend to permit independence in waves. There are likely feedback effects between the anticipated response and the choice over secessionism. This finding casts some doubt on the standard deterrence argument.

I found little evidence of endogeneity and selection effects throughout the model. Prior sovereignty or secessionism was only significant where the choice of secessionism is concerned; it did not matter at all when metropoles respond and decide whether to fight. A history of nationhood and/or nationalism may render secessionism more likely, but on its own it does not increase the chances that the metropole will permit independence. In addition, robustness checks using Heckman selection models found no evidence for selection effects between the different stages. It is possible that the anticipation of metropolitan response dissuades many potential secessionists, but probing for such nonevents will have to await the qualitative chapters.

I found no evidence for the common belief that states are more likely to fight over valuable territory. Admittedly, these results are based on limited data for the economic and strategic value of secessionist regions, and it is possible that governments value territory in idiosyncratic ways that are difficult to capture in a large-N analysis. However, these findings are consistent with my core argument: the value of territory is less important than other factors such as the need for states to downsize in an organized manner.

The results help clarify the relationship between metropolitan response and conflict. I have conjectured that metropolitan denial is a necessary condition for secessionist conflict, and the results support this claim. All cases of conflict included a nation that was denied independence. Nevertheless, not all denied cases end in violence so denial is clearly not a sufficient condition. The response of the state is a pivotal moment in the life of a secessionist movement.

The results provided evidence for the importance of geographic distance and democracy. All else being equal, geographically distant units are more likely to receive a favorable outcome from their metropole.

---

[42] Beissinger 2002; Weyland 2009.

Perhaps sundered territory provides metropoles with a way to release units even after controlling for administrative distinctions. Curiously, geographically distant units were not more likely to declare independence. However, regime type seems to matter, especially at the conflict stage. Secessionism is slightly more likely in autocracies and secessionist conflict is less likely in democracies. This is an important finding, but of course it is unclear why democracy would have these effects. I return to this relationship in the chapters to come.

There remain a number of ways in which this theory can be researched qualitatively. First, and crucially, there is the question as to whether changing conditions in the post-1945 period have affected metropoles in the way that I theorize. To what extent have a decline in conquest and changing notions regarding the economic value of peripheral units affected the cost-benefit calculation of holding territory? My analysis of both the British and Russian/Soviet metropoles sheds light on the matter. Second, this research is based largely on the argument that the administrative architecture of states actually structures their response to secessionism. In subsequent chapters I explore the ways in which metropoles conceptualize their political space, and I examine whether the selective effects of proto-states hold out in reality. All three of my case studies – UK, Russia/Soviet Union, and India – are metropoles with highly articulated internal structures, and they allow me to test my hypotheses. Finally, in the subsequent chapters I investigate two alternative explanations that showed strong statistical results: the tidal effects of secession(ism) and the consequences of regime type.

4 | The Expansion and Contraction of the British Empire

> We seem, as it were, to have conquered and peopled half the world in a fit of absence of mind.
>
> – John Robert Seeley[1]

The UK is a touchstone case in this study. Not only is its expansion and subsequent contraction consistent with the global pattern, but more than any other state it helped set that pattern. More than 15 percent of the secessionist movements were directed at the British metropole, and 32 percent of the proto-states were part of its administrative structure.[2] Beyond its sheer size, the British metropole is a useful case for several reasons. First, it existed over the entire time period, so the response of the metropole to secessionist demands in the pre-1945 era can be compared with the years that followed. Second, it emerged as a victor from World War II. Although battered and forced into a somewhat subordinate role with the USA, the UK remained a great power. This is an important consideration given that it permitted the secession of so many units in the post-1945 period. Unlike the Ottomans or the Austro-Hungarians, the contraction of the British realm cannot be simply explained away as the consequence of military defeat. Third, the metropole classified and categorized its units in a variety of ways. This articulation is useful for studying the effects of precedent setting.

The structure of this chapter follows a pattern that will recur in the subsequent case study chapters. I begin with a detailed description of the different types of British proto-states and the patterns in secessionism and secessionist conflict. This discussion gives context to my previous talk of secessionist movement and proto-state data. These are the phenomena of interest and it is important that the complexity

---

[1] Seeley 1883, 12.
[2] Of a total of 4576 secessionist movement years, 693 were connected to the UK, and the metropole accounts for 12 153 of the 38 556 proto-state years.

of British administrative design and volume of secessionism be classi-fied and made explicit. The remainder of the chapter uses this material to explore theoretical arguments. I first examine the manner in which a changing international system has influenced London's response to secessionism. I then study the effects of administrative organization on secessionist outcomes. I finish by looking at tidal effects and the conse-quences of regime type, two alternative explanations that were shown to be important in the quantitative analysis.

Although this chapter provides a qualitative complement to the quantitative work in the previous chapter, it maintains a fairly macro perspective. This is inevitable given the size and scope of the British metropole. Where possible I give the topic a closer look and try to pull apart specific instances of secessionism. Both in this chapter and the next two case studies I provide a vignette, or blow-up case, that explores a single movement or set of movements. In this chapter I dis-cuss the island of Bougainville, a fascinating case in a number of ways. Attention is given to not only how the secessionist movement started and fared, but also to the intricacies and importance of administrative design and selection.

Proto-states, Secessionism, and Conflict

Proto-states

The British Empire was the largest and most widespread in history, and it was certainly true that the sun never set on the British flag. A graph of the British proto-states depicts the expansion and contraction of this political system (see Figure 4.1). The metropole began the period in 1816 with thirty-four proto-states and ended with ten in 2011.[3] It peaked with 114 proto-states in 1893/1894 and maintained an average of 106 until 1945 when the number began to drop precipitously.

Although this expansion and contraction is altogether consistent with the patterns in state size over the past 200 years, it is important to point out that the number of proto-states does not correlate perfectly with the size of a given state.[4] It is possible for a large state to orga-nize its internal units in such a way that none of them would count

[3] See Appendix B for a list of British proto-states.
[4] See Lake and O'Mahony 2004 for a discussion of state size.

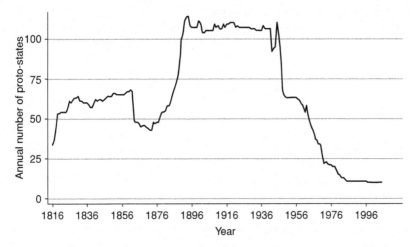

Figure 4.1 Number of British proto-states.

as proto-states – that is, none were geographically distant, indirectly ruled, nationally distinct, or recently transferred. For example, the dip in the number of British proto-states in the 1860s is not on account of a reduction in state size – on the contrary, the metropole was expanding during this period – but rather the transition from indirect to direct rule in numerous units in Africa, Southeast Asia, and, primarily, South Asia.[5] Therefore, the strength of the correlation between the number of proto-states and overall size depends on the internal construction of the state and the extent to which it is administratively articulated. As it turns out, the design of the British system developed somewhat organically and in reaction to the needs of the metropole.

I identified seven different types of British proto-states between 1816 and 2011 (see Table 4.1). The first type was the crown colony. The metropole began with twenty-five such units in 1816. The last set, including Montserrat, Turks and Caicos, Cayman Islands, British Virgin Islands, and the Falkland Islands, were reclassified in 2002 as politically internal overseas territories. In most cases, these units counted because they were more than 100 miles distant from British territory, although they sometimes counted because they were transferred units or else accorded special national distinction. These units were categorized as politically external, and they typically experienced direct rule.

[5] The reasons for this development are interesting, and I return to them later.

Table 4.1 *Types of British proto-states*

Type	Name	Geographically Distant?	Political External?	Indirect Rule?
1	Crown Colonies	yes	yes	no
2	Protectorates	yes	yes	typically
3	Viceroyalty	yes	yes	no
4	Overseas Territories	yes	no	no
5	Crown Dependencies	no	no	typically
6	Internal Countries	no	no	no
7	Dominions	yes	yes	yes

Note. Geographic distance implies at least 150 miles of noncontiguous territory from the core.

The second type of proto-state was the protectorate, a politically external unit that was generally (though not always) ruled indirectly. The British had five of these units in 1816: Hyderabad, Rewa, Travancore, Mysore, and the Ionian Islands. The metropole expanded to include more than sixty of them in the early twentieth century. However, by 1984, the last of them (Brunei) seceded peacefully. The use of these units developed alongside the crown colony, and, in some sense, was a residual type. Whereas many territories with foreign populations were "ruled from London through a governor and collectively styled crown colonies... still other areas, which it was not thought convenient to rule directly, were termed protectorates."[6] Depending on the geographic location and the local political apparatus, the government often determined that it was more cost-effective to merely appoint a "resident" and control the unit's foreign policy. "The supreme virtue of this eclectic approach is that it allowed the politicians at home to reconcile voracious expansionism with fiscal parsimony and free-trade economics."[7] In practice, however, many of these units were *de facto* directly ruled.

Although these first two types account for the majority of the British proto-states, there are five additional types. Type three is a category with only unit: the Viceroyalty of India from 1858 to 1947, "a possession so rich, so populous, so enormous, and so prestigious that it

[6] Henige 1970, 78.   [7] Darwin 1998, 64.

continued to the end of its colonial status to be treated as a category of its own."[8] The year 1858, when India commenced to be ruled directly by London rather than through the East India Company, marked the beginning of the viceroyalty, a unique type within the imperial system.[9] Its status reflected the great importance placed on the territory and the fact that the Viceroy was a sovereign of sorts over the various princely states and polities of India. Given that the Viceroy was always appointed by the British government, I coded India as having direct rule. Importantly, however, subordinate to India were a host of second- and third-order units (colonies and protectorates) that were often ruled indirectly.

The fourth type of proto-state was the overseas territory. Beginning with the British Overseas Territory Act of 2002, dependent colonies were reclassified as politically internal units. Thus, London was effectively assigning full citizenship to the overseas territories.[10] Although there are fourteen of these territories, only Montserrat, Turks and Caicos, Cayman Islands, British Virgin Islands, St. Helena, and the Falkland Islands qualify as proto-states on account of size and population criteria.

The fifth type of unit is the crown dependency, and of these there are three: Jersey, Guernsey, and the Isle of Man. These are politically internal units with high levels of autonomy and national distinction. Their relationship to the crown stretches back to feudal times. Although Guernsey is actually too small to count as a proto-state, the status of it and Jersey remained constant between 1816 and 2011. Meanwhile, crown dependency status was returned to the Isle of Man in 1828 and full indirect rule was granted in 1961. Since the category was never singular, the secession of a unit at any time would have constituted a precedence issue for the others.

The sixth type refers to the internal countries of Northern Ireland, Scotland, and Wales. Technically, England is a member of this category, but it is not counted given that it is the core of the metropole. These units are politically internal but given national distinction. Wales and Scotland count as proto-states over the entire time period. Ireland was a proto-state from 1816 until 1922 when it seceded. Northern Ireland,

---

[8] Henige 1970, 77.

[9] Prior to 1858, I coded India as a type 1 unit, along with other similarly arranged British units.

[10] Doyle 1986 refers to this move as crossing the Caracalla Threshold.

the remainder of the former British territory, was a proto-state from that point onward.

The final type was the dominion. Beginning with Canada in 1869, a special category consisted of a set of colonies that were given dominion status and accorded responsible government (indirect rule). For this group "strategic dependence, demographic links, cultural ties, and economic attraction coexisted amicably with strong provincial identities within the capacious framework of responsible government."[11] Other members of this type included Australia, New Zealand, Newfoundland, and the Cape Colony. Whenever such a unit was a lone dominion – that is, it was the only member of its kind – as Canada was for periods of time between 1869 and 1892, I coded it as not constituting an issue of precedence.

One final point pertains to the British Commonwealth. Although the organization represents an arrangement that is partly hierarchical, it is nonetheless intersovereign. The relationship between the units is conducted on the basis of formal sovereign equality. The Commonwealth is best considered as that of a confederation or perhaps a league.[12] However, as I discuss later, the Commonwealth plays an important role in the contraction of the British Empire and its expectations regarding seceding units.

Secessionism

It is not surprising that the UK faced numerous secessionist movements given its many proto-states. Figure 4.2 illustrates the number of secessionist movements over time.[13] The total number of British secessionist movement years was 693, which is 15 percent of the total (4576) around the world between 1816 and 2011. Notably, this percentage is significantly less than the share of British proto-states (32 percent), suggesting that secessionism itself was less likely in the British realm. The long-term trend shows a gradual increase in secessionism in the

---

[11] Darwin 1998, 65.

[12] Elazar defines a league as having "loose but permanent linkage for limited-purposes without common government but with some joint body or secretariat" and a confederation as having "strong self-governing constituent polities permanently linked by loose, limited-purpose common government" (Elazar 1998, 8).

[13] See Appendix A for a complete list of British secessionist movements.

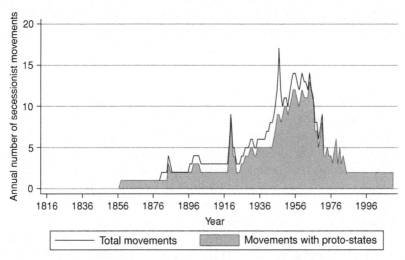

Figure 4.2 British secessionist movements.

late nineteenth century, followed by distinct upticks after World War I, in the 1930s, and after World War II. The total number of movements then began to decline in the late 1960s. Surprisingly, I found no evidence of a formal secessionist movement across the realm prior to the onset of Irish Republicanism in 1858.

All told, the UK faced a total of seventy-five secessionist movements over the entire time period. Secessionism occurred largely among the crown colonies and protectorates. India, the sole Type 3 unit, had a secessionist movement from 1885 to 1947. Ireland, Northern Ireland, and Scotland – all Type 6 units – also sponsored secessionist movements. In fact, the Irish and Scottish are the only movements the metropole has faced in the twenty-first century. Most of the dominions eventually seceded and formed sovereign states; the notable exception is Newfoundland. Finally, none of the overseas territories (Type 4) or crown dependencies (Type 5) have declared independence.

What about secessionist movements from nations that did not cohere with proto-states? As Figure 4.2 illustrates, most secessionist movements claimed proto-states. However, there were eleven exceptions: (1) Sudan from 1881 to 1886; (2) Israel from 1897 to 1949; (3) Pakistan from 1940 to 1947; (3) the Karen State from 1946 to 1948; (4) Baluchistan in 1947; (5) Buganda from 1953 to 1962; (6) Anguilla from 1967 to 1971; (7) Barotseland from 1946 to 1964;

(8) Travancore in 1947; (9) the Shan State from 1942 to 1945; (10) Nagaland in 1947; and (11) Khalistan in 1947.

Conflict

Between 1816 and 2011 the British metropole fought a total of ten secessionist conflicts. In general, these conflicts are distributed somewhat evenly across the time period. Notably, the number of conflicts remains fairly low even as secessionism soars in the early postwar period. The most discernible correspondence between secessionism and conflicts occurred shortly after World War I when a number of proto-states attempted to secede and met with British resistance. Finally, the metropole has only fought three secessionist conflicts after 1945: (1) Kenya from 1952 to 1956; (2) Malaya from 1948 to 1957; and (3) Northern Ireland from 1971 to 1991.

The International System

This section focuses on the external (or international) factors affecting British decisions regarding secession. The discussion will be structured around a set of questions. To what extent have changing international conditions affected the willingness of metropoles to permit secession? Did the end of World War II constitute a sea change in this respect? Did changing perceptions regarding the threat of conquest and the value of large economic units play a role? Have states in the postwar period been more amenable to secession because they anticipated continued relations with the emerging state?

The Pre-1945 Period

The expansion of the British Empire has been documented and studied both on its own and as part of larger investigations into imperialism. As such, the dynamics that drove British expansion are well known, if still somewhat debated. Although it is not the purpose in this study to enter into that debate, it is nevertheless useful to identify the core factors that drove expansion as they can help shed light on the post-1945 period of contraction.

In his historical analysis of empires, Michael Doyle groups competing explanations into three categories. The first, which he calls metrocentric theories, locate the cause of expansion in the dominant society. This view was particularly popular in the nineteenth and early twentieth centuries, and exponents such as Vladimir Lenin and Joseph Schumpeter sought to explain expansionism as either the result of class struggle or social-militaristic atavisms.[14] The second type of explanation, or pericentric theories, locates the cause of expansion in the periphery. In this regard, it is sociopolitical conditions in the periphery that incites the would-be empire to expand. These theories became popular in the mid twentieth century, and an early example was given by John Gallagher and Ronald Robinson, who conceived of imperial expansion as a policy option for core states to pursue when alternative methods of exploitation were less cost-effective.[15] Finally, the third category locates the source of expansion in the international system itself and contends that it is interstate competition that compels core states to acquire territory. Prominent theorists here include Benjamin Cohen and David Fieldhouse.[16]

After persuasively arguing that none of the three types can independently provide a satisfactory explanation for imperial expansion, Doyle offers a composite theory. Essentially, political expansion happens when strong, internally differentiated states run across weaker and exploitable polities in the context of a competitive international system.[17] In particular, he draws attention to the multipolar system that existed in the late nineteenth and early twentieth centuries and argues that this configuration compelled the lead states to seek formal rule over the periphery. Whereas unipolar or bipolar systems permit stable collaborations – whether on a sovereign or informal basis – between a peripheral unit and a given metropole, multipolar environments allow for those peripheral units to play metropoles off one another more easily.[18] Thus, each metropole has greater incentive to take formal control over other territories.

Doyle's composite explanation for the form of control that stronger polities take over weaker ones has been extended by other theorists.

---

[14] Lenin 1939; Schumpeter 1950.   [15] Gallagher and Robinson 1953.

[16] Cohen 1973; Fieldhouse 1961.

[17] Tony Smith combined metrocentric with pericentric theory in his notion of the "two calendars": understanding imperialism requires an appreciation of the rate of change in both the core and periphery (Smith 1981, 85–86). Taking a different but rather metrocentric approach, Snyder located the cause of imperial expansion in domestic politics (Snyder 1991).

[18] Doyle 1986, 343–344.

For example, Jeffry Frieden argues that imperial relations were likely in the late nineteenth century when peripheral expropriation was easy and cooperation among the major powers was low.[19] Conversely, when cooperation among lead states increases and expropriation becomes more difficult, as it has in the late twentieth century, then imperial relations become less likely. David Lake draws similar conclusions in his analysis of the many political relationships that exist on the spectrum running between complete anarchy and perfect hierarchy.[20] The upshot of this discussion is that conditions were ripe for political expansion in the late nineteenth and early twentieth centuries. The British metropole was blessed with the right internal features, the global periphery was largely exploitable, and the competitive pressures of the international system compelled states such as the UK to acquire territory. Not taking or actually giving up territory meant that another power might take it. Moreover, the accession of peripheral units guaranteed that resources and goods from that region could be securely extracted.

The period running from approximately the 1870s until World War I constitutes a particularly expansionist phase of the years under investigation. This was the so-called new imperialism or scramble for Africa, in which the core powers moved quickly to lay claim to the remaining areas of the world that they regarded as *terra nullius*, in much of Africa, the Pacific, and along the rim of the Indian Ocean.[21] This is the era to which Doyle is mostly referring.

However, it is important to note that the earlier period from 1816 onward was also a time of British expansion. The main difference between these periods had to do with the form of control. In the earlier era, the British often engaged in both informal (also known as unofficial) empire and formal (but indirect) rule. The difference between these concepts lies in whether the weaker party retains sovereignty. Informal empire was a loose term that described the London's practice of interacting economically with other (weaker) sovereign states. Essentially, the UK used its superior military power to back up its economic contracts with the occasional show of force. As the British saw it, free trade required the occasional demonstration of power to ensure

---

[19] Frieden 1994.   [20] Lake 1999.

[21] There were a significant number of states in these areas that were not regarded as sovereign equals by the great powers. See Griffiths and Butcher 2013 and Butcher and Griffiths 2015 for a discussion.

that markets remained open and contracts were fulfilled. When back-
ing his policies, Lord Palmerston put it as follows:

These half-civilized Governments such as those of China, Portugal, or South
America, all require a dressing down every eight or ten years to keep them
in order. Their minds are too shallow to receive an impression that will last
longer than some such period and warning is of little use. They care little
for words and they must not only see the stick but actually feel it on their
shoulders before they yield to that argument which brings conviction.[22]

The pejorative undertones aside, Palmerston's comments illustrate an
important point: during the first half of the nineteenth century, London could often pursue its economic policies without the accession of
peripheral regions.[23] The metropole still engaged in accession, both
indirectly with its protectorates and directly with its crown colonies,
but the interstate rivalries of the late 1800s had not yet arrived. To use
Doyle's terms, there were both metrocentric and pericentric forces driving British expansion, but the third element – systemic competition –
was largely absent.[24]

The cause of change in the late nineteenth century was interstate
rivalry. As Lawrence James writes, "there was little that was novel
about this phenomenon [the new imperialism] save its frenzied pace
and the participation of Germany, Italy, the USA, and Japan, states
which had previously avoided overseas expansion."[25] Coupled with
the arrival of new powers was a reduction in free trade beginning in
the 1870s. London's best response in this environment was to engage in
increasingly formalized types of accession.[26] This competitive process
possessed elements of the prisoner's dilemma; the conquest or accession of territory was not always the best outcome, but it was better
than permitting a peer competitor to seize the territory in question.[27]

The result of this international competition was that the UK
expanded dramatically in two different ways. In a horizontal sense,
it reached further out to bring more and more territories under its
flag. It was that behavior, along with the actions of other powers,

---

[22] James 1994, 174.   [23] Lugard 1893, 651.
[24] Doyle argues that prior to the scramble for Africa and the entrance of Germany
and other states into the colonial game, the global periphery was dominated by
a single pole (the UK) even though Europe was multipolar (Doyle 1986).
[25] James 1994, 201.   [26] Curzon 1892; Parliamentary Papers 1886.
[27] Fazal 2007.

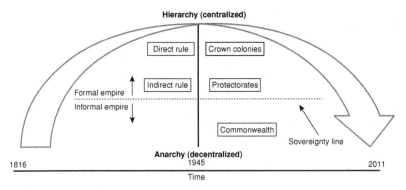

Figure 4.3 Historical arc of British rule.

which effectively brought all of the previously uncounted landmass outside Antarctica into the formal interstate system by the early years of the twentieth century. However, in a vertical sense, London also intensified its relationships by making them more hierarchical (see Figure 4.3). Informal relationships become formal, and the weaker polities forfeited their juridical sovereignty and exited the system. Likewise, indirect relationships became direct as the metropole increasingly took over control of its units.[28] Both of these patterns are depicted in Figure 4.1, where the number of British proto-states increased even as some ceased to qualify as proto-states because of the increased directness of political rule. Although many territories jumped directly from informal to direct rule as Egypt did in 1882, others traversed all three categories. The Transvaal existed as a sovereign state beneath the very shadow of the British Empire until it was annexed in 1881 on an indirect basis; later it was the fear of German encroachment from Southwest Africa, among other causes, that compelled the British to bring the Boers completely under direct rule.[29]

If international conditions compelled the British metropole to expand in the pre-1914 era, the interwar years placed matters in a holding pattern. Although the UK was the only true global power by the early 1920s – the other lead states were either in disarray or else in isolation – it was now faced with nascent nationalist movements and an uncertain international political climate. The competitive pressures to acquire territory had slackened, although they began to return

---

[28] Platt 1968.   [29] Boyce 1990, 75.

in the 1930s. Meanwhile, the cost of holding many territories had increased.

At the end of the war in 1918, London encountered secessionist movements in Palestine, India, and Ireland, and over the next decade it faced a wave of independence demands stretching from the home islands to distant colonial possessions. Although the origins of these movements varied a great deal, there are two factors that are common among many of them. The first was the perception of a weakened state on account of the war and the feeling among secessionists that the time was ripe. This was the case with Ireland, a movement that began in the late 1800s but gathered steam after the war. The second factor was the rhetoric and ideology of both nationalism and the concept of self-determination. This had clear importance with the internal countries of Ireland and Scotland, and it had caught the imagination of the educated strata in various overseas territories. This was the case in Egypt and most noticeably in India, where "after 1919 the pace of India's march towards self-rule quickened, gathering momentum, which simultaneously increased the impatience of nationalists and frightened conservatives in India and Britain."[30] The British-educated Congress-elite who had long imbibed the notion that education would lead to enlightenment were further emboldened in the wake of World War I by the Wilsonian emphasis on the principle of self-determination.[31]

How did London respond to these calls for independence? Although morally infused sympathy existed among a portion of British society, the metropole could little afford to casually give up territory. Its general response was to thwart secessionism where it could and, as a result, it fought five secessionist conflicts between 1918 and 1939. Only Afghanistan and Ireland prevailed immediately in these interwar conflicts and acquired sovereignty. The Irish case was particularly hard-fought, but despite Prime Minister David Lloyd George's position that Ireland was as vital to the UK as the confederate states had been to the USA, Ireland seceded with all but its northern counties. Notably, the Sinn Féin leadership accepted dominion status as part of the bargain, though it later abolished the associated executive position, the Governor-General, in 1936 and formally withdrew from the

[30] James 1994, 415.   [31] Manela 2007.

Commonwealth in 1947. The remaining cases of conflict were won, at least initially, by the British in Egypt, India, and Iraq.[32]

The main exception to the British response was to permit sovereignty in those cases where the emerging state would remain partially subordinate – a sovereign unit in a semi-hierarchical relationship. This was clearly the pattern with the dominions, although Newfoundland alone among this group chose to give up responsible government and its dominion status in 1934 and once more become a crown colony; this unusual decision was reversed in 1949 when Newfoundland left British rule to become a province of Canada.

Although a number of secessionist movements would endure beyond World War II in a nonviolent manner, Egypt and Iraq seceded peacefully in the 1930s. Egypt regained in 1937 the sovereignty it had lost in 1882. Whereas it had been indirectly ruled by London since 1922, the gains from full sovereignty included admission to the League of Nations and control over foreign policy. Although there were signs of nationalist sentiment prior to World War I, the movement intensified after the war. The British granted semi-autonomy in 1922, but many nationalist leaders wanted more. Young educated Egyptians such as Gamal Nasser and Anwar Sadat took part in repeated demonstrations that were generally organized by the Wafd, Egypt's largest political party. The most violent chapter in this struggle occurred early on in 1919, when about 1500 Egyptians died in more than eight weeks of fighting.[33] With Edmund Allenby's concession of self-rule in 1922, tension was reduced but not extinguished. In fact, as his critics charged, Allenby's olive branch merely placed negotiations on the slippery slope that ultimately ended with the Anglo-Egyptian Treaty of 1936. Egypt had finally and just barely regained its sovereignty, but London retained control over the Suez Canal, its garrisons and air bases in Egypt, and its naval base at Alexandria. In short, it had salvaged what it most needed: control over a highly strategic water passage and an alliance with Egypt to back it up.[34]

Iraq's path to independence followed a similar route. It too fought a secessionist conflict with the British metropole early on and it too had kept up the pressure throughout the 1920s. Iraq had been formed

---

[32] The UK fought and won secessionist conflicts in both Egypt and Iraq in the early 1920s; however, both territories would secede in the 1930s.

[33] James 1994, 389.

[34] For the Egyptians, the alliance was especially attractive given Mussolini's recent invasion of Ethiopia.

under the British during World War I after being seized from the Ottomans. It was mostly indirectly ruled until 1932 when it joined the League of Nations and became independent. As with Egypt, the chief factors that excited Iraqi nationalism were the notion of self-determination and anger over the British presence. Like Egypt, the Iraqi effort had over time worn down British resolve. However, it was also easier for the British to release Iraq given it lacked the strategic value of Egypt or Palestine, although the Anglo-Iraqi Treaty of 1930 preserved British military bases and transit routes in the new state.

In sum, the UK worked to retain territory where it could and gave it up where it must. India was the classic example of forestalling the inevitable. With its well-developed nationalist movement, vast population, and relative distance from London, it was considered by many to be only a matter of time before India seceded. Despite this awareness, the British metropole played for time with vague promises of future devolution. It could not grant India the same dominion status that it had Canada or Australia. Its value as a territory and the fear that it would be less likely to hew closely to British hegemony made this impossible. India was too thoroughly integrated militarily and economically with the UK. Unlike the dominions, "India met the costs of an Imperial garrison comprising one-third of the British army, as well as supporting a colonial army of its own available for Imperial service."[35] Dominion status was premised on the notion of cultural kinship that was presumed to only be found in the settler colonies. Moreover, dominion status would require that the Indian Congress construct a federation, and many of the vital Indian princely states, as well as Bengal and the Punjab, were beyond its control. The project, in essence, was too risky because India might follow the path of Ireland, and it was far too valuable to lose. "Whatever settlement was reached, Britain could never permit India the right to neutrality implicit in dominion status. To have done so in the international situation of the mid 1930s would have been suicidal."[36]

The Post-1945 Period

The strategic calculations that had long constrained British policy faded with the end of World War II. Several key factors led to this change. First, the international pressures driving states to acquire

---

[35] Darwin 1998, 78.   [36] James 1994, 421.

territory had disappeared. Both superpowers espoused strong anticolonial ideologies. "The dominance of the Soviet Union and the United States that took shape soon after World War II awarded primacy in the international military order to two powers that were rhetorically anticolonial, despite their own imperial legacies."[37] The USA had made clear during World War II that it was not fighting to rebuild the British Empire. Meanwhile, the Soviet Union preyed on examples of British brutality for propaganda purposes; in 1952 a Soviet paper "published a photograph of Mau Mau suspects with the caption: 'Here are two members of the Mau Mau organization, manacled like slaves. . . . They fought to liberate Kenya from the imperialist yoke, and for this they were regarded as bandits.'"[38]

Instead of acquiring territory in a formal manner, the USA and the Soviet Union sought instead to create spheres of influence and relationships of informal rule.

After World War II the doctrines of self-determination and national independence became tools of struggle in the Cold War, as the United States and the Soviet Union vied for influence over the emerging anticolonial movements of the Third World . . . the United States . . . followed a complex policy intended to court pro-Western independence movements, prevent the rise of anti-Western movements for national liberation, and to facilitate, in some regions, the transformation of West European formal empires into informal empires.[39]

In that regard, the Soviet threat actually hastened British devolution in many of its former territories.[40] The prospect that emerging states would become battlegrounds of Cold War ideology had a strong impact on policy. Whereas the British metropole had initially set out to comprehensively transition its units into well-functioning democratic states – in some cases it was calculated that the process would take decades – by 1948 it was becoming clear that delay could embolden potential and actual communist movements in these territories. By favoring the local faction that was on the right side of the Cold War, and granting independence, the metropole aimed to rescue many of these territories from communism. Thus, the importance of combating communism ended up trumping the American prerogative for ending empire; anticommunist movements seceded quickly while

---

[37] Kahler 1997, 288.   [38] James 1994, 535.
[39] Parrott 1997, 16.   [40] Cabinet Papers, *Kenya*, February 8, 1962.

communist movements were thwarted. "In the American mind anti-Communism always prevailed over anti-imperialism and thus gave the British Empire, at least, an extended lease on life."[41]

This tendency provides evidence for Doyle's argument that bipolar systems yield informal rule since the dominant faction in a peripheral unit could not easily switch allegiance to the other pole.

Since the periphery was ruled by either one domestic faction or another, associated with one metropole or the other, the stability of international alignments was reinforced by the domestic costs of change. Since the faction out of power in each periphery would attempt to establish links to the metropole not already linked to its governing collaborators, a change of allegiance would tend to require a domestic "revolution."[42]

As early as 1948, British policy began to "concentrate on the cultivation of the most influential native populations, who could be trusted to take over the reins of government in the empire's successor states."[43]

This focus on fighting communism helps explain the secessionist civil war in Malaya, one of only three such conflicts that the British fought in the post-1945 period. The chief antagonist is this conflict, which lasted from 1948 until formal secession in 1957, was the Malaysian National Liberation Army, the military wing of the Malaysian Communist Party (MCP). Although Malaya had negotiated a future independence with London in 1948, the MCP desired a communist state and began an insurgency to obtain it.[44] Because the aims of the MCP represented a less desirable future Malaya, one that was communist, the metropole chose denial. "While committed to future Malayan self-determination, Britain was prepared in 1948 to fight an extended campaign (euphemistically called an 'emergency' to avoid charges of colonial oppression) against local Communist guerrillas."[45]

In all, the advent of the Cold War and threat of Soviet nuclear and military attack shifted priorities. Prime Minister Clement Atlee signaled a growing skepticism over the value of the colonies when he said, "We shall have to consider the British Isles as an easterly extension of a strategic arc the center of which is the American continent more than as a power looking Eastwards through the Mediterranean and the East."[46] The Global Strategy of 1950 formalized this view by

---

[41] Louis 1998, 330.   [42] Doyle 1986, 343.   [43] James 1994, 539.
[44] Clayton 1998, 296.   [45] James 1994, 543.   [46] Clayton 1998, 294.

emphasizing the American nuclear umbrella and bomber squadrons based in Britain. Thus, it became clear quite early in the Cold War that British grand strategy was shifting from a reliance on territorial possession and manpower to one that emphasized the increasing importance of nuclear weaponry. To an extent, nuclear weapons obviated the need for possessing territory.[47]

This new focus was reinforced by the fact that the threat of conquest had dramatically receded. Only the Republic of Kuwait and Vietnam exited the system violently after 1945, and neither fell at the hands of a great power.[48] Regimes were, of course, periodically overthrown by the superpowers either through proxy wars or direct military intervention – for example, Hungary in 1956, Czechoslovakia in 1968, and Grenada in 1983. However, in each case formal sovereignty was maintained, even if relations between the client state and the respective superpower were quite hierarchical.

A second factor pertained to the perceived value of large economic units. Shoring up territory and securing resources had been an objective prior to World War I. During the interwar period, the internal economy of the Empire had been crucial in helping to sustain the country in an otherwise economically closed world.[49] Those same forces, however, were absent after 1945 and political conditions in the periphery now made intersovereign relations easier (and more profitable) to sustain.[50] "The dominance of the United States economy after 1945, a temporary consequence of the world wars, brought liberalization of international trade and investment. These changes in turn reduced the advantages of empires as large-scale economic units. As barriers to international trade declined, the need for large internal (imperial) markets declined as well."[51]

The economic loss of territory was partially assuaged by the perceived benefits of the emerging Commonwealth. "In a sense the Commonwealth was becoming a surrogate empire. Indeed, when plans for colonial self-government finally matured, it was assumed in London that the former colonies would automatically join the Commonwealth."[52] In more formal language, the optimal political

---

[47] Spruyt 2005.
[48] The Republic of Vietnam (South Vietnam) fell to North Vietnam in 1975; Kuwait was conquered by Iraq in 1990 (Fazal 2007, 23).
[49] Fieldhouse 1998.   [50] Chamberlain 1999, 119–124; Gallagher 1982.
[51] Kahler 1997, 288.   [52] James 1994, 534.

relationship had shifted below the sovereignty line. Holding most territories on a formal basis had become prohibitively expensive. Essentially, London now aimed for a confederal relationship with many of its former units. In reference to the fact that Burma had seceded and then left the Commonwealth while Ceylon had done the same and become a dominion, the new guiding phrase was "more Ceylons and fewer Burmas."[53]

In conclusion, the nature of the international environment had profound effects on the expansion and contraction of the British state. Blessed with the right internal features, the metropole was ideally configured to take advantage of peripheral weaknesses in the nineteenth century. The competitive pressures of international politics later in the century further spurred the metropole to expand its perimeter where it could. It expanded horizontally across space to dominate ever larger amounts of territory; and it expanded vertically to intensify its form of rule (see Figure 4.3). Thus, informal empire became formalized, and many territories that had been indirectly ruled lost their internal autonomy. This process was consonant with the general arc in the international system that resulted in fewer states and increased centralization.

If the interwar years left the state attempting to preserve the status quo, the post-1945 period and the advent of the Cold War affected the costs and benefits of holding territory. Earlier fears over territorial conquest had diminished; so too had concerns over access to economic resources. British apprehensions that the release of a territory would only pave the way for a peer competitor to seize the territory were replaced by a focus on ensuring that the emerging unit was on the right side of the Cold War. That fact that numerous emerging states would remain connected to the British metropole on a confederal basis made this process easier. The international environment had changed and, as a result, the state was much more amenable to secession. But although external factors may have driven this expansion and contraction, it was the internal organization of the state that determined which nations would become the right type of administrative unit, and which units would ultimately be positioned to secede peacefully.

---

[53] Louis 1998, 337.

Domestic Administrative Structure

The purpose of this section is to explore a set of hypotheses pertaining to state structure and the manner in which proto-states are organized. Does having a proto-state increase the likelihood of secession for a given group? To what extent are metropoles guided by issues of precedent setting? Do differences in type effectively compartmentalize these issues of precedence and permit the state to release one type of unit but not another? The British metropole is an excellent case for studying the effects of state structure. Political space begins with the English core and then expands to include the internal countries and the crown dependencies. After that, the state encompassed five types of territories spread around the world. Of these, all but the overseas territories were politically external. Taken together, these many administrative units and secessionist movements make up a large set and it is therefore impossible to pay sufficient attention to each case. However, to the greatest extent possible, I highlight the exceptional cases and the outliers, and I also provide a vignette of secessionism in Bougainville, a nation whose administrative destiny was determined by the British and Germans during the colonial era.

Secessionism without Proto-states

Between 1816 and 2011, sixty nations achieved independence from the British metropole, and all but three of them possessed a proto-state. To put that figure in perspective, roughly 16 percent of the total number of secessionist movements – the successes and the failures – did not claim a proto-state. These unlucky nations were clearly much less successful at winning their sovereignty.

Who were the three exceptions? Sudan won a brief independence in 1886 after a five-year struggle against its British and Egyptian overlords.[54] More messianic in character, the Mahdist Revolt possessed expansive territorial claims that did not cohere with any defined administrative region. Pakistan was born as part of the Indian partition in 1947. It consisted of a number of regions that were previously subordinate to the British Raj, and this is partly signified in the name itself; the name "Pakistan" is derived from Punjab, Afghania, Kashmir,

[54] Harding 1998; Fazal 2007.

Sind, and Baluchistan. The state was merely the western half of the new territory that was being given to Muslims.[55] Similarly, Israel was born in the tumult of the Palestinian transition in 1948. Palestine itself had been a proto-state, a mandate given to British control. In the aftermath of the Jewish-Palestinian conflict, part of the former territory became Israel and part was assigned to Jordan. None of these state births happened peacefully and none had London's full blessing. They were the products of complex tensions on the ground (and internationally) that overcame British intentions.

The metropole's approach to devolution favored proto-states, especially in the post-1945 period. This is because all of the countries and colonies, protectorates and provinces, territories and dominions, possessed their own administrative apparatus. The depth and detail of each system varied, but it was on these structures that the comprehensive plan for releasing states was built. Although the political calculus of the Cold War often got in the way, the British aimed to be the midwives to the birth of healthy states with sound democratic institutions.[56] This approach presented a disadvantage to those movements that did not correspond with existing administrative units. For example, the Karens of southeastern Burma had played an active role in colonial affairs and supplied more than half of the colonial recruits to the imperial army in Burma during the 1930s.[57] Unfortunately, on the run-up to Burmese independence in 1948, they were lumped together with the rest of the territory. Disappointed by the British insistence on a Burmese state to include all of its regions, the Karens mounted a secessionist movement in 1947. Under British pressure, the movement settled for a semi-autonomous relationship within the new Burma and the possibility of future independence.[58] However, when the new Burmese government rejected that bid in 1948, the Karens began a secessionist conflict that has persisted in fits and starts to this day.

The Baganda of the African lakes district possessed an independent kingdom called Buganda when the British used the pretext of a Muslim uprising to annex the territory in 1884. The Baganda were eventually grouped into the larger colony called Uganda, and, as the Uganda territory began to prepare for independence in the post-1945 period, the Baganda became concerned that the future state would be dominated

---

[55] The eastern half was Eastern Pakistan, or Bangladesh.
[56] James 1994, 544–547. [57] Minahan 1996, 290. [58] Ziegler 1985.

by the non-Bantu northern tribes. After the Baganda declared independence in 1960, London dispatched the colonial army to force them to accept federal status within a united Uganda.[59]

The story of Baluchistan is a bit different. Unlike the Karens or the many other nations that were tucked away within the larger proto-state of Burma, and unlike the Baganda who were a people within the larger unit of Uganda, the Baluchis were divided over a number of administrative units. There were a set of Baluchi princely states such as Kalat, and these were governed in a quasi-indirect manner by the British. Thus, Baluchistan itself was not a proto-state; it was a collection of units subordinate to the Raj. The chief obstacle to Baluchi secession was the lower-order status of the administrative units it claimed. Both the British administrators and the Indian nationalist movement were keen to secede with the entire territory intact.[60] Indeed, other regional secessionist movements from subunits such as Hyderabad and Travancore were denied independence for the same reason. The partition of Pakistan was the great exception to these efforts.

Empirically, these accounts bear out the claim that nations without proto-states are going to have a more difficult time seceding. Many of the nations had the sympathy of the British metropole, but their independence claims raised the issue of recursive secessionism. Permitting Travancore, Nagaland, Khalistan, and Baluchistan to secede independent of India would send a signal to other nations. Meanwhile, the cases of Israel and Pakistan illustrate the problems inherent in trying to divide territories along lines that do not adhere to previous administrative boundaries.[61] To be sure, there are other factors animating the conflict between Jews and Palestinians, and Pakistanis and Indians, but the lack of prior boundaries is certainly a factor in their ongoing border disputes.

These nations faced a problem common to those who are bereft of a proto-state. The UK aimed to downsize in a clear and organized manner and could little afford to open the door to a more general debate about where borders should be drawn.[62] Its allies in this process were those proto-states and political agents who stood to benefit from the existing administrative boundaries – for example, Burma and

---

[59] Minahan 1996, 89.   [60] Cabinet Papers, *India Policy*, May 22, 1947.
[61] Chester 2009.
[62] Cabinet Papers, *The Gold Coast. Memorandum by the Secretary of State for the Colonies*, August 29, 1956.

Uganda. These boundaries provided focal points.[63] They benefited not only the British who sought an organized devolution, but they were also reinforced by those who held the reins of power in each territory. Ian Lustick describes this process as follows:

As independent African states emerged, native elites came to power by identifying themselves with their established borders and the bureaucratic apparatus of the colonial states that operated within them. These political entrepreneurs understood the danger of challenges to their authority which could be mounted if legitimacy were granted to claims for "national self-determination" advanced by ethnic or tribal groups within their borders – movements that would be led by opposing elites with better credentials to exploit such solidarities and lead the smaller states that would be built up around them. Internationally, and in the Organization of African Unity, it was recognized that unless the "artificial" borders drawn in the colonial period were treated as sacrosanct, that is unless the idea of changing them was hegemonically excluded from political agendas, not only would the leadership position of those running the newly independent states be jeopardized, but the continent as a whole would be in danger of dissolving into fratricidal conflict.[64]

In the cases that could be classified as instances of decolonization, the collusion between the metropole and the proto-state was backed by international law and its emphasis on the principle of *uti possidetis*. New states should inherit their former administrative boundaries. Perhaps nowhere was the application of this principle to the right of self-determination more consequential than in Africa, where the Organization of African Unity reaffirmed the principle in 1964, stating "that colonial frontiers existing at the moment of decolonization constituted a tangible reality which all member states pledged themselves to respect."[65] Claims to territories that did not cohere with these former units were thus shut out of the state-making process. Their fate was controlled by these administrative distinctions.

One could argue that the assignment and creation of proto-states is purely a function of the existing national/institutional structures present at the beginning. That is, proto-states were simply assigned

---

[63] Cabinet Papers, *Malayan Policy. Memorandum by the Secretary of State for the Colonies,* June 28, 1947.

[64] Lustick 1993, 441–442.   [65] Shaw 1997, 494. Also see Bartos 1997.

to those nations who stood the best chance of becoming a sovereign state later on. I explore this line of reasoning in the next section.

Proto-states and Their Consequences

The great expansion of the British Empire resulted in a vast number of administrative units that were organized in a variety of ways. I argue that the initial assignment and typing of these units was the result of a set of factors, only one of which was the actual strength and viability of the local nation and polity at the time of creation. Although the British often took advantage of such conditions and built proto-states around existing polities, international strategic considerations as well as simple fortune also played an important part. Once set, these proto-states shaped the further development of local nations. Moreover, these units and the categories of which they were a part became increasingly fixed over time in the minds of the relevant parties. This salience had consequences given that it both affected the predisposition of some toward secession, and developed clear lines on which the metropole would ultimately discriminate between competing calls for independence.

The most obvious example that British proto-state creation possessed a simple element of arbitrariness is the map itself. It is well known that many, if not most, of the African countries possess borders whose straight lines and geometric logic defy natural contours and ethnonational fault lines. This is particularly so in the interior where the metropole would simply draw lines across the map to serve as boundaries between administrative units and/or the possessions of other metropoles. Yet these lines that were created in such a casual way served as the borders of future states and nations. "No one concerned with drawing the empire's frontiers had ever imagined that he was setting the boundaries for a future self-governing independent state. Antipathetic racial, tribal and religious groups had often been corralled together willy-nilly."[66]

Although these administrative units may have generated nations later on, the forging of those nations was often incomplete. Nigeria once consisted of a set of proto-states beginning as early as 1851. These units, which included the colony at Lagos as well as the Oil Rivers

---

[66] James 1994, 545.

Protectorate, were assigned to other proto-states in the region such as Sierra Leone and the Gold Coast. However, by 1900 the area was consolidated into two proto-states: Southern Nigeria and Northern Nigeria. These two were then merged in 1914 and the unit remained a first-order crown colony until 1960. There were generative consequences to this formation, as the ethnically diverse territory did eventually form a Nigerian secessionist movement in 1944. Of course, the creation of the Nigerian nation was never fully consolidated. Its fragmentary tensions, ethnic turmoil, and famous secessionist civil war in Biafra has been evidence of this.

Although the somewhat arbitrary provenance of territories such as Nigeria may have only generated a semi-coherent nation, the selective function of proto-states locked in its path to sovereignty. The British metropole sought to downsize along clean administrative lines in the hope that well-functioning states would be born. This was in the interest of the nationalist leaders in Lagos, who clearly did not want to see the new state fragment along tribal lines. It was also in the interest of the international community, which through the principle of *uti possidetis* made the presumption that the best guides for new states were previous administrative boundaries. It mattered "not what the provenance of such units may have been," even though "the mode of establishing boundaries was ... different in that geometric lines predominated and, on the whole, there was little reference to local ethnic or economic considerations."[67]

There was a fair amount of institutional habit in the British administrative design. One hallmark of the British system was its propensity to employ indirect forms of rule. To some extent, this was a legacy of the manner in which the empire developed. The practice of colonial indirect rule had been utilized by joint-stock companies because company officials reasoned that it was a cost-effective method for increasing profits. Like the Dutch, the British metropole more or less continued this practice after taking control from the trading companies in the latter years of the nineteenth century.[68] The absence of the same operational history in France, Spain, Portugal, Russia, and even the USA, is one of the reasons why indirect rule was less common in their administrative structures.

[67] Shaw 1997, 493, 504.   [68] Hechter 2000, 52.

Of course, the choice between direct and indirect rule, which corresponded to the distinction between a crown colony and a protectorate, often turned on the robustness of the local territory. Where the British metropole found a preexisting polity and some level of institutional development, it often calculated that indirect rule was the optimal form. Where it did not find similar structures to leverage, direct rule was often required. Thus, the conditions on the ground at the moment of creation played a role in the type of proto-state that was created. However, these conditions were unstable and often gave way to direct rule as British authority gradually took more direct control over protectorates. At times this happened in a process akin to mission creep as British advisors came to exercise *de facto* control. At times this also happened in a formal manner as it did among many of the Indian princely states between 1857 and 1862 on account of the replacement of the East India Company by the government.[69]

If the evolution in the form of rule generally ran from indirect to direct, the great exception was with the British dominions. Colonies that met certain criteria were permitted responsible government, a relationship that in most cases counted as indirect rule. These assignments were clearly built upon the right local conditions, which included large settler populations replete with a cultural and institutional life that was largely British in form. The development of the dominions was really the first step in British imperial devolution. It began in response to demands in the mid 1800s and moved through stages in which independence was gradually given.

The third factor in the creation and assignment of proto-states was interstate security. This is primarily because security concerns drove expansion itself and this resulted in the need for practically designed proto-states. "The steady expansion of the Cape Colony and India, always in search of 'stable' frontiers, are particular cases in point, but examples abound."[70] Rivalries with other powers, as well as local intrigues among smaller neighbors compelled the British metropole to expand, and in the process a myriad of political units, indirect and direct, were born. Of equal importance was the creation of political boundaries that were conjured in an attempt to determine frontiers with other states; both the Durand Line and the border separating

[69] Henige 2004.   [70] Henige 1970, 78–79.

Malaysia from Indonesia are examples of these decisions. Finally, some proto-states were simply created for highly strategic reasons; among these were the Aden Colony and Singapore.

Thus, administrative distinctions were made through a curious mix of pragmatism, strategy, institutional habit, and simple chance. These assignments were significant in the long run, not just for nations that aspired to part ways with the UK, but, as the following vignette shows, also for nations that continue to seek independence from countries that were themselves once subject to the British metropole.

Great Power Politics, Boundaries, and Administrative Design

Bougainville was the site of a bloody secessionist civil war in the 1990s that was not widely reported. It is a fascinating case that demonstrates many of the patterns common in this sort of struggle, from issues of economic grievance, to ethnic radicalization, to guerrilla warfare. It also shows the consequences of administrative design.

Although the region was inhabited by Melanesians for 30 000 years, its modern-day political status is the product of its encounter with imperialism and the expansion of the sovereign state system. The title itself was bequeathed by an eighteenth-century French explorer, Louis de Bougainville, who saw fit to name the islands and people after himself. In 1882 the area came under control of a German trading company and a dispute began between the Germans and the British over control of the Solomon Islands, of which Bougainville was the northern part (see Map 4.1). In the resulting agreement, Germany kept Bougainville, which it shortly added to its colony of German New Guinea, and the British retained the rest of the Solomon Islands as a protectorate. That critical division set the two ends of the island chain on different trajectories.

Germany lost New Guinea during World War I, along with its other colonial possessions, and the region was combined with British New Guinea and converted into a League of Nations mandate under Australian control. In this way Australia more or less inherited the colony that would eventually become Papua New Guinea (PNG), one of the most ethnically and linguistically heterogeneous countries in the world. PNG declared independence on September 16, 1975, and Australia and the rest of the international community quickly granted recognition. However, two weeks prior, on September 1, Bougainville declared

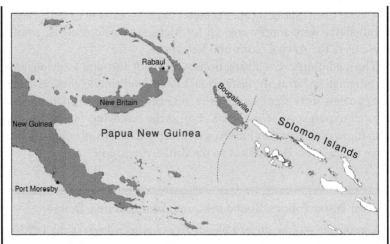

Map 4.1 Bougainville, Papua New Guinea, and the Solomon Islands.[71]

independence as the Republic of the North Solomons.[72] This demand
was denied by all parties for the simple reason that Bougainville was a
part of PNG, and its secession would threaten the integrity and orderly
process of decolonization. It was thus a casualty of the application of
uti possidetis. One of the first acts of the government of PNG was to
suspend the provincial government of Bougainville and send troops to
occupy the islands. Three years later, in 1978, the rest of the Solomon
Islands seceded peacefully and became a sovereign state.

Like many nations that found themselves unwillingly decolonized
into a state where they are a minority, the Bougainvilleans were not
content to put aside their secessionist aspirations. Tensions arose once
more in the late 1980s and independence was declared again on May
17, 1990. A ten-year civil war ensued that killed as many as 20 000
people and displaced as much as 40 percent of the Bougainville population. In 2001, Bougainville negotiated with PNG a peace agreement
with several stipulations, including the promise of an independence
referendum between 2015 and 2020 provided certain conditions are
met.[73]

The tale of Bougainville highlights the relationship between administrative distinction and secessionist outcomes. First, the simple division
of the Solomon Islands between two metropoles and subsequent assignment of Bougainville to New Guinea is a twist of fate, one with long-

---

[71] GADM 2012.   [72] Minahan 1996, 415.   [73] Wallis 2014.

lasting consequences. Second, Germany had more on its mind than the strength of local nations when it made administrative distinctions. Rather, it organized its space with an eye on good natural harbors and the potential for resource extraction. As such, it made Kokopo, and later Rabaul, on New Britain as the territorial capital, and not some preexisting polity on the main island of New Guinea. In other words, Bougainville was not made subordinate to other regions in what would become PNG because other nations were somehow more coherent or deserving. I thus find no support for the argument that initial administrative decisions merely reflect the underlying strength of the local nation.

Third, Bougainville's experience shows the relative importance of what I call the generative and selective effects of administrative units. Bougainville has twice mounted a secessionist effort in the absence of any special administrative status. One could point out that PNG has developed a sense of nationality and that this is a product of a political-administrative apparatus around which that identity could form. But was PNG recognized as sovereign, when Bougainville was not, because its national identity was more robust and its candidacy more deserving? That is the thrust of the counterargument regarding the nation-generating effects of administrative design.

I submit that in Bougainville's case the selective aspect of administrative design was far more important. This is more than just an abstract academic argument; the Bougainvillean leadership understood the importance of administrative history with respect to sovereign recognition. I interviewed several individuals who were leaders during both the secessionist struggle and in the peace-building process after 2001. James Tanis, former president of the Autonomous Bougainville Government, stated that they tried to present their case as unique given Bougainville's original imperial transfer from Germany.[74] Indeed, the leadership had learned partly by networking with the East Timorese secessionists that such arguments can win sympathy from the international community, especially when they are coupled with perceived human rights abuses. Since Bougainville and East Timor were both courting international favor around the same time, the Bougainvillean representative to the United Nations, Moses Havini, had opportunities to discuss strategies for winning recognition.[75] Ultimately, Bougainville

---

[74] Author's interview with James Tanis on October 12, 2012.
[75] Author's interview with Moses Havini, former spokesperson at the United Nations, on February 6, 2013.

failed to win its recognition by appealing to the practices of decolonization, presumably because its case was perceived as weaker than East Timor, but nationalism remains a potent force.[76] The Bougainvilleans did not need the right administrative status to generate a nation, but they needed it when they attempted and failed to gain sovereign recognition.

How has administrative organization shaped secessionist outcomes across the British realm? Prior to World War II, the only type of units the metropole was willing to permit sovereignty were the dominions. The Cape Colony technically joined the community of states in 1885, and the other three did so in 1920 after joining the League of Nations.[77] The British metropole took care when granting dominion status since it implied eventual independence. As a distinction that developed in the years before 1945, it was important that the emerging states remain close to the metropole and be part of the Commonwealth, a confederal relationship that was closed off to all but the dominions prior to 1947.[78]

Issues of precedent were very much at stake, especially during the interwar period. London could not acquiesce to the Irish demand for a republic because doing so would risk similar demands from other areas of the empire; the British logic was that if Ireland, an internal country, could secede, then so too could other types of territories. To some extent, the spike in secessionist conflicts in the interwar period was the result of increasing self-determination movements and a need by the metropole to demonstrate resolve. Those units that were not

---

[76] The application of *uti possidetis* requires that a critical date be identified: the exact date when administrative ownership should be recognized (Bartos 1997). For cases of decolonization, the critical date was typically the moment when the colony was scheduled to become independent. In 1975 East Timor was a stand-alone Portuguese colony that declared independence, only to be seized by Indonesia. As such, the East Timorese could make a strong claim for independence based on *uti possidetis*. In contrast, Bougainville had been a secondary province within greater New Guinea for the entire twentieth century. Stretching the principle to accommodate Bougainville would open the door to countless other potential applicants who had been the subject of an administrative transfer and/or reclassification.

[77] Fazal 2007. Ireland agreed to dominion status as part of its independence agreement.

[78] Henige 1970, 81.

dominions and yet still seceded did so by exhausting the metropole through low-level resistance or outright civil war.

When the metropole downsized in the post-1945 period, it elected to release three additional types of units: its crown colonies, its protectorates, and the Viceroyalty of India. The secession of India was a liminal moment for the metropole, one that had implications for many of the other territories.

The sub-continent was the first non-white area to become independent of British control, a development hardly conceived of by Indians, let alone Imperial rulers, before the First World War. . . . Once India was independent, the logistics of the Empire were radically changed. So were the credentials of colonial nationalism. Independence for the oldest and most prestigious Asian part of the Empire was to be a beacon for nationalists in other parts of the Empire, as they stove for freedom and for new national identities.[79]

Despite the fact that India was classified differently – and was a unique member of its type (a lone branch) – it nonetheless set a precedent for other overseas territories with respect to British political devolution and decolonization. In that sense, the conceptual bulkheads separating the crown colonies and protectorates from the singular viceroyalty were not quite as clear as this thesis had argued. This may well be a result of the fact that many colonies began as protectorates and then become crown colonies, and sometime vice versa. To some extent, the three types shared a common history and were lumped together in the eyes of the central government and the territories. India had its pride of place it seems, but issues of precedence did travel across type.

In the process of this postwar state contraction forty-nine nations were permitted to secede and fifteen were initially denied. Not surprisingly, the only three instances of violence took place among denied cases (Malaya, Kenya, Northern Ireland). Two of these nations possessed the right administrative status and eventually won their independence. As noted before, the Malayan case was partly the consequence of a communist movement and the political dynamics of the Cold War. Its administrative status was never the problem. In Kenya, the Mau Mau movement waged a violent insurgency in the mid 1950s. The core of the movement was the Kikuyu ethnic group, whose motives stemmed primarily from economic stress and deprivation.[80]

---

[79] Brown 1998, 421–422.
[80] Chamberlain 1999, 49–51; Clayton 1998, 301–302.

More or less a military wing of the Kikiyu Central Association, the Mau Mau movement was one part of the larger coalition of Kenyans who had declared and sought independence. British reticence on the issue stemmed from the fact that the Mau Mau used divisive methods, including terror, and they often targeted British settlers.

Although the British metropole during the post-1945 period has been prepared to release the great majority of its overseas units, the same disposition has not applied to the internal countries and crown dependencies.[81] Of these, only Northern Ireland and Scotland have launched formal secessionist movements. These are fascinating cases for several reasons. First, they are simply closer to the core of the metropole. Releasing Northern Ireland could potentially set an example for Scotland and perhaps Wales. Such fragmentation could bleed over to the crown dependencies, and basically reduce the state to its core. It is therefore easy to see why the British metropole would erect a bulwark to secession in the internal countries and deny Irish demands.

Second, there was a high degree of cognitive salience on this issue. The downsizing of the overseas territories was connected with the process of decolonization, which was supported by the superpowers and international law. In these cases, the right to secession was accorded to colonized peoples so that they could separate from a colonial power and form a sovereign state. Neither Scotland nor Northern Ireland met this criterion, and the fact that their failure to do so seems sensible to most observers is a testament to the strength of the conceptual salience between colonized lands and noncolonized lands. That distinction was of course rejected by Irish nationalists who pointed to a long history of subordination to a colonial power across the Irish Sea. They had an incentive to challenge that distinction just as the metropole had an interest in preserving it.

Nevertheless, the outcome of these movements is still being determined. An important element in the denial of Northern Ireland was sentiment for Ulster unionists as well as the feeling that the Irish secessionists were employing illegitimate methods to achieve their ends. However, the road to independence via legitimate means has become a real possibility. Indeed, as the 2014 Scottish referendum suggests, it seems the London has prepared to abide such outcomes. Overall, the British metropole is still downsizing, but it has made the process

---

[81] Note that the type six overseas territories were not created until 2002.

increasingly democratic. I return to this issue in the final section of the chapter.

What about the other nations who were denied independence in the years after World War II? Most of them simply lacked proto-status, and for groups such as the Lozi and the Sikhs, the obstacle to independence consisted of a makeshift alliance between the metropole, who preferred to downsize in an orderly manner, and emerging states such as Zambia and India, who wanted to prevent the possibility of recursive secession. Other nations, such as the Sikkimese, actually possessed administrative units, but they were of a lower-order nature and denied for the same reasons. In sum, the fate of British secessionist movements was shaped by administrative lines and categories.

Tidal Effects

An additional focus question concerns the purported tidal effects of secessionism. Chapter 3 provided statistical evidence for the alternative hypothesis that secessionism occurs in waves. Indeed, one of the best predictors of when an internal nation will declare independence is the number of other secessionist movements in the same state. In the British case, secessionism swelled in the mid twentieth century. The first sign of this increase occurred after World War I, when by 1920 the metropole faced nine movements. That number increased gradually over the next few decades and peaked at seventeen movements in 1947. From there the number of movements decreased, until in 1985 the state faced only two movements in Northern Ireland and Scotland. Not since 1881 had it faced so little secessionism.

There has been a tidal character to secessionism across the British realm. From 1918 onward, the British state was more or less trying to hold back this tide. The conflicts of the 1920s and 1930s are a testament to these efforts. Beissinger explains a tidal surge of nationalism – secessionism in this context is the consequent – as not being grounded in structurally predetermined conditions.[82] Rather, one call for independence affects another and the resulting groundswell of these movements acquires a momentum and its own causal power. These dynamics were evident in British secessionism. Some of these movements such as those in Ireland or India were indeed the outcome of local

[82] Beissinger 2002, 36.

conditions that had ripened over long periods. But in other areas of the British realm such as the Caribbean and parts of Africa, local nationalisms had not developed from the inside-out in quite the same way. There were spillover effects in which the ideology and principles of the lead secessionist movements were affecting potential secessionist movements elsewhere. By and large, there was mutual empowerment as leaders in one region supported leaders in others.

However, this mutual empowerment was partially structured by the British metropole's administrative divisions. As discussed before, the leadership in emerging states was often loath to recognize calls for self-determination from other groups within their proto-state. Doing so could undermine their authority that was often based on a somewhat superficial tie to the territorial administration, and it would certainly reduce the size of their future territory, as Karen or Shan independence would have reduced the size of Burma, or Baganda independence the size of Uganda. It seems that leaders and political entrepreneurs are selective about whom they choose to empower, and this choice is controlled to some extent by the manner in which the metropole had organized its political space.

The choice to declare independence is partly endogenous to the anticipated response of the metropole, which is in turn shaped by administrative realities. I have identified eleven nations that lacked a proto-state and still chose to declare independence (see earlier). What about the nations that never formally mounted a secessionist movement? Although such cases are hard to identify, a rough estimate can be calculated by looking at the secessionist movements that emerged in countries that recently seceded from the UK. For example, Burma has faced secessionist movements from six different nations: the Arakanese, Karenni, Karens, Shans, Kachins, and Mons. Outside of the Karens and Shans, who declared independence prior to Burmese secession, the remaining nations formed secessionist movements within a year or two of the birth of the Burmese state. All told, there were about thirty instances of recursive secessionism within states that were formerly British. Most, if not all, of these were identifiable ethnicities and coherent nations during the British period and yet they were never given a proto-state. As a consequence, they were dissuaded from mounting an independence movement.

The administrative structure of the state effectively channeled these waves of secessionism. This mechanism helps make sense of an apparent tension between two competing theories in the literature.[83] If secessionism has a tidal character and groups are inclined to declare independence when they witness others doing the same, and if metropoles are more likely to deny such attempts as the number increases, then one should expect waves of secessionist conflict. This may accurately describe the Spanish secessions in Latin America. That it did not for the most part occur across the British realm – that the wave passed without conflict – illustrates how governments can use these categories to discriminate between calls for independence. Secessionist movements are not all like types. Administrative lines and categories shape the response of the metropole and the choice to declare independence.

The Effects of Regime Type

What role has democracy played? The quantitative analysis in Chapter 3 indicated that secessionism was somewhat less likely in democracies, but once formed, secessionist movements in democracies were more likely to get a favorable response from their metropole, and significantly less likely to have a conflict over the issue. The history of the British regime since 1816 has shown a consistent upward trajectory toward full democracy. It entered the time period as a weak democracy and had reached full maturity by 1922.[84] Relative to most states in the system, it achieved full democracy quite early.

It is difficult to gauge whether British democracy has actually reduced the level of secessionism. Most of its secessionist movements have occurred after World War I, the period in which the UK has more or less been a consolidated democracy. As such, secessionism and democracy are positively correlated, but this relationship could be entirely spurious because we also know that secessionism has simply been more common around the world since 1918.

Yet there is good reason to think that democracy has influenced the core and periphery on matters of secession. Part of the literature on decolonization argues that the gradual democratization of the British state and the corresponding extension of suffrage called into question

---

[83] Beissinger 2002; Walter 2009.
[84] According to the Polity IV dataset, the UK's polity score (on a scale from 0 to 20) was 8 from 1816 to 1836, 13 from 1837 to 1879, 17 from 1880 to 1900, 18 from 1901 to 1921, and 20 from 1922 onward (Polity IV Project 2011).

the moral basis of empire. Critics charged that imperial relations were antiliberal and antidemocratic, and that London had a moral responsibility for the welfare of its many territories.[85] Lawrence James writes that "during this period, Britain became a democracy and so the empire could not have been sustained without the general approval of the British people."[86] The British electorate had become significantly larger by the mid twentieth century, and public opinion mattered. As M. E. Chamberlain observes, "Indian nationalists had discerned from a very early date that it was worth appealing directly to the British electorate, bypassing the vested interests in Calcutta or London."[87] The importance of social change with respect to core-periphery relations has been highlighted in the literature.[88]

Although these principles almost certainly mattered, it is unclear how much they mattered and how exactly they interacted with other forces governing state contraction. After all, the UK was a fairly democratic state in the late 1800s, but that did not stop it from engaging in the "new imperialism" of the time.[89] Clearly, external fears regarding interstate rivalry as well as internal concerns over secessionist precedent setting often trumped the importance that these metropoles placed on liberal democratic values.

A review of the cases shows that secessionist tactics have mattered to the British metropole. One of the weaknesses of the Mau Mau movement was the belief that the group used terror to achieve its ends rather than institutional channels. By and large, the British populace had a "preference for movements which had proved their representativeness and progressive intentions, and shown themselves prepared to negotiate with the British in the interest of gradual reform, than for those impatient for power, defiant of foreign rule, and prepared to resort to civil disobedience" or even violence.[90] This emphasis on institutional channels and democratic legitimacy is echoed in the more recent Anglo-Irish Agreement of 1985 that outlined a constitutional route to devolution and confirmed that secession would be permitted once a majority of the Northern Irish voted for it. At the heart of the British attention to proper devolution is an issue of control. The metropole has aimed

---

[85] Owen 1998, 208.   [86] James 1994, xiv.   [87] Chamberlain 1999, 119.
[88] Finnemore 1996; Crawford 2002.
[89] Similarly, the USA was a full democracy by 1871 (Polity IV) and it also participated in imperialist expansion at the turn of the century.
[90] Owen 1998, 209.

to downsize in a peaceful manner that establishes viable states and reduces the risk of precedent setting. It has also wanted to maintain a close confederal relationship with the new sovereigns. Since the entire process had to be on London's terms, it makes sense that it would favor those units that sought independence through legitimate and institutional channels.

These observations lead to several tentative conclusions regarding the relationship between democracy and secessionist outcomes in the British system. First, it is unclear whether democracy has reduced secessionism. On one hand, the democratic features of the state may have placated potential secessionists and precluded them from declaring independence. On the other hand, liberal democratic norms seem to have generated a somewhat sympathetic core population, and this could have incentivized secessionists. It is hard to know how these two countervailing forces balance out. Second, toleration and recognition are not the same thing, and the British metropole has denied independence to many nations because of security issues and/or administrative status. Third, and perhaps most importantly, that tolerance for secessionist movements and preference for democratic tactics may help prevent conflict for denied nations. This approach has transformed the situation in Northern Ireland and it permitted Scotland an independence referendum in September 2014. Democracy has diverse effects on secessionist outcomes, but its ability to reduce conflict is arguably the most salient.

Conclusion

The general pattern of expansion and contraction of the British metropole is consistent with the central argument of this manuscript. To a large extent, the state responded to external factors when it expanded, particularly in the late nineteenth century. Likewise, its subsequent contraction in the post-1945 period was in many ways the mirror image of its initial expansion; the forces that made it beneficial to expand in the earlier era had changed after World War II and now made it beneficial to contract. System-level factors had changed and the importance of shoring up territory against rivals had diminished. Although we cannot simply isolate all of the other factors that fed into this process and only vary certain parameters at the international level, the analysis in this chapter indicates that the British metropole was being influenced by the invisible hand of the international system.

However, the pattern by which the state contracted was also guided by its internal structure. The manner in which it was originally organized had downstream consequences during the period of contraction. A significant number of the eventual candidates were merely artifacts of the British administrative design, and the calls for independence from these units were built upon nations that were effectively conjured by that design. This is the generative function of proto-states. However, more important is the selective function of proto-states. As I have shown, those units that lacked a proto-state were shut out by both the metropole and, importantly, other proto-states. The exceptions to this rule were the violent partitions in Palestine and South Asia. In addition, the type of proto-state that a secessionist group laid claim to also mattered. Being a dominion was clearly a special status that led to a different fate – at least in the short run – than being a colony or protectorate or viceroyalty. This was so even though all of these units either began as a colony or as a protectorate. Of course, being an internal country or dependency implied a different future, one that is still being worked out.

Finally, the British case shows some support for the importance of tidal effects and democracy, two alternative hypotheses that were significant in the quantitative analysis. First, the metropole experienced a secessionist wave, and there is evidence of mutual empowerment and learning among the aspiring nations. However, as the Baganda and the Karens learned, not having a proto-state meant that the efforts of secessionists would not be accepted by those who did have a proto-state. In effect, the state's administrative structure channeled the surge of secessionism, motivating some to pursue independence while dissuading others from attempting to do the same. Second, democracy likely encouraged and discouraged secessionism, made the metropole a bit more tolerant of secessionist groups, and channeled secessionists groups away from violent tactics into a more legitimate and democratic bargaining process.

5 | *The Arc of Russian Rule*

It's getting to the point where sooner or later someone is going to declare his apartment an independent state.

– Mikhail Gorbachev[1]

Russia is a useful case study for studying the dynamics of secessionism for a number of reasons. First, it is a large multinational state. It surpassed the British in terms of territorial size at some point in the early twentieth century, and its great size has encompassed a substantial number of different nations and ethnic groups, languages, and religions.[2] At the heart of this polyglot state is a core group, the Russians, who have over time exercised their power over subordinate nations in a variety of ways. Second, the Russian state has also existed over the entire range of years from 1816 to 2011. This permits me to look at patterns in secessionism in different eras, including both the pre- and post-1945 periods. Third, it is also useful to look at Russia because, unlike the UK, it was essentially a land-based empire. As I observe later, there appears to be different tendencies between sea-based and land-based empires with respect to administrative organization. Finally, the state has gone through three incarnations since 1816: the Empire, the Soviet Union, and the Federation. As I show in this chapter, these different lives of the state have had important consequences for proto-state formation and secessionist outcomes.

This chapter has the same structure as the previous chapter on the UK. I begin with an extended analysis and cataloging of Russian/Soviet administrative design, secessionism, and secessionist conflict. In some ways the administrative architecture of the state is quite different from

---

[1] Curtis 1996, 196.

[2] In general, I use the term "Russian" when referring to the metropole, unless I am specifically discussing the Soviet government from 1922 to 1991. This is a common approach when evaluating the state over different periods (see Bunce 1993; Lake 1997).

the British system. In the Soviet era, in particular, there are novel and experimental attempts at ethnographic management that are fascinating and sometimes tragic. However, the British and the Russian/Soviet case studies both reveal the underlying importance of administrative lines and categories in regard to secessionist outcomes.

The remainder of the chapter is ordered around the core research questions. I first discuss the role that the international system has played in the expansion and contraction of the metropole. I then look inside the state and examine the consequences of administrative organization. Like the British case, I zoom in wherever possible to highlight specific regions and secessionist groups, and I provide a vignette describing the devastating role that chance and punishment played in Soviet administrative design. Although I cannot pay equal attention to all cases, these close-up examinations of Finland, Circassia, and others, are useful for building the argument. The chapter culminates with a discussion of secessionist waves and the effects of regime type, two alternative explanations that found support in the quantitative analysis.

Proto-states, Secessionism, and Conflict

Proto-states

I identified nine types of proto-states for the Russian metropole, which are divided out over the three phases of the state between 1816 and 2011: there were two types for the Russian Empire, four types for the Soviet Union, and three types for the Russian Federation.[3] Each of these incarnations had important consequences on the number and ordering of proto-states, and this is illustrated in Figure 5.1. The Russian metropole possessed only two proto-states in 1816 – Poland and Finland – and until 1917 the average number per year was a little more than three. After the revolution, the number of proto-states increased dramatically and averaged more than forty units per year until the downsizing of the state in 1991. Since the early 1990s, the average number has been twenty-three.

As Figure 5.1 illustrates, there is a striking difference between the number of proto-states during the Russian Empire and the Soviet

[3] See Appendix B for a list of Russian proto-states.

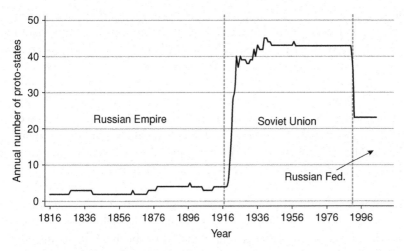

Figure 5.1 Number of Russian/Soviet proto-states.

Union. However, this is not on account of the size of the state; one might think that the state expanded dramatically after World War I and then contracted in an equally abrupt manner in 1991. Only in the latter transition did the size of the state correspond to the number of proto-states. The first and more dramatic transition had to do with the reorganization of the state during the transition from Tsarist Russia into the Soviet Union. Indeed, Russian territorial expansion had already reached its zenith by the mid to late nineteenth century.[4]

Why then did the Russian metropole generate so few proto-states during the nineteenth century when rival states like the UK created so many? One reason for this difference is geography. The UK was a maritime empire in which the territories were disconnected and far-flung; in contrast, Russia was a classic land empire. To some extent that territorial noncontiguousness resulted in more proto-states for the UK given the criterion that units are proto-states when they are separated by more than 100 miles of water or foreign soil. There is another element to this comparison, however, that speaks to the different ways

---

[4] Outside of minor alterations following the Treaty of Paris (1856) and the Congress of Berlin (1878), little would change on the western and southwestern borders of the Russian realm. The final significant phase of imperial expansion began with the annexation of the left bank of the Amur River and the Maritime Province in 1858–1860, followed shortly thereafter by the invasion of Central Asia that began in 1864 (Ledonne 2004, 235).

in which sea-based and land-based metropoles organize their political space.[5] As I showed in Chapter 4, the British developed a complex and enduring system of colonies, protectorates, and client states, a great many of which enjoyed indirect rule. For Russia, similar attempts at a client system were inherently unstable and the government tended toward direct rule. First, just demographically, ethnic Russians tended to expand with the state, particularly into the Black Sea region. Second, Russia tended to garrison its frontier territories on a permanent basis. Third, the formerly peripheral units were gradually integrated into the metropole by a process of social differentiation that created local elites whose interests became tied to the metropole.[6] Finally, these geographic realities combined with the highly centrist Tsarist regime to favor direct rule. It was for these reasons that D. K. Fieldhouse summed up the status of the Russian Empire as "a problem of distinguishing between colonies and the metropolis."[7]

The first type of proto-state, the autonomous union, consisted of two members: the Grand Duchy of Finland from 1809 to 1917 and the Kingdom of Poland (Congress Poland) from 1815 to 1864 (see Table 5.1). Both units were born during (and at the end of) the Napoleonic wars that, among other things, had resulted in a reshuf-fling and reordering of territory across Europe. The Russian metropole regarded these two regions as politically external and nationally dis-tinct. They were also meant to be indirectly ruled; although this was taken away from the Finns in the 1890s, and for Poland it was always a fiction.[8]

The creation of these units was the result of Tsarist whim built upon the recognition of the preexisting societies. This emphasis on "recog-nizing the regional identity of border territories based on their histo-ries, religion, economy, and customs," was a disposition introduced during the short reign of Paul I (1796–1801). For his part, Paul was partly reacting to the policies of his mother, Catherine II (1762–1796), who had always aimed to "replace dependence on client states and societies with direct rule by members of the elite dispatched to bor-der regions to take over management and integrate them immediately into the empire."[9] Alexander I (1801–1825), the first Tsar of the period

[5] See Kohn 1974 for an interesting comparison of Russian and American expansion.
[6] Ledonne 2004, 227. See also Hosking 1997, 39–40.
[7] Fieldhouse 1966, 334.   [8] Hatton 1974, 126.   [9] Ledonne 2004, 205.

Table 5.1 *Types of Russian/Soviet proto-states*

Type	Name	National Distinction?	Political External?	Indirect Rule?
1	Autonomous Union[a]	yes	yes	sometimes
2	Protectorates[a]	no	yes	yes
3	Soviet Socialist Republic[b]	yes	no	no
4	Autonomous Republic[b]	yes	no	no
5	Autonomous Oblast[b]	yes	no	no
6	Autonomous Okrug[b]	yes	no	no
7	Autonomous Republic[c]	yes	no	no
8	Autonomou Oblast[c]	yes	no	no
9	Autonomou Okrug[c]	yes	no	no

[a] Russian Imperial unit. [b] Soviet unit. [c] Russian Federation unit.

examined in this study, followed Paul I's lead with the annexations of Finland and Poland. Alexander I evidently pursued these policies out of sympathy for the respective regions and a desire to implement new forms of political control in the Empire. Indeed, he contemplated alternative plans for reorganizing the imperial administrative architecture. One plan "consisted in using the Polish Charter of 1815 and the organization of the Finnish central administration as models for carving out large regions everywhere else."[10] Whatever the aspirations, these additional schemes were not put into place, and the ascension of the more traditional Nicholas I (1825–1855) put an end to them.

The second type of unit was the protectorate, units that were politically external and indirectly ruled. This set included the Emirate of Bukhara, the Khanate of Khiva, and Tannu Tuva. These territories were not juridically assigned to a particular people. Rather, they were built on existing state structures and enabled the Russian state to maintain political control in a cost-effective manner. Khiva and Bukhara came under the Russian flag in the last stage of Russian imperialism that finally reached beyond the deserts of Central Asia. Both units were established using older social structures "that were carefully preserved

[10] Ledonne 2004, 211.

through methods of indirect rule."[11] The choice of indirect rule was the result of their remoteness and the politics of the Great Game, which, as discussed later, encouraged the Russians to rule at arm's length. Both units endured until 1924 when the Soviet government dissolved them in an effort to reorganize the region.

The situation of Tannu Tuva was somewhat different. Since the 1700s it had been a vassal to Mongolia, which was itself a vassal to China.[12] With Russian assistance it declared independence in 1911 at the same time that the Mongolians were also seceding from China. However, despite Tuvan hopes for sovereignty, the Russians exercised *de facto* control over the region until 1914 when it was made into a protectorate.[13] Whether the Tuvans would have kept this status under Tsarist rule is difficult to say, but the advent of World War I and the Russian Revolution set the region on a different path. The turmoil of the revolution left the region in a limbo until 1921 when Bolshevik and Tuvan leadership proclaimed it the Tuvan People's Republic. According to the Russians and later the Mongolians, this was a sovereign state, though it was not recognized by any other country. However, given that its foreign relations were entrusted to the Russians, I extended its protectorate status until 1944 when the territory was transformed into the Tuvan Oblast, a politically internal unit of the Soviet Union. Until that time it was one of a kind within the Soviet system, a relic of sorts from the days of the Tsar.

The creation of the Soviet Union resulted in a significant number of proto-states that were organized along ethnonational lines – they were politically internal, directly ruled, but nationally distinct.[14] This transformation was largely the consequence of the emphasis that Vladimir Lenin and others placed on ethnonational self-determination. In 1917, shortly after the October Revolution, Lenin issued the "Declaration of the Rights of the Peoples of Russia," which highlighted several important principles such as, for example, the right to free self-determination including secession and the formation of independent states.[15] Of course, by recognizing such rights Lenin opened the door to potential fragmentation, but he never intended for regions to actually secede. Rather, he felt that by giving minority nations distinct juridical rights

---

[11] Sarkisyanz 1974, 77–78. See also Harding 1998.
[12] Harding 1998, 235.   [13] Alatalu 1992.   [14] Simon 1991; Slezkine 1994.
[15] Nahaylo and Swoboda 1989, 18–19. Also see Roeder 2007, 57.

(and administrations) including that of secession, they would naturally prefer to remain with the Soviet Union "because big states afford indisputable advantages."[16] To some extent, Lenin's actions foreshadowed the dynamics of decentralization that have characterized center-periphery relations in many states during the latter twentieth century.

The result was a classification scheme during the Soviet era with four types of proto-states. The Type 3 unit was the Soviet socialist republic (SSR), also known as the union republic. This was the highest-level unit in the metropole's administrative architecture. Each republic supposedly had the right to secession, and this was enshrined in both the Soviet constitution and those of each republic.[17] The next unit (Type 4) was the autonomous Soviet socialist republic (ASSR). These were also administrative jurisdictions that were assigned to a specific nation. Like all of the Soviet proto-states, the specific name of the unit referenced a specific people (for example, the Ukrainian SSR, the Tatar ASSR). In terms of rank, these were considered the second-order units in the state's classification scheme, and were subordinate to union republics. The Type 5 unit was the autonomous oblast. These provincial units were given to specific nations and constituted the third rung on the so-called nationalities ladder.[18] There were only eight of these units when the metropole downsized in 1991. The final unit, Type 6, was the autonomous okrug, or area. These were administrative jurisdictions given to indigenous peoples located along the Arctic or in Siberia.

The final three types have existed in the Russian Federation since its transition from the Soviet Union in 1991. These units are in many ways an extension and legacy of the former Soviet classification scheme. The Type 7 unit is the autonomous republic, which now constitutes the first-order unit of the Russian state. Each unit is allocated to a particular minority nation, permitted a level of local governance, and allowed to decide its own language policy. The units are made up of the former ASSRs and the autonomous oblasts – the two categories were merged and upgraded after 1991. As of March 21, 2014, there were twenty-two autonomous republics. However, the most recent addition to this rank, Crimea, is disputed by Ukraine and regarded as Ukrainian by

---

[16] Nahaylo and Swoboda 1989, 15. According to Roeder, Lenin chose a federal system partly as a way to limit the expanding central bureaucracy (Roeder 2007, 57).

[17] Both Belarus and the Ukraine were members of the United Nations.

[18] Shabad 1945.

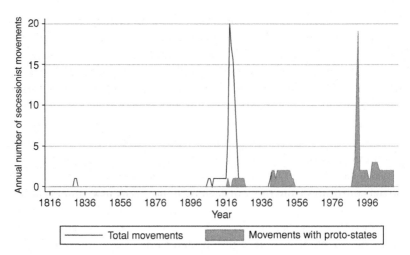

Figure 5.2 Russian/Soviet secessionist movements.

the great majority of the international community. The Type 8 unit is
the autonomous oblast, and there is only one member of this category:
the Jewish Autonomous Oblast. This was the only Soviet autonomous
oblast to not be upgraded to the status of autonomous region – the
current Jewish population in the territory is deemed too small and too
much of a minority to be given the higher status. The Type 9 unit is
the so-called autonomous okrug, an extension of the former Soviet
administrative region for indigenous peoples. Many of these have been
broken up since the early 1990s; currently there are only four.

It is worth mentioning the Commonwealth of Independent States
(CIS), which includes most of the former Soviet republics. Somewhat
like the British Commonwealth, the CIS is a confederacy of sovereign
states.[19] Although it does possess a few common political organs, its
powers are too decentralized to count as a state. As such, the respective
members are not proto-states.

Secessionism

The Russian/Soviet metropole faced a total of fifty-three secessionist
movements over the period from 1816 to 2011 (see Figure 5.2).[20] The

[19] Elazar 1994.
[20] Note that several nations mounted more than one movement (for example,
Ajaria). See Appendix B for the complete list of secessionist movements.

total number of secessionist movement years was 189, which means that the average movement lasted 3.5 years. Aside from brief efforts in Poland in the early 1830s and Gagauzia in 1906, secessionism in Russia was quite rare until World War I.[21] There was, however, a veritable tidal wave of secessionism beginning in 1917. The metropole faced twenty-five secessionist movements between 1917 and 1922, peaking at twenty movements in 1918. This striking spike in independence demands provides support for the claim made by Erez Manela that the so-called Wilsonian Moment fired the imagination of stateless nations.[22]

The government faced two subsequent waves of secessionism. The first, more of a ripple, began in 1941 and endured in some regions until the early 1950s. There were five movements during this period: Western Ukraine, Kalmykia, Karachay-Balkaria, Lithuania, and Ukraine. The final peak began in 1988 and corresponded with the downsizing of the state. Between 1988 and 2011 the government confronted twenty-two secessionist movements with a peak of nineteen movements in 1991. As of 2011, the end of the period under examination, there were two ongoing efforts in Chechnya and Dagestan.

One interesting aspect of Figure 5.2 is the contrast between the secessionist waves with respect to proto-state status. Whereas the earlier wave consisted almost entirely of nations that lacked administrative status, the second wave was dominated by proto-states. The chief cause of this contrast was the difference in administrative design. The Soviets created proto-states where few had existed before and, as I show, that approach to organization has ultimately shaped (and continues to shape) secessionist outcomes.

Conflict

There were thirty-seven secessionist conflicts over the entire time period. All told, secessionist movements in Russia were fighting the state 63 percent of the time.[23] That figure is significantly different from the 9 percent rate of conflict in the British realm.[24] Relatively speaking, secessionism in Russia has been quite violent, but the trend has

---

[21] Sarkisyanz 1974, 71.
[22] Manela 2007. In the Russian sphere, there was somewhat of a parallel Leninist Moment.
[23] Of the 189 secessionist movement years, 119 involved conflict.
[24] Of the 693 secessionist movement years, 62 involved conflict.

varied over time. The spike after World War I was essentially a wave of secessionist civil war, with nearly every movement taking the field against the state. In contrast, the majority of the secessionist efforts in the 1990s were concluded nonviolently.

The International System

This section focuses on the first part of the structured analysis: the external environment. To what extent was the expansion and contraction of the Russian state driven by the invisible hand of the international system? Did the threat of conquest and the perceived value of large economic units affect Russian calculations on territorial possession? Was World War II some sort of sea change?

The Pre-1945 Period

The expansion of the Russian state has been well documented. In Russian historiography there is a strong emphasis placed on the relationship between geography and expansion.[25] As John Ledonne states, "Russia was always on the defensive, surrounded and threatened by enemies, real and imaginary... the creation of a vast empire covering eleven time zones resulted from the need to secure protection against the encroachments of malevolent neighbors."[26] Observers of Russian history such as Robert Kerner and Boris Brutzkus stressed the psychological and political impact of the long unprotected Eurasian steppe.[27] Self-preservation incited the Russians to expand and entrench themselves in the habitats of those they conquered. However, since these new regions were themselves open for attack, the Russians were encouraged to expand further. As expansion gradually drew in Russian settlers, the boundaries between core and periphery were always fuzzy and in flux. This narrative has elements of geographic determinism: the vast open territory pushed the nation to continuously expand in search of greater security. It also resonates with the idea that powerful states will often

---

[25] Importantly, expansion did not always occur in a ratchet-like pattern, and retrenchment did take place. In 1637 the Don Cossacks captured Azov and offered it to the Tsar. But after being counseled that holding the fort would cost too much, the Tsar returned it to the Ottomans (Boeck 2009, 21–22).

[26] Ledonne 2004, 4.   [27] Kerner 1942; Brutzkus 1953.

move outward in an attempt to reach a more defensible perimeter, a concept discussed in the literatures on empires and hegemonic stability theory.[28] According to Geoffrey Hosking, this was a "characteristic feature of Russian imperialism: its tendency to forestall possible danger by expanding to fill the space it is able to dominate."[29]

Another related element of the effects of geography was the so-called urge to the sea.[30] Obtaining access to the Baltic, Black Sea, and the Pacific had long been a strategic imperative of the Russian state and it found expression in the saying that "Moscow must either dominate or suffocate."[31] From the "Volga-Oka Mesopotamia," the Russians expanded along the natural waterways connecting the Baltic, Black, and Caspian basins.[32] Expansion was common until it "ran up against natural moats such as the Gulf of Bothnia, the Danube, the Araks, and the mountains of Central Asia."

It may be that geography had a strong effect on Russian expansion, but, like the UK, we can also see Michael Doyle's pericentric and systemic factors at work.[33] Pericentric explanations locate the source of expansion in the periphery and typically point to weak sociopolitical conditions that incite the would-be empire to expand. In his 1864 defense of Russian imperialism, Foreign Minister Alexander Gorchakov evinced this way of thinking:

The situation of Russia in Central Asia is similar to that of all civilized states which come into contact with half-savage nomadic tribes without a firm social organization. In such cases, the interests of border security and trade relations always require that the more civilized state have certain authority over its neighbors, whose wild and unruly customs render them very troublesome. It begins first by curbing raids and pillaging. To put an end to these, it is often compelled to reduce its neighboring tribes to some degree of close subordination.[34]

Much like the rhetoric of superiority that took hold in Western Europe, Russian chauvinism differentiated between the less-developed societies of the hinterland and the more institutionalized polities along its southern and western perimeters. "In Central Asia, tsarist imperialism of the

---

[28] Doyle 1986; Gilpin 1981. [29] Hosking 1997, 13–14. [30] Kerner 1942.
[31] Hatton 1974, 107. [32] Ledonne 2004, 220. [33] Doyle 1986.
[34] Hosking 1997, 38.

nineteenth century used the argument that the vicinity of nomads was bound to force civilized states to expand until they reached the frontier of another civilized state."[35]

However, it is where the Russian state ran up against peer competitors that we see the effects that interstate rivalry can have on metropolitan perceptions of the value of territory. Intervention and expansion into the Caucasus was partly "motivated by the fear … that otherwise the region, already unstable, would become the base of operation of another power, Asiatic or conceivably even European."[36] Over the mountains were the Ottomans and the Persians, and by the mid nineteenth century the British lurked just beyond.

The Anglo-Russian contest for mastery of Central Asia, the so-called Great Game, is a classic illustration of how interstate rivalry can generate expansionist tendencies. It was also contemporaneous with the new imperialism of the later nineteenth century when most of the rest of the world was effectively brought into the interstate system as rival powers competed for new territory. The Russian push beyond the Aral Sea began in earnest in the 1860s and by 1884 had reached its furthest extent. Between 1864 and 1873 it subdued the successor states of the Timurid Empire: Kokand, Bukhara, and Khiva. Although the latter two remained protectorates and would outlive the Russian monarchy, Kokand was directly annexed. The effect of Russian expansion into the Pamirs and the foothills of the Hindu Kush partly resulted in the imposition of British control over Afghanistan. Russian failure to back Shaw Ali's resistance against the British – which they had encouraged – resulted in a British victory in 1879 and the Treaty of Gandamark that made Afghanistan into a British protectorate.[37] Meanwhile, Eastern Turkestan (Sinkiang), which had seceded from China in 1870 and joined the sovereign state system in 1874, was brought back under Manchu control in 1877.[38] In this way, the handful of polities that formerly composed the area had been consolidated by the 1880s under the control of three metropoles: Russia, China, and the UK. Thus the great buffer regions of Central Asia were absorbed as each state defended its perceived "legitimate interests" against the "intrigues" of its rivals.[39]

Outside of the concurrent gains across the Amur River and along the Pacific coast, the Russian frontier had mostly peaked by the late

[35] Sarkisyanz 1974, 49.   [36] Hosking 1997, 19.   [37] Sarkisyanz 1974, 62–63.
[38] Fazal 2007; Griffiths and Butcher 2013.   [39] Sarkisyanz 1974, 48.

1800s.[40] Russian expansion, which had proceeded largely by swallowing up the politically unrecognized and institutionally thin landmass along the Eurasian steppe, had finally come against natural barriers and the borders of other recognized sovereign states that the metropole could not easily push aside. The Tsar did, however, toy with other more far-flung gains that were akin to the overseas acquisitions of the Western European powers, but nothing materialized. The only African possession was the short-lived Sagallo, a small Russian settlement on the Red Sea founded by a Cossack soldier of fortune and an orthodox Archimandrite. However, this settlement was quickly bombarded into submission by the French who claimed that the Russians were violating their territorial rights.[41]

Although the security motive was probably paramount, obtaining land also brought economic benefits. It provided the state with access to the sea and a wide variety of resources. For example, obtaining preferential access to Central Asian wheat was one of the reasons for the seizure of Kokand, Bukhara, and Khiva, particularly as prices skyrocketed in the context of the American Civil War.[42] Although some goods could be gotten through trade, the optimal political arrangement was to subordinate other states where possible to nonsovereign status.

Russia preferred direct rule and rarely settled for less hierarchical relationships. Unlike the British metropole, where hegemonic relations over weaker but sovereign polities were common, Russia had less experience with informal empire. One example prior to 1945 was the fur tribute, or *iasaq*, that the Tsar demanded of many Siberian peoples.[43] However, Russian ethnic migration made these relations inherently unstable and they gradually gave way to more formalized relations of control.[44] Indirect rule was arguably even less common for the Russian state, a rarity that has endured to this day. Outside of Finland, which enjoyed indirect rule into the 1890s, only Khiva, Bukhara, and Tannu Tuva were governed in this manner. With respect to Khiva and Bukhara, the main reason given in the historical accounts for this choice of control was to placate the UK, "which regarded the

---

[40] Its most significant territorial contraction at the time was the sale of Alaska in 1867.

[41] Harding 1998, 307. Sagallo does not qualify as a proto-state because it was too small.

[42] Becker 1968, 21–23.   [43] Slezkine 1992.

[44] See Sarkisyanz 1974, 72; Hosking 1997, 14.

extent of Russia's advance with considerable apprehension."[45] Similarly, Afghanistan was absorbed in the 1870s and ruled indirectly by the British until 1920. That these buffer states were stripped of their sovereignty as part of the Great Game is not surprising given the inherent commitment problems that arise in such cases.[46]

The standard Russian calculation regarding territory survived the revolution and persisted throughout the interwar period. This is reflected both in the manner in which the state dealt with secessionism and the way in which it expanded in the 1930s. The wave of secessionism that arose between 1917 and 1923 was extremely violent – the metropole was clearly bent on retaining territory. In only five instances did the breakaway region successfully form a sovereign state: Finland, Poland, Lithuania, Latvia, and Estonia. These births were a direct consequence of World War I. As the fortunes of war ebbed and flowed on the eastern front, these nations were repeatedly courted by the neighboring powers and promised future political relationships based on autonomy and self-determination. A darling of sorts, Poland in particular was given promises by Germany, Austria-Hungary, as well as the struggling Bolsheviks.[47] The Russian state then formally surrendered these territories with the Treaty of Brest-Litovsk in 1918, along with Belarus and the Ukraine. The revocation of the treaty after the German defeat later that year set the stage for a Russian invasion, one that succeeded in retaking Belarus and the Ukraine but was repulsed by the Poles, Lithuanians, Latvians, and Estonians. Though this resurgence was successful elsewhere across the realm, most notably in the Caucuses, it was checked in Poland and along the Baltic Sea.

Only in Finland was secession peaceful insofar as Russia did not violently contest it. The Finns declared independence on December 6, 1917, in the context of the Russian Revolution and German victory on the eastern front.[48] Within weeks the declaration was accepted by Lenin who, evidently thought the emerging communist state would want to join the Soviet Union.[49] The Russian acceptance was formalized yet again a few months later at Brest-Litovsk. The birth of the Finnish state then set in motion the violent Finnish civil war in which the German-sponsored Whites overcame the Bolshevik-sponsored Reds. Although historians speculate that Finland might have

[45] Wheeler 1974, 274.   [46] Doyle 1986; Fazal 2007.   [47] Fazal 2007, 164.
[48] Armitage 2007, 151.   [49] Nahaylo and Swoboda 1989, 21.

remained a German protectorate of sorts under its new appointed monarch, the German Prince Frederick Charles of Hesse, the defeat of Germany later that year resolved the issue. Finland established a republic that was internationally recognized. Importantly, although the birth of the state was violent, I do not code it as a violent secession since the civil war was an internal one.[50]

Throughout the interwar period the perceived costs and benefits of holding territory differed little from the days of the Tsar. The state fought to deny secession where it could. In addition, it acquired new territory where possible. Although the borders were relatively static after the Soviets consolidated power in the early 1920s, the heightened interstate tensions of the latter 1930s demonstrated the peril of buffer states in the pre-1945 era. Against the odds, Poland had been resurrected in 1918, but it was situated between two states that resented its existence. Although the German and Soviet animosity toward the new state were motivated largely by a desire to regain lost territory, the heightened tension between Adolph Hitler and Joseph Stalin in the late 1930s led to its partition.[51] A similar death befell Lithuania, Latvia, and Estonia the following year when the Soviets annexed them. Memories of earlier invasions and the resulting Russian instinct to expand as a means to protect were once again at work. "Such memories go part of the way to explain the Soviet decision to occupy and reabsorb Estonia, Latvia, and Lithuania in 1939 and 1940. . . . They would serve as a shield for a German attack on the U.S.S.R."[52] In sum, the standard policy for the metropole was to obtain and hold territory.

The Post-1945 Period

How then did the end of World War II affect the metropole's perceptions regarding the value of territory? An observer of Stalin and the early postwar period would almost certainly challenge the argument that conditions had changed. The state was clearly concerned with conquest. The long history of invasion coupled with the epic struggle of the Great Patriotic War against the Germans had emphasized the need for self-preservation. Nevertheless, when viewed from a greater distance,

---

[50] Both Germany and Russia supported their respective sides and even provided small numbers of troops (Jusilla et al. 1999).
[51] Fazal 2007.   [52] Hatton 1974, 129.

certain key factors had changed after 1945, and having sovereign control over large territories decreased as both a security and an economic asset.[53] This was a consequence of the new bipolar system, the emphasis on territorial integrity, the development of nuclear weaponry, and the burgeoning liberal economic order. Although the full realization of these changes did not occur overnight, and their cumulative effect would not be felt until the state downsized in 1991, the year 1945 was the important pivot; it was the beginning of the Cold War, the nuclear age, and the postwar economic order. These effects can be examined by looking at how the state expanded (or did not expand) and how it dealt with internal calls for independence.

It is striking that the Soviet Union acquired barely any new territory after 1945. Outside of tiny acquisitions from Poland in 1951 and Estonia in 1999, the size of the state did not increase.[54] Of course, the acquisitions during the war were dramatic. The three Baltic republics were overrun and forced into nonsovereign status as union republics. In addition, sizeable portions of Germany, Poland, Czechoslovakia, Finland, Romania, and Japan were added to the Soviet Union. Importantly, however, Moscow chose not to annex the remaining Eastern European states even though its armies had penetrated deep into Central Europe. Here, the Soviets chose a form of control that was effectively informal empire.[55] That is, it exerted a tremendous amount of control over Poland, East Germany, Hungary, Czechoslovakia, Bulgaria, Romania, and Albania, but the states retained their international legal sovereignty. Why did Russia choose this form of control instead of formal rule? After all, security was arguably the central reason for maintaining a buffer zone.[56] If, as David Lake points out, the cost of acquiring these lands was already sunk insofar as the end of World War II had left the Russians in military control, why did it not bring these states under its flag?[57]

Essentially, the metropole did in Eastern Europe something that it had rarely done previously: it permitted conquered territories to maintain their sovereignty. There is no doubt that these satellite states were subordinate and engaged in a highly hegemonic relationship, but the

[53] Pravda 1992, 5.
[54] There were two sizeable additions in 1947, one from Romania and the other from Finland. However, both were de facto Russian possessions stemming from the war. In each case ownership was only formalized in 1947 (Tir et al. 1998).
[55] Lake 1999.   [56] Liberman 1996, 122.   [57] Lake 1997, 43.

relationship was intersovereign. This was evidently the preferred form of rule and the consequence was that instead of an enlarged Soviet Union there were a handful of sovereign states. Three of them – Hungary, Romania, and Bulgaria – were aligned with the Axis powers and had fought against the Soviets. None of them had formally lost their sovereignty during the conflict despite the fact that they had been overrun by Soviet forces. In contrast, Czechoslovakia, Poland, Albania, and (East) Germany had effectively died as states – that is, they exited the international community of countries. However, between 1944 and 1954, Moscow permitted the restoration of their sovereign status.

Informal empire was the optimal political relationship. "Since free elections in Eastern Europe would have produced anti-Soviet governments, and since outright annexation might have provoked another war, informal control through puppet regimes appeared the best way to protect Soviet security."[58] According to Valerie Bunce, Moscow's satellites in Eastern Europe were ideally suited for a relationship of this kind. They would be reliable allies and, crucially, they would contribute to Soviet security in the context of European conflict. Economically, informal rule would not incur the same administrative costs as more direct rule, and yet it would still provide the metropole "with greater economic stability through assured, stable, and malleable markets and through a growing and easily transferred surplus; needed primary and secondary products at low cost; and favorable terms of trade."[59] Similarly, Peter Liberman says that, "In addition to offering a territorial buffer between the West and Soviet homeland, East Germany, Czechoslovakia, Poland, and Hungary also provided economic security in the form of guaranteed trading partners and an industrial base that could be mobilized in the event of another world war."[60] Moscow could exploit and dominate these countries in a cost-effective manner even while it supported their territorial integrity as sovereign states. Not unlike the Monroe Doctrine and the American informal empire in Latin America, the Soviet relationship with these states was summed up the Brezhnev Doctrine, which reserved for the Soviets the right to intervene and support socialist regimes from internal foes.[61]

---

[58] Liberman 1996, 121. [59] Bunce 1985, 3. [60] Liberman 1996, 123.
[61] Lake 1999, 30.

This choice over the form of control once again bears out Doyle's argument that bipolar systems permit informal rule. The dominant factions in each satellite state could not easily switch allegiance to the West, nor casually shop around for a different patron. The Czech, Polish, and Hungarian leadership became tied to their Soviets sponsors in a way that was different in the pre-1945 period. When attempts at regime change from within did occur, as they did in Hungary in 1956 and Czechoslovakia in 1968, the Soviets stepped in to quell dissent. It is telling that the Soviet invasion of Afghanistan in 1979 was considered an intervention, much as Vietnam had been to the USA. The emphasis was not on annexation or the taking of sovereignty – violations of territorial integrity – but rather on the maintenance of a communist Afghanistan. This was a pattern that played out again and again around the world in the proxy wars between Soviet Union and the USA.[62] Moreover, the bipolar configuration had ripple effects on weaker states such as the UK, who had less say in the manner of rule in the periphery than did the USA and Russia. Since London had hitched its security strategy to the USA and its nuclear umbrella, it was encouraged to release former colonies provided they were on the correct side of the Cold War.

This tendency toward more decentralized forms of rule was reinforced by the introduction of nuclear weapons. In the early days of the Cold War, the satellite states in Eastern Europe augmented Soviet forces with as many as eighty divisions. Furthermore, these territories enabled Moscow to forward-deploy about 100 Soviet divisions.[63] However, as early as the government of Nikita Khrushchev, it began to sink in that nuclear weapons were transforming security strategy.[64] As John Herz put it, the old hard shell of states was broken.[65] Since large standing armies and deep territory could no longer protect against a nuclear attack, their relative importance was decreased. Granted, this realization evolved slowly – and debates persisted into the 1980s – but even early on there were signs of awareness. According to Liberman, "Beria and Malenkov were both believers in the efficacy of nuclear

---

[62] Fry 1997.   [63] Spruyt 2005, 61–62.

[64] Shenfield 1987; Catudal 1988; Lynch 1989; Garthoff 1990; Blacker 1991; Nation 1992.

[65] Herz 1976; Deudney 1995.

deterrence, which reduces the importance of territory and economic size to security."[66] Decades into the Cold War this was clearly felt.

Nuclear deterrence had long decreased the importance to Soviet security of East European territory, armies, and military-industrial capacity. Although the Soviet Union first acquired a survivable intercontinental nuclear deterrent in the 1960s and achieved nuclear parity in the 1970s, it took time for the significance of the nuclear revolution to take hold. Stalin himself denied that nuclear weapons had transformed war. Khrushchev's enthusiasm for nuclearizing the Soviet military met with stiff resistance from the High Command, and under Brezhnev Soviet doctrine went the other way, toward preparing for nonnuclear or limited nuclear war. But Gorbachev's generation, which had little or no direct experience with World War II, appears to have concluded that nuclear deterrence was enough.[67]

The effects of the global economy on the Soviet metropole are more difficult to assess. Whereas the UK and other similar states could benefit from the international economy, the Soviets were effectively cut off from it by the competitive nature of the Cold War and by the state's own internal economic logic. Just as the perceived value of large economic units declined in the eyes of the British or the French, this awareness was probably slow to come to the Soviet Union on account of the fact that it was not so integrated into the global economy nor tuned to take advantage of increasing free trade and capital mobility.[68] In that sense, changing global conditions did not have the same impact on Soviet calculations regarding territory as the other factors pertaining to security. Clearly, Moscow did not choose informal empire in Eastern Europe because the global economy enabled free trade between sovereign states. Overall, the purported effects of the global economy on territorial calculations, particularly where secession is concerned, were not present until rather late. However, it is when the Soviet leadership began to appreciate the importance of the global economy and turn toward it that secession became a possibility.

Although the collapse of the Soviet state in 1990–1991 was mostly unpredicted, scholars have subsequently been able to outline several of the most salient causes.[69] Chief among these was the feeling that the state was overstretched, that its economic model was not working,

---

[66] Liberman 1996, 123.   [67] Liberman 1996, 125.   [68] Zubok 2007, 323.
[69] Gaddis 1992/93.

and that it was outclassed by Western capitalism and the resources the West could muster. By the mid 1980s the Soviet Union was experiencing "downward mobility in the international system because of military weakness and economic deficiencies," and these problems were intertwined.[70]

Thus, when Mikhail Gorbachev took power in March 1985, he confronted a failing foreign policy just as surely as he faced a failed economy. The two were linked because it was clear to Soviet reformers that the economy would never recover in isolation from the trade, credits, and technological know-how that the international system could provide. Yet a Soviet foreign policy that so clearly challenged the interests of economic giants like Japan, the United States, and China only deepened that isolation. Gorbachev, in his first major address to the Party Congress in February 1986, called for "new thinking" in foreign policy to parallel perestroika at home.[71]

Thus began the Soviet effort at retrenchment that aimed to bring the costs of empire in line with the benefits.[72]

For Gorbachev the aim was not to give up territory. Rather, it was to open up the society and implement liberal reforms. As he saw it, the crisis that Moscow faced "reflected the interaction between two developments. One was the long-term costs of having pursued a very ambitious foreign policy. The other was more of a short-term nature. It was the failure of the Soviet Union to undergo what in the West occurred during . . . the 1970s: namely, a combined industrial and military revolution."[73] For him the solution was clear: "make the government, the economy, and the foreign policy more efficient."[74] However, as is well known, these efforts set in motion a series of events that included not only regime change in several satellite states, but also a wave of secessionism. By and large, these events happened without conflict.

I argue that a condition for secessionist civil war is that a region demands independence and the central government denies it. Why did Moscow not deny the secession of the fourteen republics? Part of the answer is that the costs and benefits of retaining territory had changed.[75] As James Goldgeier and Michael McFaul put it, the "major difference between the new and old worlds of state behavior is the role of territory in great power politics. The great powers gain neither more

---

[70] Bunce 1993, 116.   [71] Rice 1991, 160.   [72] Wolhforth 1994/95.
[73] Bunce 1993, 112.   [74] Bunce 1993, 119.   [75] Kokoshin 1998, 184–192.

secure borders nor increased wealth by adding territory."[76] Daniel
Deudney and John Ikenberry argue that the Soviet response to secessionism was shaped by the international environment.

Important sources of the new Soviet behavior lie in the world system in
which the Soviet Union is positioned. This international environment has
a paradoxical character: although the West had grown more militarily and
economically powerful, it has presented the Soviet Union with a more
benign and attractive face. With similar effect, nuclear weapons have eased
the Soviet's territorial security problem while producing new incentives for
accommodation.[77]

Liberman strikes a similar chord when he argues that the "dissolution of the Soviet Union was permitted because it was costing too
much in Western antipathy, had become less essential for Soviet security in the nuclear era, and was irreconcilable with Soviet domestic
liberalization."[78] Appreciation of these changes made it easier for Gorbachev to reorient state policy from defense to the economy.[79] "Gorbachev's primary concern was to solve Soviet domestic economic
problems, which had been compounded by high military spending and
economic isolation.[80] Ending the Cold War and improving relations
with the West would not only dampen the arms race, but would also
open foreign economic barriers."[81]

Essentially, the conditions in the international system made it easier
for the state to give up territory. First, Gorbachev made a positive decision not to intervene in the regime transitions underway in East Germany or Poland.[82] Second, by 1991, the state had decided to not use
force to attempt to deny most attempts at internal secession – although
there were a few exceptions to this that I address in the next section.

Of course, the degree to which the state deliberately downsized is
a debatable topic. For his part, Gorbachev was more interested in
holding the state together, albeit in a more decentralized, federal manner. Importantly, state leaders offered a set of opinions as to how the
state should respond to secessionism, ranging from total reassertion of
the centralized Soviet state to complete fragmentation.[83] It was only

---

[76] Goldgeier and McFaul 1992, 484.   [77] Deudney and Ikenberry 1992/93, 117.
[78] Liberman 1996, 121. Also see Levesque 1997; Bennett 1999.
[79] Nation 1992, 293.   [80] Zubok 2007.   [81] Liberman 1996, 125.
[82] Wolhforth 1994/95, 116–119.
[83] There was even discussion of implementing indirect rule in the union republics
(Nahaylo and Swoboda 1989, 312).

after the failed August coup of 1991, when Boris Yeltsin emerged as the hero, that the fate of secessionism, at least among the union republics, was sealed. Both Gorbachev and the conservatives were now discredited, and Yeltsin was free to pursue policies that accommodated secessionism. This perception further ignited independence movements and Yeltsin acknowledged the separation of the union republics that December. The process that began in the mid 1980s more or less snowballed until secessionism was very much on the table. Nevertheless, once on the table, the state did not fight to deny these demands like it did throughout its history.

One potential critique of the preceding argument is that Moscow did not accommodate all of its secessionist movements. The Chechens, Ossetians, Ajars, Abkhazians, and Tatars declared independence at the same time and yet sovereignty was not permitted to them. Moreover, the state has worked to deny all attempts since 1991. If international conditions permit states to give up territory, why has the metropole not done so in these cases? The answer, as I address in the next section, has to do with the manner in which these territorial units were organized.

In conclusion, the nature of the international system has had strong effects on the expansion and contraction of the Russian/Soviet state, much as it did the British empire. By all accounts, the aggregation of states goes back centuries, and the long expansion of Russia across Eurasia was a part of that process.[84] Conditioned by factors such as geography and perhaps just good fortune, the hand of the international system was at work in that expansion. Likewise, the system influenced the contraction of the state in the latter part of the twentieth century. Of course, that contraction came later than the UK's, and lagged the end of World War II by more than forty years, but the key international factors that permitted it were all part of the post-1945 period. Changing conditions in the international system played in a role in enabling the metropole to downsize in a peaceful manner, something it never did in an earlier period.

Domestic Administrative Structure

The guiding argument in this section is that although the external environment has altered the costs and benefits of holding territory, it

---

[84] Tilly 1975; Greengrass 1991.

is the internal structure of the state that governs how it downsizes. I now examine the consequences of state structure by pursuing the same focus questions as the previous chapter. Does having a proto-state increase the likelihood of secession for a given group? Has the Russian metropole been guided by issues of precedent setting? Does the type of proto-state matter insofar as it creates focal points in the eyes of the relevant parties?

Secessionism without Proto-states

In the Russian metropole, secessionist movements from groups with no proto-states were confined almost entirely to the early years of the twentieth century. The one exception appears to be an unsuccessful independence effort in the Western Ukraine in 1941. Strikingly, metropolitan denial *and* violence were the outcomes in every single case of secessionism from a nation that lacked a proto-state. Moreover, in only four instances did the breakaway nation succeed in establishing a sovereign state: Poland, Lithuania, Latvia, and Estonia. These were four of the five states born in the tumult of World War I and the Russian Revolution; the other was Finland. Like other minority nations throughout the country, these groups sought their statehood in the context of the war and the revolution, as well as the general collapse of the government. Unlike most of the other minority nations, the Poles and the Baltic nations had the advantage of being temporarily ceded to the Central Powers as part of the Treaty of Brest-Litovsk. In that sense, their emergence was complicated and aided by the war. Although Ukraine had also been ceded and also declared independence in 1918, it was not able to withstand a Russian invasion to retake the territory.[85] Overall, the success rate among this group was quite low as twenty-three nations were thwarted in their attempts to gain sovereign independence. Empirically, these findings support the argument that peaceful secession is less likely when the group in question does not lay claim to a proto-state. The only instances of peaceful secession in Russia between 1816 and 2011 were Finland in 1917 and the union republics in 1991, and these were all proto-states.

More generally, however, is the question as to whether these secessionist groups that lacked a proto-state were at a disadvantage? In

---

[85] Belarus had been ceded as well, but it never officially declared independence.

the British case, it was easier to detect this dynamic because there was evidence that both the metropole and seceding regions were discounting calls for independence from places such as Buganda because they were not proper administrative units. Acceptance of such calls by the British could undermine the orderly process of downsizing its colonies and protectorates along administrative lines. Moreover, acceptance by Uganda, the proto-state in which Buganda was located, risked the territorial reduction of their emerging state along lines that were ill-defined. Thus, these administrative units and their corresponding boundaries provided focal points, and they were supported by both the British metropole and the units that benefited from them.

If these dynamics were at work in the Russian case, they are harder to detect for several reasons. First, the nations that lacked proto-states existed in the pre-1945 era when a clear goal of the state was to retain territory, and the related benefits of territory were still very much appreciated. Second, a comprehensive analysis requires that one compares the fate of proto-states with non-proto-states. The difficulty, however, is that there are so few proto-states during this time. Of these, three of the former imperial units did form secessionist movements: Finland, Bukhara, and Tannu Tuva. Only Finland seceded without a conflict with the Russian state; Bukhara was put down and administratively dismembered, and Tannu Tuva merely endured until 1944 when it was reclassified. That Russia fought to retain Bukhara suggests that it was not willing to downsize its protectorates. That it released Finland, an autonomous union and the only member of its type, is an intriguing topic and I return to it subsequently. In addition, there were several secessionist conflicts among newly formed Soviet proto-states such as Bashkiria and Kalmykia. Here, the metropole was also keen to prevent any fragmentation.

I contend that administrative lines and categories have mattered greatly in the post-1945 years because this was the age of secession. Since there was an absence of secessionism from nations that lacked proto-states in these years, it is hard to test the argument that secessionist movements that lack a proto-state are less likely to be recognized and more likely to experience conflict. However, the Russian case provides an excellent opportunity to examine the consequences of different types of proto-states.

Proto-states and Their Consequences

I have argued that the formation and classification of proto-states have downstream consequences for a people and their chances of founding a sovereign state. The creation of these units is the product of geography, international strategic considerations, local political/institutional conditions, and simple chance. Once a proto-state is typed, it is set on a trajectory that affects its long-term chances at becoming independent. There is some flexibility here as units were often reclassified, dismembered, upgraded, or downgraded. In fact, some types of units appear to be stickier than others. As it turns out, the administrative units during the Soviet era – types three through six – were somewhat less sticky than British proto-states. But what matters in the end is the type of the unit when the metropole decides how to respond to its call for sovereign independence.

The establishment of the autonomous unions and the protectorates during Tsarist times is an interesting example of proto-state design. In part, it was the good fortune of Poland and Finland to have come under the Russian flag during the reign of Alexander I, a man who was sympathetic to those nations and a Tsar who expressed a keen interest in forms of rule that differed from traditional Russian methods. These units were the product of one man's sensibilities and his recognition of, and appreciation for, the preexisting societies and their corresponding political institutions. Although his hopes for implementing similar administrative arrangements elsewhere never materialized, he did grant the Finns and the Poles national distinction and a degree of indirect rule. Perhaps more of these units would have been created with time had it not been for the more conservative leanings of his successor, Nicholas I, who emphasized policies of russification.[86]

Intriguingly, the longevity of these units was inversely proportional to the degree of national consciousness at the time the proto-states were created.[87] By the early 1800s, Poland was a well-developed nation. It had been a sovereign state at various points in the past, and it had once been a dominant power in the region. In comparison, Finland had long been a possession of Sweden, and, by the early 1800s, the culture demonstrated a class divide in which a Swedish-speaking aristocracy

---

[86] Sarkisyanz 1974, 54.   [87] Ledonne 2004, 210.

lorded over a Finish-speaking peasantry. Ironically, greater national consciousness in the Polish case motivated the Poles to attempt secession and fight a series of conflicts that resulted in their defeat and administrative reorganization. In a sense, they overreached.

Meanwhile, Finnish nationalism was initially weak, but the Russians encouraged it throughout much of the nineteenth century as part of an effort to strip the territory of its Swedish identity.[88] Finland is a clear example of the identity-generating capacity of proto-states.[89] From a society that exhibited a classic pattern of diglossia in 1809, the Finnish nation and language gradually took hold in the imaginations of the people over the course of the century. Recognition of the Finnish nation by the Tsar permitted the institutionalization of the language and an emphasis on Finnish culture and texts such as the Kalevala. Whereas prior to the 1860s the idea of a state for the Finns was more of a seventeenth-century princely state, with some level of local autonomy, the notion of full sovereign independence began to emerge in the minds of the elites.

The crucial question is whether Finland was permitted to secede because of its unique status. How did Finland avoid Russian denial (and conflict) like every other secessionist movement at the time? Note that this case did support the statistical results in Chapter 3 since Finland was the only unit of its type in 1917 – a lone branch – and it did secede peacefully. There are some indications that its status mattered. Osmo Jusilla argues that Stalin "clearly recognized Finland as a state separate from Russia," and this position was held by various other leaders at the time. When evaluating the legitimacy of Estonian secession, one general stated "There is no such thing as Estonia"; there was no institutional system or political apparatus like in Finland. Indeed, years later at the Tehran Conference in the midst of World War II, Stalin would justify the "incorporation of the Baltic lands into the Soviet Union by virtue of the fact that they had not enjoyed autonomous status during the final period of Tsarist rule."[90] Thus, Finland's unique distinction had some cognitive salience and would provide an explanation for why some territories could be sovereign when others could not.

To assign all of the causal explanation to these factors, however, would probably overdraw the argument. It was also Finland's good

---

[88] Hosking 1997, 38.   [89] Roeder 2007.   [90] Jusilla 1989, 85.

fortune to declare independence relatively early, before the Bolsheviks began to suffer a string of defeats at the hands of the Whites, and before the real torrent of secessionism began. Within weeks of declaring independence on December, Finnish representatives met with Lenin in St. Petersburg and received his written acceptance.[91] Although Lenin's intentions on the matter remain an interesting and debated topic, the general consensus seems to be that he felt his recognition would "encourage the Finnish working people to engage in revolution," forge a sister state, and "freely join" the emerging Soviet state.[92] Whatever the reasons, this acceptance was vital since, as the Finns well knew, other countries would not recognize Finland until Russia did.[93] Even then recognition came slowly; in a discussion that presaged similar debates later in the twentieth and twenty-first centuries, various world leaders questioned the viability of the aspiring state.[94] Over the few next years, Finland managed to avoid any military contestation to its sovereignty by Russia. In October 1920, it signed a second treaty with Russia that recognized its independence. Two months later it joined the League of Nations. By the time Russia could have attempted a reconquest, the Finns were united and "European powers had made it clear to the Bolsheviks that that they would help in the defense of Finnish independence against any westward expansion of Bolshevism."[95]

Overall, Finland's status as a proto-state had strong generative dynamics and moderate selective consequences insofar as its status was somewhat focal in the eyes of key leaders. However, it does not seem that the Russian metropole released the unit in an attempt to downsize, like some sort of pressure valve, knowing that it could justify its denial elsewhere because of administrative categorization. There is nothing to indicate that this was Lenin's motive, although such reasoning was used later to discredit other movements. Finland's administrative status clearly helped, but so did other situational factors.

The origins of Russia's protectorates in Central Asia were different than that of Poland and Finland, and so too were the eventual outcomes. The formal accession of Khiva and Bukhara are a classic

---

[91] Note that St. Petersburg was actually called Petrograd at this point. But to avoid any confusion between those names and Leningrad, I use St. Petersburg over the entire time period.

[92] Nevakivi 1989; Jusilla et al. 1999, 105.   [93] Jusilla 1989, 90.

[94] Engman 1989, 102; Szporluk 1997, 77.   [95] Roeder 2007, 322.

illustration of the peril that buffer states faced in earlier times. "Russia's primary interest in the khanates of Central Asia ... was to ensure the friendly disposition of their governments in order to facilitate the maintenance of law and order along the Russian frontier and to prevent the penetration of British influence into the areas adjacent to that frontier."[96] In this region of Asia, the protectorate status was chosen because it could make use of the existing political structures, and because Russian leadership felt that direct control would be provocative for the British, their rival in the area.[97] As Khiva and Bukhara became embroiled in the Russian civil war conflict, both looked to assert their independence.[98] However, by 1920, both regions had been reconquered and within a few years their fate was determined by a small commission headed by Stalin. Claiming that the special status of the two territories was anomalous within the Soviet state, that the mercantile histories of the two protectorates were at odds with communism, and that, by Stalin's definition, these were really multinational units, the commission decided on a new institutional solution: "a completely new system of national republics and national oblasts to replace the traditional political divisions in the area."[99] Their political existence was terminated and the respective regions were folded into a number of new administrative units, most notably Uzbekistan.[100]

The other protectorate, Tannu Tuva, followed a different path. Unlike Khiva or Bukhara, the fact that Tannu Tuva was made into a protectorate between 1911 and 1914 had little to do with local political and institutional conditions; the traditional inhabitants of the remote region were nomadic groups of hunters and reindeer herders.[101] The metropole decision making in this case was largely strategic. The Russians were responding to a Tuvan declaration of independence – which they had actually encouraged – from China, its suzerain. China's refusal and the onset of World War I and the Russian Revolution left the situation in limbo until 1921 when the region once again declared independence as the People's Republic of Tannu Tuva. In the face of conflicting claims with China, Moscow decided to formally recognize Tuvan independence despite the fact that it maintained *de facto* control over its external relations. Mongolia followed suit, though no other country did mostly because Russian recognition was suspect. Thus, Tannu Tuva

---

[96] Becker 1968, 45.   [97] Sarkisyanz 1974; Wheeler 1974.
[98] Bukhara formed a secessionist movement.   [99] Becker 1968, 309.
[100] Allworth 1990; Slezkine 1994, 428.
[101] Ballis 1941; Mongush 1993; Minahan 1996; Harding 1998.

never joined the list of sovereign states and from that point until 1944 the unit's status was truly unique within the Soviet state. Its reorganization came during World War II when local groups, under Soviet pressure, requested annexation by the state and status as an autonomous oblast. Although the people have not again declared independence, a nationalist movement has gradually evolved and they did unilaterally declare themselves a first-order republic in 1992.

To recapitulate, there were few proto-states during the imperial period. Those that existed were created for reasons pertaining to interstate relations, the preferences of the designer, and because it was useful to build on existing nations and institutions. Most of the earlier cases demonstrate the generative function of proto-states, but perhaps only Finland shows their selective importance. However, matters changed with the reorganization of the Russian state under communism. Not only was there a proliferation in the number of proto-states, but the Soviet designers applied an administrative scheme that had far-reaching consequences for the development and successes of secessionist movements down the line.[102]

An important aspect of the Soviet administrative architecture was its vertical orientation.[103] Units were ranked in levels – first order, second order, and so on – in such a way that denoted hierarchy and status. This is different from the imperial period when the distinction between an autonomous nation and a protectorate was not clearly hierarchical. These were merely different types separated in more of a horizontal/spatial sense. As a comparison, the British architecture possessed both orientations as some types clearly possessed a higher rank – for example, the Viceroyalty of India versus the crown colonies – whereas others did not – for example, the crown colonies versus the protectorates versus the crown dependencies. The Soviet design was vertical and highly rationalized, and, as a consequence, the importance of type was reinforced. To be a first-order unit was to have a clear edge in terms of rank and the possibility of secession. Phil Roeder's notion of the "administrative upgrade" is particularly accurate in describing this arrangement. When a territory was reclassified from an autonomous republic (Type 4) to a union republic (Type 3), it experienced an administrative upgrade; the opposite was a downgrade. An upgrade from a union republic to a sovereign state was essentially an upgrade that brought full independence with it. When the entire set

---

[102] See Hale 2005 for a related discussion.   [103] Simon 1991.

of union republics seceded in 1991, the units below them experienced an upgrade of a kind since they now became the highest level.

Recognition as a union republic was particularly prestigious given that these units had the legal right to secede.[104] When granting the right, Lenin evidently felt or hoped that constituent nations would elect to remain part of the emerging Soviet federation on account of ideology as well as the fact that big states conferred undeniable advantages. However, when key units effectively called his bet, he (and the larger regime) was forced to deny any attempts in an effort to hold off state fragmentation. Thus, the right of secession was more or less a fiction until the end. It was, however, the line on which the state would make a stand in 1991.

Chance and Punishment in Soviet Administrative Designations

An important counterargument with respect to the purported effects of proto-states is simply that the long-term chances of a nation to secede peacefully have nothing to do with their administrative status. This is more or less a null hypothesis that holds that administrative designations merely reflect the underlying strength of the nation. The nations that were given proto-states during the Russian Revolution were simply the most coherent nations at that time. The type (or level) of proto-state given was merely a function of the intensity, coherence, or basic viability of the corresponding nation. Likewise, administrative upgrades (or downgrades) during the Soviet era were a function of the group's level of national development. Taken to its logical extent, this argument holds that the fourteen states that seceded in 1991 were built on the most coherent and developed nations inside the metropole when they were originally typed. The second rung down the "nationalities ladder" were likewise the second most-developed group, and so on.

I contend that the preceding argument greatly underestimates the causal impact of administrative design. In fact, the assignment and eventual consequences of national distinction in Soviet times are a marvelous illustration of the effects of administrative choice. Initial assignments were made for reasons pertaining to local conditions, punishment, and simple chance. From the beginning and throughout most of the Soviet era, the primary goal was to create an efficient structure that harnessed national energies and that could be prevented from fragmentation. In the end, these categories created a degree of cognitive salience

---

[104] Nahaylo and Swoboda 1989, 15–22.

regarding the right to secession, and the state used these categorical distinctions when responding to secessionist movements.

Many of the secessionist movements that failed to win a proto-state during the revolution were actually developed and coherent nations. After declaring independence in 1918, the Don Cossacks allied with the Whites in opposition to Bolshevik forces. Although the Cossacks sent a delegation to the Paris Peace Conference in 1919 to plead their case for sovereignty, and were one of the most powerful military units in the anti-Bolshevik forces, their attempted secession was put down violently by 1920. "The Soviet authorities, determined to end the Cossack threat to their control, ended all traditional Cossack privileges, prohibited military training, and banned the use of the Cossack language and forbade all references to Cossack culture or history."[105] They were then reclassified as ethnic Russians. A similar fate befell the Kuban and Terek Cossacks, two nations that also declared independence in 1918. The unfortunate alignment of many Cossacks with the Germans in World War II resulted in even further suppression. Despite a national revival beginning in the 1980s and an ongoing effort to wrest greater autonomy from the state, the Don Cossacks have not been given a proto-state.

Circassia was a fairly well known nation and territory in earlier times, and it had a long history of conflict against the Tsar. Map 5.1

Map 5.1 Circassia and surrounding administrative units.[106]

[105] Minahan 1996, 158.
[106] GADM 2012; map adapted from Putin's Party, *National Geographic*, January 2014.

illustrates the extent of the Circassian nation in 1855, superimposed on administrative boundaries that would be created during the Soviet era. Like many groups the Circassians made a bid for independence in 1918 that ended in military defeat. In the aftermath of the Civil War, the metropole chose to divide the nation over several administrative units that combined other local nations in an effort to dilute the national identity. Such efforts by Moscow to manage its nations have been somewhat successful in reducing independence efforts, though calls for an autonomous Greater Circassia have become more common in recent years

Many nations with a developed institutional structure and international support fared badly in the awarding of administrative status. Consisting of a frontier culture built on the fusion of Slavic and Germanic immigrants mixed with local Evenki, Chukot, and Koryak, the Far Eastern Republic attempted to secede in 1918. In a breathtaking struggle at the far end of the Trans-Siberian Railroad, the Far Easterners fought for independence alongside White and Japanese forces, with smaller contingents of American, British, Canadian, French, and Italian troops, as well as the famous Czechoslovak Legion that had essentially fought its way from Europe all the way to Vladivostok. When defeat came in 1920, all calls for autonomy were ignored as the region was absorbed administratively into the Russian Republic.

Of the nations that were assigned a proto-state, there were a considerable number of upgrades, downgrades, and general reformations. Although they had fought vigorously against the Bolsheviks between 1917 and 1919, and had allied with the Terek Cossacks for a time, the Chechens were given an autonomous oblast in 1922. Chechnya was then combined with Ingushetia in 1936 and made into an autonomous republic. The unit was later downgraded in 1944 as a punishment because numerous Chechens had collaborated with Nazi Germany. Then, as part of a rehabilitation effort in 1957, the unit was upgraded back to the level of autonomous republic. It remained that way until 1991 when the Chechens and Ingushetians divided into two separate autonomous republics (see Map 5.1).

These administrative changes can have enormous consequences down the line. Although it was initially made a union republic in 1919, Crimea was downgraded to the status of autonomous republic in 1921.[107] Then, in 1954, it was made a gift from the Russian to the Ukrainian union republics as part of the 300th anniversary of their

---

[107] Minahan 1996, 139.

union. The reasoning behind that administrative transfer has been challenged recently by Russian secessionists in Crimea, who objected to the fact that the peninsula was part of an emerging Ukraine in 1991, and not Russia.

The consequence of an administrative change is well illustrated by the case of Karelia. After the Winter War of 1940, the autonomous republic of Eastern Karelia was joined with the Finnish lands acquired during the war to become a union republic. Later, in 1956, the unit was downgraded once again to the level of autonomous republic. Had it kept its status for the remainder of the Soviet era and remained a first-order unit until 1991, it would likely have enjoyed the fate of Tajikistan, Kyrgyzstan, and the other union republics and become a sovereign state.

The point behind these examples is to emphasize the manner in which these units were created and changed. For administrative designers such as Stalin, the goal of economic efficiency as well as the managing of national loyalties was an objective. "The dominant principle governing this administrative reorganization was the conversion of the arbitrary and economically shapeless pre-Soviet divisions into units closely integrated according to natural, cultural, and, above all, economic criteria."[108] For that matter, the punishment of nations deemed disloyal was also an important factor, though the line between spite and efficiency could be blurry.

For purposes of this study, it is the rationale behind union republic status that deserves the most scrutiny. Although these were supposed to be the highest rung on the nationalities ladder, the line between them and second- or even third-order units was vague and periodically crossed. Being granted a union republic was not a clear indicator of population size. Tatarstan, an autonomous republic, possessed more than 6 million inhabitants in 1990; whereas, Estonia, a union republic, possessed barely a million.[109] One explanation focused on external boundaries: "Stalin refused to grant the Tatars the status of a union republic on the spurious argument that Tatarstan did not border on a foreign territory and thus would not be able to exercise its constitutional right of secession."[110] Even if this was Stalin's true reason and not simply a convenient explanation, it is not clear that it does justice to state viability. After all, Uzbekistan has one outside border with Afghanistan, and now has the interesting distinction of being one of

[108] Shabad 1945, 304.   [109] Nahaylo and Swoboda 1989, 4.
[110] Szporluk 1997, 77.

the two doubly landlocked countries in the world.[111] Although another
explanation insisted that union republics recognize a majority nation,
the Kazakhs were themselves a minority in Kazakhstan in 1991.[112]
In sum, there was a fair amount of administrative whim in the design
and recognition of these units. This is not to say that those nations that
got union republic status did not deserve it. It is just that others were
probably equally deserving.

In the long run, the primary reason these distinctions mattered is
that Moscow used them to select which groups could secede from those
who could not. In late 1991 it recognized the independence of the union
republics, citing their legal right to secession. Meanwhile, it refused to
recognize lower-order units such as Tatarstan, Dagestan, and Chechnya
even though they had declared independence prior to several of the
union republics. The metropole effectively downsized by permitting
the secession of its first-order units only. Importantly, that distinction
was focal insofar as it provided a measure of cognitive salience and a
clear line on which it would resist any further attempts at secession.

Of course, the conceptual distinction between a union republic and
an autonomous republic should not be overstated. The difference was
not as salient as, say, the perceived difference between a British dominion or internal country and a crown colony. The Soviet classification
system, after all, allowed mobility up and down the nationalities ladder. In fact, Gorbachev attempted to elevate the status of autonomous
republics such as Tatarstan and Chechnya in his final days of power.
His reasons were simple.[113] Unlike Yeltsin, he wanted to hold the state
together in a federal manner. Upgrading the autonomous republics
would provide them with the legal right to secede and, thus, deter the
metropole from permitting any secession since now it stood to lose an
additionally nontrivial amount of territory. Although it is unclear what
would have happened had he succeeded, the efforts itself speaks to the
focal nature of proto-states. These types provided the metropole with
a clean way in which it could downsize.

The government's choice as to who could secede was then backed
by international law and the other union republics. Whereas decolonization had made use of (and slightly modified) the principle of

---

[111] The other is Liechtenstein.   [112] Roeder 2007, 304.   [113] Toft 2002, 94–95.

uti possidetis, the collapse of communism paved the way for the most recent iteration of the principle: the privileging of higher-order administrative units.[114] Although the Soviet Union did not fit within the traditional colonial framework, its union republics now had the right to secession on account of consent. The manner of that secession was to be guided by *uti possidetis*, which naturally alighted on clearly defined territorial units regardless of their provenance. Moscow's choice was thus reinforced by international law; its lower-order units had neither consent nor the domestic legal right to secession. Moreover, their acceptance would threaten the territorial integrity of the emerging states.

This last point was clearly one of the reasons that Moscow's decision was supported by the other union republics. Article 5 of the Agreement Establishing the Commonwealth of Independent States (CIS) held that each member state would hold as inviolate their respective territorial integrity. Many of the new states were of course born with their breakaway proto-states – for example, South Ossetia, Gagauzia. Just as many of the former British proto-states worked with the metropole to deny internal groups the right to secession, the same patterns of collusion existed between Moscow and its union republics.

Although other explanations for secession from the Soviet Union help complete the picture, they tend to elide the selective importance of proto-states. One argument for why the first-order units seceded when the second- and third-order units did not focuses purely on the generative importance of proto-states. As Roeder argues, the union republics had greater autonomy and were thus better positioned to become a sovereign state.[115] This is certainly true and it speaks to the downstream consequences of type, but there is more to the story. A number of territories have generated strong nationalist movements and have fought to obtain independence. Nations such as Chechnya are clearly determined, and the effort to suppress them has proven costly for Russia. Therefore, there must be other characteristics beyond the local capabilities of proto-states that influence which units the metropole selects for release. This is not simply a function of the number of other movements, as Barbara Walter argues. After all, Moscow was "willing to grant independence to the Kazakhs, Kirghiz, Moldavians,

---

[114] Bartos 1997; Radan 2002.   [115] Roeder 2007.

Tadzhiks, Ukrainians, and Uzbeks even though these territories contained valuable strategic features," and, for that matter, it was simultaneously denying independence for arguably less valuable autonomous republics.[116]

Walter's argument is best suited for explaining the dynamics of secessionism when the units in question are the same type. Since 1991 the Russian Federation has faced secessionist movements in Chechnya, Dagestan, and Tatarstan. The government's position has been to refuse these demands, and conflict has resulted in Chechnya and Dagestan. Importantly, Moscow often uses language that evokes the problem of precedent setting and the need to demonstrate resolve. The loss of Dagestan could produce a "domino effect" that would embolden other republics in the Russian Federation to seek independence.[117] Additionally, "Putin has vowed to relentlessly defend the 'links in the chain' that make up the Russian Federation." Given that Russia currently has twenty-one autonomous republics (excluding Crimea), its first-order units, and many of these had secessionist movements in the past and could in the future, it clearly has a need to demonstrate its resolve. It could downsize this category as it did the union republics in 1991, but of course that would greatly reduce the size of the state again.[118]

Unfortunately, international law currently works against the secessionist movements in the Russian Federation and in the former Union republics.

According to the overwhelmingly accepted *uti possidetis* principle, only former constituent republics such as Georgia but not territorial sub-units such as South Ossetia or Abhazia are granted independence in case of dismemberment of a larger entity such as the Soviet Union. Hence, South Ossetia did not have the right to secede from Georgia, and the same holds for Abkhazia for much of the same reasons. Recognition of breakaway entities such as Abkhazia and South Ossetia by a third country is consequently contrary to international law in terms of an unlawful interference in the sovereignty and territorial integrity of the affected country, which is Georgia.[119]

---

[116] Walter 2009, 6.   [117] Holmes 1999, 3; Walter 2009, 22.

[118] Hale argues that the current administrative structure makes it harder for Russia to fragment (Hale 2005). I discuss this argument in Chapter 7.

[119] Council of the European Union 2009, 17.

The current international legal debate on secession attempts to find a middle ground between the principle of self-determination and the principle of territorial integrity. I have argued that states often solve this dilemma by discriminating between types of internal movements, thus raising the right to self-determination in some cases, and subverting it to their need for territorial integrity in others. Administrative distinctions provide states with a useful mechanism for making these decisions, and these distinctions can endure beyond the state that created them and control the destiny of subordinate nations.

Tidal Effects

Like the UK, the Russian case demonstrates the tidal character of secessionism. Between 1917 and 1991 there were two significant waves and one small wave after World War II. These waves were not simply the result of predetermined structural conditions. Rather, as Mark Beissinger argues, there was groundswell that rippled through various nations and motivated them to seek independence.[120] In addition, there were common triggers in each episode that initiated the wave: the revolution, the German invasion during World War II, and the reform policies of Gorbachev.

The massive wave of secessionist violence that attended the Russian Revolution is consistent with the theories of both Beissinger and Walter. The trigger was the collapse of the monarchy, but this set off a wave of secessionism as one nation after another responded to the emerging anarchy by declaring independence. Such declarations and the resulting violence furthered the perception of anarchy and encouraged other nations to attempt the same. That such a high number of nations resorted to making formal declarations of independence speaks to the spread and spillover of self-determination rhetoric – only two such declarations had been made against the Russian state in the previous 100 years. In addition, there was mutual empowerment as various nations allied with one another against the central government. However, because Lenin and his comrades sought to hold the state together by whatever means possible, violence was almost always the outcome.

---

[120] Beissinger 2002.

The second wave that occurred during World War II was much smaller and the tidal effects were not as pronounced. The clear trigger was the war, but the attempts at secession were more isolated. The recently reconquered Baltic states attempted to secede at the end of the war, but they were unsuccessful. Meanwhile, a handful of other nations, particularly in the Caucasus, declared independence. For example, both the Karachay and the Kalmyks declared independence once again in 1942. However, the clear connection between these two groups was not so much other secessionist nations as it was the German army that had overrun the area and encouraged grievance-bearing groups to rise up. There may have been some spillover here as one group observed the other, but it seems that it was the Germans who did the empowering.

The third wave is, of course, a great example of nationalist mobilization and the tidal effects of secessionism. Beissinger describes these events in detail and chronicles how independence movements developed their own momentum and how they each leveraged the attempts of others. Nevertheless, one wonders if the state would have shown greater resolve had the perceived value of territory not diminished in the post-1945 period. Moreover, the state did show resolve in several cases, and its choice as to where to do so fell along administrative lines. In a sense, the Soviet architecture provided the metropole with a release valve: it permitted the wave among the union republics but withstood it among the autonomous republics. Notably, this choice was supported by the union republics, which points out the limits of mutual empowerment.

How secessionism would have played out in the absence of that administrative structure is quite another question, fascinating to speculate upon and difficult to answer. I have argued that the choice to declare independence is partly endogenous to the anticipated response of the metropole, which is in turn shaped by administrative realities. As such, nations that possess the right status, such as the Kazakhstan, may find secession thrust upon them and declare independence half-heartedly. Conversely, desiring nations that lack the correct status may decide to forego a secessionist bid. Five lower-order units declared independence in the final days of the Soviet Union – Adjaria, Abkhazia, South Ossetia, Tatarstan, and Chechnya – and all were denied. Would others have declared independence if the administrative obstacles were absent? One way to answer this question is to identify secessionist movements that emerged after the Soviet breakup. My dataset shows six cases: Dagestan, Transnistria, Gagauzia, Nagorno-Karabakh, Talysh-Murhan Republic, and Crimea. With the exception of Dagestan, which is part of Russia, all of these movements withheld their secessionist bids against Moscow and took them up instead against their new sovereigns. Indeed, recent events have shown that that ambition endures in Crimea.[121]

The Effects of Regime Type

What were the effects of democracy (or autocracy) on secessionist outcomes? Russia's level of democracy over time has been much lower than the UK's and it has been characterized by movements both away and toward greater autocracy. For the entire nineteenth century, the regime was perfectly autocratic. It then began to become less autocratic in 1905 and during the revolution years. However, consolidation of the state resulted in a highly autocratic regime and remained so until Stalin's death in 1953.[122] Although it became slightly less autocratic over the next few decades, as measured by the Polity IV index, it was not until 1988 that real democratic institutions were introduced. The state began to transition in 1991 and 1992, and since then it has persisted as a transitional democracy.

At first glance, it is unclear whether the Russian regime rendered secessionism more or less likely. The secessionist rate among proto-states was slightly lower in Russia (3 percent) than when compared with the UK (6 percent). However, 43 percent of Russian secessionist movements did not cohere with proto-states, whereas in the UK 16 percent did. This pattern makes sense given that much of the secessionists in Russia took the field before the Soviet era when proto-states were rare.

Interestingly, the two main secessionist waves occurred during a move away from autocracy in the general, albeit limited, direction

---

[121] The Russian Crimeans mounted a short-lived secessionist movement against Ukraine in 1992.

[122] According to the Polity IV dataset, Russia's polity score (on a scale from 0 to 20) was 0 from 1816 to 1904, 2 in 1905, 4 from 1906 to 1916, 9 from 1917 to 1921, 3 from 1922 to 1926, 2 from 1927 to 1932, 1 from 1933 to 1952, 3 from 1953 to 1987, 4 in 1988, 6 in 1989, 10 from 1990 to 1991, 15 in 1992, 13 from 1993 to 1999, 16 from 2000 to 2006, and 14 from 2007 to 2011.

of democracy.[123] Lenin's issuance of the Declaration of the Rights and the Peoples of Russia provided the principle and the exit option for national groups, and it no doubt incited the Finns and others to seize the opportunity.[124] Similarly, the liberalization of the state under Gorbachev acted as a catalyst in the late 1980s. Bruce Parrott argues that liberalization makes peaceful secession possible, and that it appears to be a necessary but not sufficient condition.[125] Although necessity is probably too strong a claim – peaceful secession has occurred in fairly autocratic settings (Norway from Sweden in 1905) – there may be something to the relationship between democratization and secessionism.[126] Perhaps liberalization and democratization removes repressive constraints, introduces uncertainty, and mobilizes ethnic identity though vote-seeking. I return to this notion in the next chapter.

How does regime type in this case influence metropolitan response and the possibility of conflict? Since democratic norms and institutions were either missing or absent over the period in question, it is useful to compare Russia/Soviet Union with the UK. Secessionists in the British realm often appealed to liberal norms when pitching their cause and one of their targets was the core population of the British state. It is not clear that similar appeals have resonated with the Russian state and society in quite the same way. However, a more salient difference centers on institutions and democratic procedures. Whereas the British metropole preferred movements that followed proper institutional channels, such channels did not really exist for secessionists in the Russian/Soviet metropole. They could not really vote their way out as some of the British proto-states did, and as the Scots almost did and may still do. Democratic institutions can prevent conflict by encouraging secessionists to bargain in the political arena. These possibilities are mostly absent in contemporary Russia where bargaining is weak and the metropole takes a more muscular approach. For regions such as Chechnya, whose path to independence is blocked by the state and international law, the only recourse is to give up or fight.

---

[123] The change in polity score provides evidence for these transitions (see previous footnote).
[124] Nahaylo and Swoboda 1989, 18–19.   [125] Parrott 1997, 19.
[126] Kohli 1997.

This conjecture explains the finding in the quantitative analysis that democracy is most significant in relation to conflict. Democracy matters for denied movements because it presents the group with more options. In advanced democracies, secessionist movements should be more inclined to seek peaceful devolution and peaceful secessionism. As long as the state holds out a hand, the relative cost of doing otherwise is expensive and the more violent factions of the movement can be marginalized. In nondemocracies, these channels are either absent or else too weak to build confidence. Without an outlet other than the status quo, power is shifted within the movement to those more willing to use violence. I explore this conjecture in the chapters to come.

Conclusion

A close examination of the Russian case yields the following narrative. Like many states, Russia experienced a long period of expansion throughout the eighteenth and nineteenth centuries. Security and economic motives were clearly a cause of this expansion as Russia's geographic position on the exposed Eurasian axis interacted with pericentric and systemic factors to push the state outward. These pressures then subsided in the post-1945 period as bipolarity, nuclear weapons, globalization, and the near disappearance in territorial conquest gradually affected the perceived costs and benefits of controlling territory.

For much of its history the state chose direct forms of rule and thus created few proto-states. However, in many ways the Russian Revolution was an inflection point in the trajectory of the state, and not least was the way in which it organized its political space. Previous proto-states such as its Central Asian protectorates were deconstructed in hopes of creating more manageable nationalities. More dramatically, the so-called prison of nations was transformed into an administrative system that recognized minority nations and, in theory, awarded them a degree of local autonomy. This was all done in a curious attempt to empower revolutionaries, to discredit the russocentric policies of the Tsar, and, perhaps most importantly, to hold the state together. The effects of these decisions had enormous downstream consequences with respect to both the shaping of national identities and their eventual chances for peaceful secession.

Overall, the Russian case supports nearly all of the central hypotheses. External factors affected Russian calculations much as predicted, though economic considerations generally took a back seat to security concerns. If the Russian case is particularly supportive of my central argument, it is with respect to the importance of proto-states. It demonstrates how metropoles can discriminate between movements when faced with a tidal surge of secessionism.

6 | *India and Its Many Nations*

There is not, and never was an India, or even any country of India, possessing, according to European ideas, any sort of unity, physical, political, social or religious.

– John Strachey[1]

Despite the fact that India has only existed as a sovereign state since 1947 – and thus cannot be analyzed in the pre-1945 era – it is an appropriate case study for several reasons. First, there is the great diversity in terms of nation and ethnicity. Most (if not all) of the world's major religions are found in India. Linguistically, the state is remarkably varied: when the state was born in 1947, there were twenty-seven languages with a million or more speakers each, and many of these possessed mutually unintelligible scripts.[2] Superimposed upon the religious and linguistic cleavages are complex differences in caste and ethnicity. To a large extent, the very existence of the Indian state is the artifact of the pre-1945 expansionary period. When the British gradually made inroads into the subcontinent during the eighteenth and nineteenth centuries, they pieced together, and brought under one flag, a veritable international system of polities, tribal groups, and princely states. Observation of this fact led British Administrator John Strachey to make the preceding comment regarding India's origins. In that sense the history of India is consonant with the general pattern of expansion and contraction that has characterized world politics in recent centuries: from a very large number of polities in 1800, the subcontinent was reduced to a single proto-state under a distant metropole.[3] Since then, it has fragmented into four sovereign states – India, Pakistan,

---

[1] Strachey 1888, 5–8.　　[2] Dasgupta 1970, 31–68.

[3] Griffiths and Butcher identify twenty-eight independent states in the region in 1816, but a significant number had only recently exited the system through conquest and formal accession (Griffiths and Butcher 2013). Indeed, Henige identifies 291 princely states that existed around 1800, though many of these

Bangladesh, and Bhutan – and the possibility of further fragmentation is far from remote.[4]

The consequence of this diversity presents the Indian state with the difficult task of holding together and/or managing the process of downsizing. In fact, holding together has been one of country's central challenges. As one scholar notes, its 1950 constitution was "a federal reaction to a federal situation."[5] After achieving its independence from the British in 1947, the central government "attempted to carve a federal polity out of a system which was administratively unitary (as it had evolved under British rule)."[6] Recognizing the difficulty in maintaining a large ethnically and linguistically diverse population, the central government opted for a federal arrangement that could maintain unity and yet grant a degree of regional autonomy. Mohit Bhattacharya writes that what "ultimately emerged was a devolutionary federation as a fundamentally unitary state devolved power on the units through a long process of evolution . . . attention was focused on the central authority that would hold the nation together."[7] During its relatively short life span, the Indian state has faced eleven formal secessionist movements, and five of these still existed in 2011 (see Table 6.1). India is one of the most secessionist-prone countries in the world. This, coupled with the number of potential movements and the mosaic of religions, languages, and cultures, makes India an important region for the analysis of secessionism.[8]

The second reason India is a good case study is that the political-administrative architecture is articulated. The federal structure is asymmetric and, as will be discussed later, not all of the proto-states are categorized in the same way. This articulation lets one compare outcomes and examine whether the metropole has responded to secessionist movements in the manner theorized. Since its inception, India has dealt with a number of secessionist movements, it has fought a handful of secessionist civil wars, and it has seen the secession of one unit, Bhutan, which was born as a sovereign state in 1971.

were subordinate to other polities (Henige 2004, 2). Also see Butcher and Griffiths 2015.
[4] Both Sri Lanka and the Maldives are also sovereign states, but neither was previously subordinate to India.
[5] Sawyer 1969, 46.   [6] Tummala 1996, 374.
[7] Bhattacharya 1992, 101–102.
[8] There have been numerous potential and nearly formal movements like Dravidistan (Kohli 1997, 334).

Table 6.1 *Indian secessionist movements*

Secessionist Movement	Year	Proto-state?	Conflict?
Jammu-Kashmir	1947–1949	yes	no
Jammu-Kashmir	1989–2011	yes	1989–2011
Hyderabad	1948	yes	1948
Nagaland	1948–2011	yes	1956–1959, 1961–1968, 1992–1997, 1999, 2005–2007
Manipur	1964–2011	yes	1982–1988, 1992–2000, 2003–2009
Mizoram	1966–1986	no	1966–1968
Bhutan	1971	yes	no
Tripura	1978–2011	yes	1978–1988, 1992–1993, 1995, 1997–2004, 2006
Assam	1979–2010	yes	1983–1991, 1994–2010
Khalistan (Sikh)	1981–1993	no	1983–1993
Bodoland	1986–2011	no	1989–1990, 1993–2004, 2009–2010

Finally, India is a good case study insofar as it is somewhat representative of a set of states that have faced multiple secessionist movements over the postwar period. India was not a great power such as Russia or the UK. It did not participate in the great expansion of the lead states in earlier times, and thus it has only suffered secessionism in the international climate of the post-1945 period. Like Ethiopia, Indonesia, or Burma, a primary goal of the state has been to hold together its various national groups.[9] Scholars of India routinely point out the remarkable ability of the state to balance its centrifugal tendencies and often placate secessionist demands.[10] India thus provides an appropriate case in which to analyze how governments manage simultaneous independence movements.

The structure of this chapter is nearly identical to the previous two chapters. I start with a description of Indian proto-states, secessionist movements, and the related conflicts. I next explore the degree to which international systemic factors have influenced the state with respect to

[9] For consistency, I use the name Burma rather than Myanmar since it was the name over the majority of the period in question.

[10] Kohli 2001; Chandra 2005; Stepan et al. 2011.

territorial expansion and contraction. However, unlike the previous chapters, I do not analyze the response of the Indian metropole in the pre-1945 era for the simple reason that it was not yet a sovereign state. I then turn to the state's domestic administrative structure, investigating how it has shaped secessionist outcomes, and I provide a vignette that looks at the consequences of administrative design in the northeast of India. Finally, I examine two alternative explanations that were supported in the quantitative analysis and in the previous two case study chapters: the tidal effects of secessionism, and the influence of regime type.

Proto-states, Secessionism, and Conflict

Proto-states

The Indian metropole has structured its units into three categories.[11] Of these, the dominant type is the state. As of 2011, there were twenty-eight Indian states that are organized along linguistic lines. Given that each state is meant to denote a particular ethnic or national group, all of these units meet the criteria for being a proto-state.[12] The concept of linguistically defined states began with the States Reorganization Act of 1956. Between 1947 and 1956, the Indian states were organized in a somewhat different manner that reflected the facts on the ground when in 1947 the fledgling Indian state inherited a bewildering array of different types of units that had all been subordinate to British Raj. Through various combinations of existing polities, the young state organized its states into three roughly equal categories that reflected whether the state was formerly a princely state, a governor's province, or a commissioner's province. Of these units, only the former princely states were coded as having national distinction and, thus, were accorded proto-state status.[13] However, after the State Reorganization Act of 1956, all states counted as proto-states.

---

[11] None of the Schedule 6 autonomous areas met the criteria for being a proto-state. These are typically too small, lacking in national distinction, or absent a discrete administrative area.

[12] Each unit also meets the necessary size criteria (Elazar 1994, 105).

[13] "Princely State" was the name given to the members of a large set of states existing across South Asia during the period of British acquisition and control of the region (Roy 1981; Yvas 1991). Quite diverse in kind, these states varied in terms of political status. Some were independent, some were ruled as

The second category of units includes the seven union territories. Unlike the states, which elect their own governments, the Indian president directly appoints the chief executive of the union territories.[14] The details of the units vary. Some units such as Pondicherry, Dadra and Negra Haveli, and Daman and Diu were territorial transfers from the French and Portuguese. Delhi and Chandigarh are capital territories.[15] Others, such as Lakshadweep and the Andaman and Nicobar Islands, are centrally administered archipelagos. However, only two of the territories count as proto-states: (1) Pondicherry for its special French-speaking status; and (2) Andaman and Nicobar Islands on account of their distance from the mainland.

The third category consisted of two proto-states: Bhutan and Sikkim. Both of these were indirectly ruled, politically external units that enjoyed protectorate status. However, this arrangement ended in 1971 and 1975 when, respectively, Bhutan seceded and Sikkim became an Indian state. The special status of these units was a holdover from the British period and persisted for nearly thirty years under the Indian metropole.

Secessionism

The data show eleven secessionist movements between 1947 and 2011 (see Table 6.1). One of the movements was a repeat attempt – Jammu-Kashmir.[16] Three of the movements did not stem from or lay claim to a proto-state. These include the Sikh efforts at creating an independent Khalistan, a region that draws on various other states within the greater Punjab. In addition, neither Bodoland nor Mizoram were proto-states, although Mizoram became a state in 1986 partly as a result of the secessionist efforts. Except for Bhutan, all of these movements occurred within type one units (states). There were no secessionist movements within the union territories. Interestingly, however, the only unit to actually secede was Bhutan, a Type 3 unit.

protectorates, and many were involved in complex patterns of hierarchy that could be traced to the Mughal Empire (Butcher and Griffiths 2015).

[14] According to the system discussed in Appendix B, the states enjoy direct-local rule and the union territories have direct-appointed rule. The states have greater autonomy, but are not indirectly ruled.

[15] Chandigarh is the capital territory of two provinces: Haryana and Punjab.

[16] The Sikhs had also tried for independence (from the British) just prior to the birth of India.

Map 6.1 India and its federal states.[17]

Conflict

Finally, conflict between these movements and the Indian metropole were common. The only cases in which conflict did not occur were Bhutan and the early movement in Jammu-Kashmir. Collectively, these movements can be placed into several groups (see Map 6.1). The issue of Jammu-Kashmir represents a long-standing issue in the northwest of India, one that serves as a point of contestation between Pakistan and India. The Sikh movement in the northwest, which aimed at forming the state of Khalistan, flashed briefly in 1947 under British rule and was reborn in the early 1980s. Khalistan, however, is not shown on a political map of India because it is not coterminous with an administrative

[17] GADM 2012.

unit. The claimed area encompasses the greater Punjab and includes eastern portions of Pakistan. It does not qualify as a proto-state.

The south of India has also experienced secessionism. During the first few years of the Indian sovereign, the princely states of Hyderabad attempted to secede, as did Travancore immediately before the birth of India. Tamil Nadu has also flirted with separatism over the years, but the principal groups have never declared independence and thus do not qualify as secessionists. Finally, the northeast of India has been the location of multiple independence movements and one secession (Bhutan); in total, four of the seven sister states of the northeast have formed secessionist movements (Assam, Nagaland, Manipur, Tripura).[18] Bodoland encompasses a section of northwestern Assam, along the Bhutanese border. It is not an administrative unit and is not counted as a proto-state.

The International System

In this section I study the ways in which international systemic factors have influenced the Indian metropole with respect to territorial possession. As I have illustrated in the British and Russian cases, the hand of the international system played a significant role in driving expansion and contraction. Are those same factors present in the Indian case? Did the threat of conquest and the perceived value of large economic units affect Indian calculations on territorial possession? India is a challenging case in which to study these dynamics for at least two reasons. First, the state was only born in 1947 and therefore there is no pre-1945 period and no historical pivot to examine how the government responded to changing international conditions. Second, India has had numerous territorial disputes including its long-running contest with Pakistan over Kashmir and its competition with China over regions in the Himalayas. Nevertheless, I contend that India's behavior is broadly consistent with my argument.

A useful starting point is with the one instance of full secession. The overall trajectory of Bhutanese sovereignty fits the general pattern of expansion and contraction that has characterized the world

---

[18] Mizoram's secessionist movement ended with the establishment of the state. Neither Meghalaya nor Arunachal Pradesh has formed a secessionist movement.

over the past several centuries. Like neighboring Sikkim, Bhutan sat on the boundaries of the British, Tibetan, and Chinese spheres of influence. As with so many of the political units located on the rim of British India, Bhutan was eventually brought under the Raj as a protectorate. Indeed, Ugyen Wangchuk's consolidation of power as king at the turn of the century was aided by British support and recognition. For Wangchuk, the 1910 treaty was partly a refutation of Chinese influence. For the British, "the main objective behind the treaty was to contain all foreign influence, particularly that of the Chinese in the south of the Himalayas."[19] Bhutan is thus a demonstration of Tanisha Fazal's argument regarding the peril of buffer states in the pre-1945 era: the chances of conquest or accession – that is, sovereign state death – increases for buffer states caught between two larger countries.[20]

Although this rivalry receded in the first half of the twentieth century as the Chinese state underwent revolution, it returned again with the establishment of communist China in 1949. Only this time the suzerain was India rather than the UK. With the formalization of Indo-Bhutanese relations in 1949, the state of Bhutan began its diplomatic balancing act that aimed to avoid deeper association with India, and yet keep its distance from an expanding China. The period from 1949 until 1962 was thus a somewhat precarious time as China first acquired Tibet in 1950 and then applied pressure along the Himalayan rim, culminating in the Sino-Indian War of 1962. Despite Chinese efforts at courting Bhutanese leadership, it seems that India generally had the upper hand, with Bhutan content to maintain its quasi-dependent relationship in which they stated "we do not consider ourselves dependent. But we are not one hundred per cent independent because of the 1949 treaty."[21] Indian financial aid and diplomacy effectively secured Bhutan from Chinese encroachment. In sum, this was balance of power politics.

Yet curiously, Bhutan began to open up in the 1960s and gradually signaled its desire to join the United Nations.[22] That it achieved this goal by 1971 given it geostrategic position between India and China is noteworthy. In part, Bhutan's success in doing so is attributable to its king, Jigme Dorji Wangchuck, who deftly managed Indian concerns

[19] Kohli 1993, 63.   [20] Fazal 2007.   [21] Kohli 1993, 85.
[22] The state modernized in various ways during this time. For example, it transitioned from an absolute monarchy into a constitutional monarchy.

over security and signaled Bhutanese confidence in Indian relations. In effect, he gradually strengthened relations with India even as he moved Bhutan toward full independence.

A striking feature of Bhutan's sovereign emergence was India's support. India sponsored Bhutan in its bid to become a member of the Colombo Plan in 1963 and the Universal Post Union in 1969.[23] When a United Nations committee met on February 9, 1971, to discuss Bhutan's admission, the Indian representative supported Bhutan's case by saying that independence was the "final manifestation of Bhutan's independent stature and nationhood," and pledged India's "full support to work in cooperation with Bhutan."[24] This support from India was later acknowledged by Pema Wangchuk who noted the key role that India played in "ushering Bhutan into the modern era." With membership into the club, Bhutan proceeded to increase its diplomatic relations with other states. Overall, the emergence of Bhutan in 1971 is noteworthy given its buffer state status and hostility between the neighboring powers. Once again, this supports Fazal's argument that international conditions were different in the post-1945 period and that buffer states could survive and, by extension, secede and form a sovereign state.

What compelled India to grant Bhutan control over its foreign relations? The general position in the literature is that Indian leadership was sympathetic to Bhutanese desires and relatively unconcerned about the consequences of granting those desires. Bhutan was clearly aligned with India rather than China and evidently had little fear over future Chinese influence. Some scholars argue that the political conditions in 1971 were ripe insofar as India had just seen a victory in East Pakistan and, in addition, the landslide election of Prime Minister Indira Gandhi that year could secure the government from internal criticism.[25] In effect, India felt confident that its special relationship with Bhutan would endure, even though it was permitting it to diversify its foreign relations.[26]

India's perception of the situation supports some of the arguments regarding the invisible hand of the international system. It had little to lose economically from Bhutanese independence. India already had trade links with the territory and was taking an active role in

---

[23] Verma 1988.   [24] Kohli 1993, 117–118.   [25] Kohli 1993.
[26] Rose 1977, 91.

developing Bhutan's infrastructure and economy, and it supported its economic diversification in terms of trade and financial aid. India did this despite the reality that it would lose formal control over Bhutan's foreign economic policy. Of course, the fact that Bhutan was land-locked and dependent on India for access to the sea no doubt helped. India could retain a measure of hegemony and that evidently was enough.

However, the related security concerns constitute a puzzle. After all, the preceding decades had been a turbulent time for the Himalayan region. China showed its willingness to seize territory in Tibet and in Arunachal Pradesh (just east of Bhutan) during the 1962 conflict. India did not yet have a nuclear deterrent, so why was the Chinese seizure of an independent Bhutan regarded as unlikely?

This is a hard case for my theory but I contend that the territorial integrity norm and related perceptions regarding the legitimacy of conquest played a role. Unlike Tibet or Arunachal Pradesh, Bhutan did not present China with a historical precedent on which is could make a territorial claim. China argues that Tibet was a formal vassal, not a sovereign state, and its dispute over the so-called McMahan Line forms the basis of its claim to Arunachal Pradesh. These claims are the result of complex historical developments and they are not groundless. It is in this gray area of ongoing boundary disputes that the territorial integrity norm is neutralized since both sides feel they can invoke it. In contrast, all parties agree that Bhutan was part of India and formerly subject to the Raj. That distinction is no small matter as it shapes the expectations and behavior of the relevant actors. The result of these factors was the consensual secession of Bhutan. India was relatively unconcerned that China would seize the fledgling state, and it was confident that its near hegemonic influence over Bhutan would endure.

The combined importance of these factors is well illustrated by the case of Sikkim. Under the Indian state, Sikkim and Bhutan constituted two members of a unique class of administrative unit. Although they shared similarities in terms of their historical relationship with the UK, their outcomes were different as Sikkim was eventually transformed into a core Indian state in 1975. Sikkim was originally brought under the British flag with the Treaty of 1861, and it was actually stripped of indirect rule by the Convention of 1890.[27] However, with the

---

[27] Rao 1978, 6.

accession of British-educated Tashi Namgyal to the throne of Sikkim, internal sovereignty was restored in 1914. Sikkim's elites considered a full break at various points and even declared independence in 1947,[28] but the British Raj insisted that the political relationship be transferred to India. In a referendum in 1949, the Sikkimese voted against becoming a member state of the Indian union and opted to retain their protectorate status. Overall, Indo-Sikkimese relations had traditionally been closer than Indo-Bhutanese, and this difference explains, in part, their contrasting fates.

However, the political realities of the 1970s were different in Sikkim. The territory was less stable than Bhutan and more susceptible to Nepalese influence on account of the shared border and large Nepalese minority population.[29] The internal strife in the early 1970s concerned India as it was unclear how an independent state might receive political overtures from both Nepal and China. That the Chogyal met with less support from New Delhi in his intimations of independence is partly the result of his less tactful approach to reassuring India of his objectives.[30] Regardless, when an antiroyalty movement acquired power in 1975, it petitioned India for statehood and was accepted, thus ending the last of India's protectorates. Sikkim never formally sought full independence from India, and it seems that part of the reason is that India did not encourage it. The best interpretation of these events is that India was somewhat amenable to secession of the protectorates. It did not fear conquest of these states, but their emergence had to be on Indian terms – that is, the resulting state would cleave to the Indian sphere of influence. Bhutan satisfied these concerns; Sikkim did not.

Critics might contend that India's support of the territorial integrity norm is self-serving. It did after all seize Goa from Portugal in 1961, a controversial accession that resulted in the death of more than fifty combatants. In fact, in its appeal to the international community Portugal accused India of violating its territorial integrity. However, the response of the international community was decidedly mixed. Portugal was widely perceived as recalcitrant where the release of colonies was concerned, it had refused to negotiate with India on the transfer of Portuguese India, and territorial integrity was often subordinated to self-determination in the process of decolonization. This was a gray area that India used to its advantage. The norm against conquest has

[28] Minahan 2012, 294.   [29] Rose 1977.   [30] Rao 1978.

less traction in such matters; it is in the absence of this ambiguity that it shapes behavior.

Moving onto secessionism in the core states, to what extent was India's consistent denial a function of external factors? A hard case for my theory is Jammu-Kashmir, which had a secessionist movement in the very early days of the Indian state from 1947 to 1949 and again from 1989 onward. The history of the disputed region is well known and has been a source of Indo-Pakistani conflict since at least its accession to India on October 17, 1947. Formerly a princely state that came under direct British rule in 1862, the region of Kashmir became a flashpoint in the latter 1940s partly on account of its Muslim majority and Hindu Maharajah, Hari Singh, who set history on a specific course when he famously acceded to India in the midst of a Muslim insurgency.[31] Since then Indian policy has been that Jammu-Kashmir is a core state of the union. Pakistani policy has been that at a minimum the Kashmiris should decide their own fate. Internally, citizens have been split between remaining with India, joining Pakistan, and forming an independent state, Azad Kashmir.

Although some historians contend that India would have let Kashmir join Pakistan had it voted to do so, territorial calculations have clearly played a role in the subsequent years.[32] Despite the desires for an independent and sovereign Azad Kashmir, the secession of the state of Jammu-Kashmir would have deprived India of a potential buffer zone between it and its rival. Worse, Kashmir may well have been swallowed up by Pakistan. There are other factors that help explain Indian resistance on the Kashmiri issue, including symbolic meaning assigned to the history of the region and, as I discuss in the next section, important precedence-setting issues with other Indian states. However, in general, this case presents a partial challenge to my hypotheses regarding changing international conditions in the post-1945 period.

The remaining cases are less problematic. It is difficult to argue that external security issues drove India to retain its northeastern units even though it was releasing Bhutan, a neighboring territory of at least equal strategic importance. The early movement in Hyderabad is also an unlikely case because it is not clear what foreign power might seize it – after all, the previous suzerain (the UK) was departing. At best, the Khalistan case might suggest external factors given its proximity

---

[31] Henige 2004, 99.   [32] Talreja 1996, 207.

to Pakistan. But as I discuss later, the main reason India sought to keep these territories had more to do with its efforts at holding the nation together than it did over external threats.

Taken as a whole, I assert that the invisible hand of the international system has influenced the size of the Indian state. Like Russia and the UK, but to a much smaller degree, the Indian metropole has downsized. It permitted the independence of a region that went on to become a buffer state, and it did so, in part, because the territorial commitment problems that characterized the pre-1945 period were absent. Of course, Bhutan's independence was assisted by the fact that India had confidence that its influence over the mountain kingdom would endure. Similar factors were at play with Russia and the UK; metropoles are more amenable to secession when they expect a privileged and/or confederal relationship after independence. Indeed, such expectations are reinforced in times of bipolarity and unipolarity. No doubt Kashmir's lack of success is attributable, in part, to the fact that secession was unlikely to be on Indian terms, and that the emerging unit would move closer to Pakistani influence. Of course, this is not the entire explanation. We also need to understand why India would permit Bhutanese secession so readily while it simultaneously fought hard to thwart similar ambitions in other areas of the country, including the regions bordering on Bhutan.

Domestic Administrative Structure

The purpose of this section is to explore whether administrative design can help explain the dynamics of secessionism in India. I ask the same questions in this section that I asked in the British and Russian chapters. Does having a proto-state increase the likelihood of secession for a given group? To what extent do issues of precedent setting affect governmental decisions? Moreover, do differences in type effectively compartmentalize these issues of precedence and permit the state to release one type of unit but not another?

Secessionism without Proto-states

It is more difficult to assess the consequences of not having a proto-state in the case of India than it was with Russia and the UK. There are two reasons for this. First, India has only had one instance of secession and a relatively smaller number of secessionist movements. There is thus a smaller sample size and less variation within the Indian case. Second, the Indian metropole has denied independence to all of its Type 1 units – the core states – and many of these denials have resulted in violence. This, as I discuss later, is partly a consequence of the firm position the state has taken on account of its concerns over fragmentation. It has simultaneously denied independence to the three movements not claiming a proto-state: Bodoland, Mizoram, and Khalistan. Overall, it is difficult to discern a difference in the treatment of secessionists possessing proto-states versus those that do not since denial (and often conflict) was always the outcome. With the exception of the protectorates, the metropole has erected a firewall against secession from any group regardless of whether they possess a proto-state.

An interesting dynamic of Indian secessionism is that the government's resolve on the issue channels groups toward increased forms of autonomy that fall short of full sovereignty, and this has resulted in more proto-states. The story of Mizoram is an interesting illustration. Occupying the hill country wedged between Bangladesh and Burma, the Mizo had been assigned to Assam under British rule. Like many other nations across the British realm, the Mizo lobbied for independence separate from the emerging state of which they happened to be a part. The British rejected the Mizo movement for the same reason that groups such as the Karens of Burma were denied independence: the metropole wanted to downsize in an orderly manner along administrative lines and the Indian government colluded in an attempt to prevent internal fragmentation. Thus, the Mizo represent yet another example of how the actions of potential secessionists are endogenous to the expected response of the metropole, which is in turn shaped by administrative organization. For this reason the Mizo did not formally declare independence prior to Indian independence. That decision was delayed for twenty years.

Mizoram's quest for self-determination after 1947 has taken a familiar path. At first the Mizo sought increased autonomy, and for that purpose the Mizo National Front (MNF) was organized in 1954.[33] Frustrated in their attempts, the Mizo leadership then declared independence in 1966, which resulted in two years of open civil war and two decades of tension. Finally, in 1986 the nation was awarded its

[33] Minahan 1996, 368–370.

own state within the Republic of India. Although this fell short of full sovereignty – and indeed one faction of the MNF still called for an independent Mizoram – secessionism gradually subsided.

Lest one conclude that the Indian political system is structured in such a way that all groups can eventually become member states through bargaining processes (which may include a bid for independence), there is at least one problem pertaining to administrative boundaries. The formation of a new federal state inevitably involves a territorial subtraction from some other state, unless of course the country of India acquires territory from another sovereign. The states that stand to lose land are typically unwilling for the usual reasons, not the least of which is the problem of where to draw the new boundaries. Part of the problem for the Sikh independence movement was that Khalistan was not coterminous with the Punjabi state.[34] Since the referenced territory drew on other neighboring states such as Haryana and Rajasthan, Sikh independence was further complicated by the problem of multiple borders. This was a major stumbling block in the negotiations between the Akali party and the central government with respect to greater Punjabi autonomy. All of the solutions for redrawing the state borders gave "zero-sum results: Punjab's gain is Haryana's and/or Rajasthan's loss."[35] Similar issues have arisen in the past as Assamese territory was gradually broken off, and it is currently a problem in the effort to secure an independent Bodoland; both the Indian metropole and the Assamese state are unwilling to acquiesce. Administrative boundaries are focal in nature, and they can present an obstacle to acquiring not just sovereign states, but also proto-states.

But in regard to the original question, does not having a protostate make independence less likely? Does Bodoland stand a poorer chance than Mizoram on simple administrative grounds? The British and Russian cases indicate that the answer is yes. If the state decides to release units, Mizoram and the core states are currently in the best position. If the application of *uti possidetis* to the Russian secessions is any example, then international law would likely admit Mizoram but not Bodoland. However, as I discuss in the next section, it is hard to imagine India releasing any of its states because doing so would set a precedent that could literally dissolve the country. Unlike Russia or the UK, India has no outer belt of territories that it can release. Thus,

[34] Brass 1991, 203–204.   [35] Brass 1991, 211–212.

Mizo independence may well come in the context of the death of the Indian state, or at least a greatly reduced one. Still, winning a federal state for the Bodos would place them in a better position later on. In the meantime, it would also permit a greater level of local autonomy.

This distinction between proto-states and non-proto-states highlights a question that was raised in previous chapters: to what extent are the dynamics of decentralization continuous with the dynamics of secessionism? As I demonstrated with the British and Russian metropoles were aware that reclassifying India as a dominion, or Tatarstan as a union republic, would present those regions with improved possibilities for independence, and at key points they chose not to make these changes so that denial could be defended on administrative grounds. Although this sort of decision making suggests an integrated bargaining space where secession constitutes one endpoint, the strategic dynamics may change depending on the status (or lack thereof) of the unit in question and on the administrative architecture of the metropole. There is no indication that India denies federal statehood to Bodoland, or once did to Mizoram, because it fears that such status upgrades will position them to secede down the road. The barrier in this case is made up of local political issues (Assamese interests), the tactics of the separatist movements (violent, locally legitimate, etc.), and perhaps a precedent-setting problem where Delhi fears that awarding one group with statehood will encourage others.[36] However, there is a countervailing factor that is that Delhi may have cause to ally with the Mizo or Bodos against Assam because it could strengthen the center at the expense of a strong federal unit. Guy Grossman and Janet Lewis argue that these incentives explain administrative unit proliferation in some countries.[37] These conflicting patterns and incentives suggest that unit proliferation will be more common in symmetric federations that lack an outer belt because the metropole is less concerned over eventual secession and therefore freer to collude against it core units. I explore this conjecture later and in the conclusion to the book.

Proto-states and Their Consequences

The origin of proto-states in India is somewhat different from that of Russian and the UK. I have argued that proto-states in those two

---

[36] Forsberg finds no evidence for such domino effects in a large-N study (Forsberg 2013).
[37] Grossman and Lewis 2014.

metropoles were created for reasons pertaining to geography, simple fortune, interstate diplomacy, and to harness the capabilities of local nations and institutions. In contrast, India was born in the post-1945 period when conquest was rare and borders were more fixed. Whereas many of the British and Russian proto-states were created during their periods of expansion, none of the Indian proto-states were. There were no administrative units created in an attempt to organize new frontiers, there were no security concerns drawing the state outward and conditioning its choice of direct and indirect rule, and, as a result, there was less arbitrariness in the determination of boundaries and the choice of administrative design. This is not to say that such factors are completely absent, but where present they are typically the legacy of choices that predate the Indian state. That the plains of Assam were categorized differently from the neighboring hill regions such as Mizoram, and that all of these lands were treated different than the neighboring Himalayan lands of Sikkim or Bhutan is an artifact of British administrative choice. The legacies that truly stand out appear to be inherited.

India was primarily guided by local conditions when it created its core proto-states. Between 1947 and 1956 it possessed a tripartite administrative architecture that classified its internal units depending on their status under the British Raj. All of these units were ruled directly, though many of the former princely states had national distinction. However, this system was meant to be transitional. In 1956, the Reorganization Commission created the primary administrative unit, the Type 1 state, which was in each case assigned to a linguistic group. In addition, it created the Type 2 unit, the union territory, which are typically small, centrally controlled, and not involved in issues of secessionism. The creation of the linguistically defined states signaled somewhat of a retreat from the ideas of earlier Indian independence leaders who sought to create a more homogenous national consciousness. The new design aimed to build a composite nationalism that balanced local linguistic, cultural, and religious preferences with a larger Indian identity.[38] It was also a reaction to calls for greater autonomy and/or independence from various internal groups. It has been a key factor in the attempt to balance India's centrifugal tendencies.

The Indian approach to proto-state formation is consistent with the general global pattern since the mid twentieth century. In the

---

[38] Brass 1991, 147.

nineteenth century the biggest determining factor for being a proto-state was geographic distance. After that, the most commonly met criteria were national distinction followed closely by indirect rule. These factors began to change after World War I through a confluence of two developments. First, the contraction of states after 1945 tended to reduce the number of geographically distant territories. Evidently, contraction brought contiguousness. Meanwhile, and perhaps for related reasons, the number of indirectly ruled units began to decline as well. Second, beginning in 1918, states began to accord national distinction to minority nations on a much more frequent basis. The Soviet regime was an early example. States such as China and Burma implemented similar policies shortly after World War II, and other states adopted them later as a solution to problems related to fragmentation. For example, Ethiopia reorganized its political space in 1991 and gave autonomous status to its five largest nations. Overall, the proliferation of nationally distinct proto-states is a more modern phenomenon, and a driving purpose behind their creation is typically to hold states together.[39]

To summarize, the primary factor guiding the creation of India's proto-states were local cultural conditions. Like the early Soviet regime and many metropoles in the post-1945 period, India built its core units – the Type 1 state – with local groups in mind. Different metropoles may be guided by different criteria – a language, a nation, and ethnicity – but such units are all part of the same general category, which is different in form from the strictly secular administrative unit that the American federal system emphasizes.

Where one sees the hand of arbitrariness and interstate security concerns at work in the Indian administrative design, it is usually a legacy of the British. The Himalayan states of Bhutan and Sikkim were the prime examples, and the result was a type of Indian unit different in conception. In the vignette that follows I contrast the perceptions of Bhutan and Sikkim with their neighbors in northeastern India, and trace those perceptions and their selective consequences to early administrative choices.

---

[39] Although the proliferation of such units is modern, their use is ancient. The satrapies of the Achaemenid Empire were built around local nations and typically given indirect rule.

The Long Arm of Geography and Administrative Whim

The creation and fate of indirectly ruled units is well illustrated by the case of Bhutan. It became a British protectorate and forfeit its sovereignty in 1910 when it signed a treaty with the British government that granted control over Bhutanese foreign affairs.[40] Until 1949, it remained a British proto-state – a first-order, indirectly ruled unit – at which time it signed a treaty of peace and friendship with the Indian government, an arrangement that was more or less the same as the 1910 treaty. After 1947, it along with Sikkim constituted a unique type of proto-state within the Indian system. The fact that they had the option of remaining protectorates in the newly formed Indian state is striking given the speed with which India consolidated the numerous princely states elsewhere on the subcontinent. The reason this was permitted was that the territories were perceived as different. This treatment was inherited from the British, and it was on this conceptual difference that the young Indian state could build its contrasting policies vis-à-vis the Himalayan and subcontinent proto-states.

This difference underscores the importance of initial administrative choice. Two factors guided the British in their treatment of Sikkim and Bhutan (see Map 6.1). First, their approach to the Himalayan kingdoms was to establish a buffer zone between India and China. They wanted "autonomous political entities to which they owed only limited responsibility as far as internal order was concerned but over which they exercised substantial influence with respect to external relations."[41] This objective formed the basis of its treaties with the two units.

The second factor was administrative whim. British administration of the northeast centered on the Brahmaputra Valley. The primary, directly rule province was Assam, and "the initial decision on Assam's boundaries was based on considerations of administrative convenience and on the whims of colonial administrators . . . [and] the reasons why those borders were more or less maintained throughout the colonial period were no less accidental."[42] Despite the fact that it had never before been connected politically to India, Assam was brought directly under British control because it was a province characterized by plains, which the British felt was directly attached to the core of the subcontinent. In contrast, the hill regions to the south and east of Assam (Meghalaya, Mizoram, Nagaland, and Manipur) were indirectly ruled

---

[40] Griffiths and Butcher 2013.   [41] Rose 1977, 66–72.
[42] Baruah 1999, 26. See Scott 2010 for a discussion on the relationship between state-making and the valleys and hill country of Southeast Asia.

because the British "came to believe that the hills and plains were different entities." Crucially, the princely states of Bhutan and Sikkim were conceived as being one step further out. Although they were closer geographically to the heart of Assam than some of the eastern hill regions, their position along the Himalayan rim was considered different. They were never subject to the Raj as their neighbors were, or as the other more powerful princely states further south were.

These administrative designations shed light on the potential for endogeneity that was raised in Chapter 2. Bhutan and Sikkim were not granted a special status because the British recognized them as more coherent or deserving nations. Indeed, there were clearly more coherent and developed nations elsewhere on the subcontinent and they were not classified in the same manner as the Himalayan kingdoms. Therefore, I find no support for the first type of endogeneity where administrative designations merely reflect the prior coherence of the nation in question.

However, these cases do provide evidence for the second type of endogeneity, which is that proto-states help generate nations. In the case of Bhutan, administrative status helped foster a sense of identity. Prior to British meddling, the region was more politically decentralized. This is understandable, riven as it is by the many spurs of the Himalayas running from north to south and effectively partitioning the region into valley systems.[43] British support of Ugyen Wangchuk helped to centralize power around a new Bhutanese monarch. In that sense, the demarcation of the territory of Bhutan and its centralization of power helped to build a political apparatus around which a Bhutanese identity could coalesce. This is a testament to the generative effects of proto-states, but it does not undermine my argument regarding the selective importance of administrative design. After all, was the Bhutanese nation really more developed than the Assamese? Did Delhi deny Assam even as it permitted Bhutan because it saw the latter as a more coherent and more viable nation? Assam is far more populous and fertile and it too was once an independent state.[44] Rather, Bhutan's good fortune was its mountainous location and the resulting belief of early British administrators that it should retain a special administrative status.

The downstream consequence of that administrative decision was the creation of a conceptual distinction between outer territories such as Bhutan and core units such as Assam. Cognitive salience on this

[43] Rose 1977.   [44] Griffiths and Butcher 2013.

point developed under the Raj and it was inherited by the Indian state. Ian Lustick argues that states generally downsize along ideological thresholds – does the secession threaten the core?[45] I contend that such thresholds usually fall along administrative lines, and these lines can be surprisingly arbitrary. In the discussion to follow, I demonstrate India's strong concerns over internal fragmentation, and show how these concerns ended at the line separating the protectorates from the rest of the country.

How has India responded to calls for independence? The metropole has taken on a policy in which "secessionist movements would not be tolerated and would be suppressed by force wherever necessary."[46] A central objective in its 1956 Reorganization Act was to reorganize the states along linguistic lines – and permit a measure of decentralization – and thus consolidate the "process of dual nationalism, the comfortable accommodation of most Indians to a recognition of themselves as members of two nations: a Sikh, Bengali, or Tamil nation at one level of identity and an Indian nation at another."[47] This was the "holding together" project, and it persists to this day.[48] Although it was a central aim in the 1950 constitution, it was bolstered with the 1956 act. To a large extent, the legacy of partition helped solidify the Indian position with respect to secessionism: negotiation was off the table. In fact, groups are typically labeled as terrorists if they call for sovereign independence, and they will not be negotiated with unless the secessionist demands are dropped. In his critique of the government's handling of the United Liberation Front of Assam (ULFA), Sunil Nath argues that the emphasis on antisecessionism comes at a price: the ULFA had to renounce its secessionist demands, not its armed activities.[49]

Implicit in the government's position on secessionism was a concern over uncontrolled fragmentation. Erecting a zero-tolerance barrier to secessionist negotiations was a means to maintain the unity of the country. Recognizing that negotiations with the Nagas in 1947 over the proposed Hydari Agreement would set a precedent for the Mizo,

---

[45] Lustick 1993; O'Leary et al. 2001.
[46] Brass 1991, 168–169. See also Nag 1999, 210.   [47] Brass 1991, 168–169.
[48] Stepan 2001.   [49] Nath 2009.

the Assamese, the Tamils, and the Nizam of Hyderabad, Jawaharlal Nehru stated the Congress policy clearly when he said:

We can give you complete autonomy, but never independence. You can never hope to be independent. No state, big or small, in India will be allowed to remain independent. We will use all our influence and power to suppress such tendencies.[50]

Some historians argue that secessionism in Jammu-Kashmir helped encourage secessionism elsewhere.[51] These concerns were quite sharp during the Sikh crisis of the 1980s when Indian leaders genuinely felt that the "unity of the country was endangered."[52] This uniform policy has applied to both high-value territories such as the Punjab and to remote low-value units such as Nagaland, where the state has repeatedly denied independence out of concern that secession among the Nagas would set a precedent for other Indian groups.[53] In essence, Indian policy from the beginning has been to show a credible commitment to thwarting secessionism. Sumit Ganguly in his analysis of Kashmir aptly summarizes the stakes in this effort:[54]

Virtually all Indians consider Kashmir to be part of India. The Kashmiri insurgent claim of national self-determination, if allowed to prevail, could lead to the disintegration of the Indian state. The demonstration effects of Kashmir seceding from India would be profound.

Strikingly, the protectorates were excluded from this policy. In the eyes of Indian metropole and the relevant parties, the protectorates were in a class of their own. If there were fears over setting precedents, they were not made in relation to the Indian states, but, instead, with respect to each other. As Manorama Kohli notes, it was felt that "any concessions to Bhutan . . . would encourage the Sikkimese also for demanding somewhat identical concessions from New Delhi."[55] Concerns over precedent setting were partitioned by administrative category, and the metropole could effectively entertain secessionism in its protectorates without concerns of spillover into state-based movements. In other words, the issue of precedence did not travel across type and motivate other internal proto-states to also seek secession. The fact that such

[50] Bartkus 1999, 58.   [51] Talreja 1996, 232.   [52] Brass 1991, 198.
[53] Yonuo 1974; Sambanis 2006.   [54] Ganguly 1997, 128–129.
[55] Kohli 1993, 102.

across-type precedence issues are absent in the public discourse suggests a measure of cognitive salience. The initial choice of the British set a pattern in motion that left little room for dispute later on. Indeed, it does not appear that the Indian metropole actually had to defend its contrasting policies by pointing to these differences in type. The conceptual distinction was sufficiently entrenched.

My theory holds that administrative categories condition a metropole's concerns over precedent setting. In the case of India, such concerns are particularly salient. With the demise of its Type 3 protectorates, the best candidates for secessionism are the states. However, its federal structure makes it virtually impossible to downsize this category. This is because India has no core political unit in the same way that Russia or the UK does.[56] It may possess a semblance of a heartland, centered mostly in the central northern portion of the country across the Gangetic plain.[57] Certainly, secessionism is more common on the margins of this area, where "Hinduism does not have a foothold (Nagaland, Mizoram, Kashmir, and Punjab), where non-Aryan race was dominant (Tamil Nadu, Manipur), and where Bhaminic ideology has made a weak and late penetration (Tripura, Assam)."[58] But that heartland does not correspond to any administrative unit like England does within the UK. India is a federation akin in form to the USA. Therefore, when searching for the rump state, one either has to settle for the Union Territory of Delhi, which is unsatisfactory, or else all twenty-eight states in their entirety. The analogue for the USA would be the choice between Washington, DC, or else all fifty states.[59] Since neither India nor the USA could plausibly endure if they were reduced to merely their capital territories (Delhi and Washington, DC), each state has to erect a firewall to secession at the state level – that is, around the core states. They cannot level down as London can by giving up Northern Ireland, Scotland, and Wales, and still possess the English core. They cannot release the other republics as Russia can and still have the core central state, which is vast. Precedence issues for states such as India are a more serious problem – it cannot downsize its central units without risking dissolution.

---

[56] See Brass 1991, 329, for a comparison of the Russian core with the Indian core.
[57] This is sometimes referred to as the Hindi Belt.
[58] Nag 1999, 32.   [59] See Chapter 3 for discussion on coding federations.

The realities of Indian federalism raise several points. First, it would seem that peaceful secession is less likely in this type of federation, all else equal. There are a number of metropoles that currently possess a set of nation-based proto-states. For some, such as China, Russia, or Burma, these units constitute a category that is different from the core of the state. In each of these cases the metropole has precedent-setting problems with respect to these units, and is therefore compelled to show resolve vis-à-vis groups such as the Tibetans, Chechens, or the Karens. In theory, however, each country could still downsize these types and yet retain the rump state. That option is not available to countries that are more purely federal in form such as India, Ethiopia, or the USA. Therefore, those who have an interest in preserving the state ought to fight harder to prevent secession.

Second, it is, of course, possible that India could grant added autonomy to key states and, over time, transform them into new types of units. In doing so, it might eventually produce new conceptual differences between units that the metropole could then exploit when discriminating between competing independence claims. In the language of Phil Roeder, this would be an administrative upgrade.[60] However, unlike the upgrade from a Russian autonomous republic to a union republic – a vertical move with enormous consequences – India does not currently possess a category into which it could upgrade its selected states. In that sense, the process would be more exploratory. It might resemble recent Spanish efforts to appease separatist ambitions in Catalonia and the Basque Country. But negotiating that slippery slope is not easy, and it is unclear how long it takes to build a salient conceptual distinction between the most autonomous type of units and the category from which they devolved. At the moment devolution occurs in India, but it is halted at the level of the federal unit.

Tidal Effects

What about the tidal effects of secessionism? Temporally speaking, there are two somewhat discernible waves to secessionism in India. The first occurred around the time of state birth in the late 1940s, in the northwest (Kashmir), the south (Hyderabad, Travancore), and the

---

[60] Roeder 2007.

northeast (Nagaland). To these movements one might add independence demands made to the British Raj right before Indian independence in Baluchistan, Khalistan, Travancore, Sikkim, and Nagaland. These early movements represented dissatisfaction with the political arrangement bequeathed by the British and a rejection of the emerging Indian national consciousness. The Pakistan movement was the strongest manifestation of this rejection.

The second wave of secessionism gathered in the 1960s and 1970s and grew to encompass and/or reinvigorate Kashmir and Khalistan once again, as well as the set of movements in the northeast (Assam, Manipur, Nagaland, Tripura, Bodoland, and Mizoram). Only Nagaland has possessed a secessionist movement throughout the entire period from 1947 to 2005.[61] To be sure, many of the groups possessed long-running secessionist aspirations. Elements of the Assamese intelligentsia had been advocating for secessionism since at least the 1930s, pointing to, among other things, Bengali encroachment.[62] Similarly, the Meithei and Mizo had long-running struggles with the central government that predated the Indian state. Although there is no single cause for this second wave, two factors stand out. The first was Indira Gandhi's centrist policies in the 1970s that alienated and agitated minority groups. The second was just the general unrest in the northeast, stemming partly from Muslim migration out of Bangladesh, and the shifting state boundaries as the central government gradually awarded statehood to some groups and simultaneously stripped existing states of their land.[63]

An analysis of these waves uncovers dynamics that were found in the earlier chapters. Many of these movements occurred around the same time because of common triggers – for example, the birth of the Indian state, the centrist policies of Gandhi. Moreover, early movers constitute demonstration effects that influence others – the Mizo National Front (MNF) learned from the example of Naga secessionists.[64] I conclude that it is proximate factors such as these that explain the statistical findings where nations are actually more likely to declare independence when there are other parallel movements.

---

[61] I code two movements for Nagaland: one against the Raj in 1947; one against India from 1948 onward.

[62] Nag 1999, 168. During much of the British period, the region of Assam was subordinate to the province of Bengal.

[63] Minahan 1996.   [64] Dasgupta 1997, 365.

However, these waves are partially channeled by the administrative design of the state. There is mutual empowerment among like types, and mimicry is conditioned by the perception of likeness. Assam was quite unsupportive of independence movements in its hill regions that threatened to reduce its territory.[65] As Nath writes, "the Assamese had neither empathy nor sympathy for the secessionist insurgency launched by Naga leadership immediately after the advent of independent India."[66] Likewise, on the approach to independence India itself lobbied against the secession of Travancore, Nagaland, and numerous others because they were lower-order units that were internal parts of India. Knowledge of this administrative pecking order can inspire nations to mimic other similar candidates and make a formal bid for independence, or turn away from secession and settle for local autonomy, as the Mizo did in 1947. I argue that the resulting selection effects help explain the related statistical finding that metropoles are more likely to permit secession when they face multiple movements; many of the movements who anticipated denial never declared independence.

The Effects of Regime Type

India has been a fairly stable democracy since 1947. The most noticeable authoritarian turn occurred during Indira Gandhi's state of emergency from 1975 to 1977. By the mid 1990s, India had regained its democratic legitimacy and was nearly perfect according to the Polity IV index.[67] How has the level of democracy interacted with secessionist outcomes over time?

Where the choice of secession is concerned – that is, the decision by a proto-state to form a secessionist movement – India's level of democracy appears to have had some effect. The low point in India's democracy came in the mid 1970s during Gandhi's imposed state of emergency from June 25, 1975, until March 21, 1977.[68] The resulting

---

[65] Ganguly 1997, 129.   [66] Nath 2009.

[67] According to the Polity IV dataset, India's polity score (on a scale from 0 to 20) was 19 from 1947 to 1974; 17 from 1975 to 1976; 18 from 1977 to 1994; and 19 from 1995 onward.

[68] Note that a state of emergency had been declared twice before. The first time was during the conflict with China during the mid 1960s; the second time was during the conflict with Pakistan during the early 1970s. Unlike these two cases in which external threats were cited as the problem, the emergency between 1975 and 1977 was built on internal disturbances.

crackdown on civil liberties and political opposition, and the legacy of those actions, helped fuel the drive to secession among the Sikhs, as well as in Assam and Tripura.[69] However, the effects are lagged rather than tightly chronological given that none of the three stated movements – those dealing with Khalistan, Assam, and Tripura – actually formalized their movements until 1978 at the earliest. Indeed, there are good reasons to think that the attribution of Indian secessionism to weak democracy is only telling part of the story. Many of the secessionist movements began before the mid 1970s and two, Bodoland and Jammu-Kashmir, began in the late 1980s and were fueled largely by local issues.

A more complex explanation focuses on the features of the Indian state and its level of development. Atul Kohli has argued forcefully that is was only natural for self-determination movements to form in multicultural, developing democracies.

A democratic polity in a developing country encourages group mobilization, heightening group identities and facilitating a sense of increased group efficacy; mobilized groups then confront state authority, followed by a more-or-less prolonged process of power negotiation; and such movements eventually decline as exhaustion sets in, some leaders are repressed, others are co-opted, and modicum of genuine power sharing and mutual accommodation between the movement and the central state is reached.[70]

The upshot of Kohli's inverted U-curve argument is that democracy in developing states actually creates the conditions for secessionism – at least for a time. This argument resembles an explanation put forth by Ganguly who states that economic modernization, institutional development, and increased political awareness all contribute to increased political mobilization. Ganguly is himself echoing Samuel Huntington when he claims that "this heightened political awareness will inevitably contribute to greater political demands."[71]

Although intriguing, this argument may overstate the degree to which secessionism is part of a linear process from political mobilization to secessionism to political enfranchisement. Many Indian secessionist movements have endured for long periods, particularly in the northeast. Some movements recur, and others appear among new minority groups in regions that were formerly attempting to secede.

[69] Brass 1991, 334; Manor 2001, 92–93.   [70] Kohli 1997, 326.
[71] Huntington 1968; Ganguly 1996, 77.

Recurrence suggests that prior agreements that assuaged secessionist groups can deteriorate and that the entire process is better conceptualized as an ongoing bargain rather than a linear process. Moreover, the appearance of new groups within formerly breakaway regions speaks to the ethnic complexity of India and the potential for ongoing fragmentation.

Overall, as with the other case studies, the evidence from India shows a complex relationship between democracy and the choice of secessionism. Indian democracy may reduce the incidence of secessionism but it is not enough to prevent the periodic declaration of independence. Moreover, it may be that such declarations are a mechanism for engaging the political process to acquire greater autonomy.

What about the relationship between democracy and secessionist conflict? Scholars of Indian democracy generally argue for the beneficial effects that it has on secession. According to Kohli, a well-institutionalized and democratic state will, in the long run, co-opt secessionist leaders, dull the overall movement, and find a balance. Paul Brass takes this argument in a slightly different direction to say that "parties play independent roles in creating, shaping, and moderating ethnic group loyalties and antagonisms. They do not merely reflect the existing cleavages of society. They may sometimes create new ones, shape old ones in new political directions, or moderate tensions."[72] According to Jyotirindra Dasgupta, the institutional design of India is meant to process and convert demands for independence and autonomy. It does this by "preempting and preventing conflict by creating in advance ways of inducting people into the processes of identification with national, developmental, civic, or other cooperative norms of values."[73] The co-option of secessionist leaders has been common in India – for example, the United Liberation Front of Assam (ULFA) and Asom Gana Parishad. Furthermore, the nested ethnicities or "heterogeneities within heterogeneities" has made it difficult to develop the kind of statewide solidarity that secessionism requires.[74] "The various cross-cutting fault lines prevent tension and conflict from building up along a single fault line in society." More recently, Kanchan Chandra has argued that with its multiple cleavages, Indian democracy actually creates equilibrium conditions that avoid outbidding and fragmentation.[75]

---

[72] Brass 1991, 344.   [73] Dasgupta 1997, 368.   [74] Manor 2001, 81–82.
[75] Chandra 2005.

If the consensus in this scholarship is that democracy has enabled India to hold together, how do we explain the frequency of secessionist conflict? One answer is that the Indian system does a fair job of placating potential secessionists but takes a firm position against formal secessionist movements. Like the UK, it provides institutional mechanisms that can draw many minority nations into the political process. Unlike the UK, however, India generally has a zero-tolerance policy toward formal secessionist movements. Whereas Scottish secessionists can form a political party and appeal to the population through institutional channels, Assamese secessionists are branded as terrorists and forced outside the political process. That is unless, of course, they lower their demands. This disposition of the metropole should have two effects: it should reduce the longevity of secessionist movements but increase the rate of violence. Only a small number of secessionist groups will go the full distance and declare independence, and conflict is likely for those who do. Indian democracy curbs centrifugal tendencies by placating groups prior to a declaration of independence. However, it cannot afford to permit secession and is therefore quick to show its resolve. Once again, there are clear elements of anticipation: the choice of secession is controlled to some extent by the disposition and anticipated reaction of the metropole.

If, however, the government shows its resolve on the issue of secession, why do secessionist groups still declare independence? One answer is that secessionism seems to arise when groups are closed off from the political process. As Brass write, "the principle dangers of violent conflict arise when all routes to power in an existing system seem closed to an organized force. . . . It is when both options are closed, access to power and the right to self-determination, or when it is feared that they will be closed, that political leaders are likely to raise secessionist demands."[76] To its credit, the Indian government has worked to draw breakaway groups into the political process and "groups that have been disinclined to take part in normal electoral politics are commonly encouraged to abandon their reluctance."[77] Indeed, such efforts by the government are often pursued at the same time as Indian security forces are engaged in conflict with other members of the same group – a carrot-and-stick approach.

There are several situations in which potential secessionists could be cut off from the political process. The first is in times of political

[76] Brass 1991, 344–345.   [77] Manor 2001, 83.

centralization when the state oversteps. Ganguly claims that it was institutional decay in the Indian government and "a reckless disregard for constitutional procedures" that spurred many Kashmiris to take up arms in the mid 1980s.[78] Empirically, secessionist ambitions did arise with Gandhi's centralization policies. Second, some groups may be cut off from the political process because they are embedded within larger proto-states. This was the case with the Mizo, who won a proto-state through their efforts. In the long run, it may be groups such as these that are the best candidates for secessionism since the proto-states of which they are part are often reluctant to give up more territory. This is part of the problem with the Bodo with respect to Assam. Finally, secessionist movements are not always monolithic. Divided leadership can prolong a secessionist effort as one faction continues the fight. This appears to be part of the explanation for Nagaland, where divided leadership has prevented consensus.[79]

In sum, the relationship between regime Indian democracy and secession is complex. It appears that the regime does a fair job of dampening secessionist aspirations. It does so by both drawing nations into the political process and by showing its resolve for those who cross the line. Importantly, there is good reason to think that its position on the issue is partly controlled by its administrative structure. It permits devolution to the level of the federal state, but it denies the full secession of any core unit because doing otherwise could introduce a potentially fatal precedent.

Conclusion

The invisible hand of the international system influences the contraction of states, but it is the domestic administrative structure of states that determine how they contract. India is in many ways a fine example of how states address territorial issues in the post-1945 era. At first glance this may seem like an odd claim given India's territorial disputes with Pakistan and China, and for these reasons India is a hard case for my theory. However, India has not engaged in the type of naked territorial conquest that characterized earlier times, and it has committed no clear violation of the territorial integrity norm. Its territorial disputes were present at the birth of the state, and they represent a gray

[78] Ganguly 1997, 88.   [79] Stepan et al. 2011.

area of possession in which both sides actually invoke the territorial integrity norm. It is when these conflicting claims of ownership are absent that modern states may choose to permit secession because the costs of doing so are not what they used to be. I contend that this was the case with Bhutan, a buffer state that was originally stripped of sovereignty in the pre-1945 period when the British metropole was expanding its territorial control.

India's release of Bhutan may seem a small matter, particularly when compared with the great British and Russian contractions, but in that comparison we can see the consequences of administrative design. A core directive of the Indian state since 1947 has been holding together. Given its diversity in terms of nation, language, religion, and caste, as well as its federal structure, the metropole has had to erect a wall to secession or else face potential dissolution. It has no inner core to fall back on as London and Moscow do. It is therefore not surprising that antisecessionism has become a paramount policy, at times even superseding the issue of armed insurgency. Moreover, it is altogether striking then that the central government released Bhutan with such grace in the early 1970s. The best explanation for its accommodation there, and the lack of it with the remaining units, is administrative rank. India could permit the secession of its protectorate without sending a signal to its core states. It was the structure of its units that was inherited from the British that determined their fate.

The analysis in this chapter reinforced several observations made elsewhere in the book. First, there is something of a tidal character to secessionism and this is largely because secessionist movements are often responding to local triggers such as simple regime change. In addition, these waves are partly channeled by administrative architecture. Higher-order administrative units tend to support other movements if they are the same type, and withhold support from lower units or groups that lack any status at all. Thus, these architectures shape the patterns of mutual empowerment and mimicry that we often see among secessionists. These patterns are then reinforced by metropolitan response, which generally falls along administrative/categorical lines.

These dynamics possess elements of endogeneity, but in ways that are either nonthreatening or supportive of my central theory. Administrative status is not simply given to the fittest nations. Indeed, it was administrative whim that controlled the contrasting fates of Bhutan and Assam. Once created, administrative units do have generative consequences, but the selective effects of administrative design have enormous consequences for aspiring nations.

Finally, democracy does matter, but in complicated ways. It can placate potential and actual secessionist movements by bringing them back into the fold and by bargaining with them. However, it seems that these effects are best at curbing secessionism, and not at preventing it in the first place or even obviating the need to use violence. Furthermore, decreased or weakened democracy, as was evident in India in the mid 1970s, can aggravate secessionist movements and incite them to mobilize. It is important to remember that a state's response to secessionism is governed by its administrative structure, regardless of regime type. Even democratic states will deny independence and fight when they are presented with a precedent-setting problem. This appears to be a motivating force for the Indian policy on secession.

7 | Conclusion

When the President talks of Self-Determination what unit has he in mind? Does he mean a race, a territorial area, or a community? Without a definite unit which is practical, application of this principle is dangerous to peace and stability.

– Robert Lansing[1]

Just as the concept of individual human liberty carried to its logical extreme would mean anarchy, so the principle of self-determination of peoples given unrestricted application could result in chaos.

– Eleanor Roosevelt[2]

This book began with a discussion of the historical pattern in the global number of states, the trend toward state fragmentation and proliferation that has characterized the post-1945 era, and the danger that secessionism poses for sovereign states. I then defined the central puzzle of this study: What are the factors that determine how metropoles respond to demands for independence? To answer this question and explain the related phenomena I offered a two-part explanation that ties together key aspects of the international system with the domestic structure of states. The historical transition from state expansion to contraction is the result of important changes at the international level. Just as security and economic pressures drove lead states to expand during the nineteenth and early twentieth centuries, changing conditions in the post-1945 period led to a contraction in state size. Reduced fears over territorial conquest amidst a burgeoning global economy affected the costs and benefits of holding territory and enabled metropoles to permit secession more frequently. To a large extent, state size and political boundaries are endogenous to

---

[1] "Self-Determination," *Saturday Evening Post*, April 9, 1921, 7. Also see Lansing 1921.
[2] Black 2000, 179.

international conditions. However, if states are guided by system-level constraints, it is their internal structures that determine how they contract. States aim to downsize in a controlled manner, in a way that is mindful of administrative lines and categories. Secessionist groups that do not cohere with proto-states stand a poor chance of seceding peacefully. Those that possess a proto-state are in a much better position to gain independence, and those that represent a unique type or special category are particularly fortunate because their release leaves less chance of setting a precedent.

The analysis of the British metropole helped contextualize this theory. The long arc of British expansion and contraction fits the overall global pattern. The UK continued to acquire territory up until the early twentieth century for the stated reasons pertaining to competition. Then, changing security and economic conditions in the postwar period led to an unwinding process as the metropole began to downsize its vast realm. However, the manner of that downsizing was prescheduled by the way in which the state had originally composed its administrative space. Proto-states were created for reasons pertaining to pragmatism, strategy, and simple fortune. Nations that were not given a proto-state were cut out from the state-making business, as were second- and third-order proto-states. In many instances, the establishment of a proto-state generated nations where none existed before. It was on these designs that the British metropole would essentially collude with first-order proto-states when creating new countries.

The British case study also clarified two of the unexpected findings in the quantitative analysis. First, there was a clear tidal character to British secessionism, but that tide was channeled by the metropole's administrative architecture; secessionist movements empowered and supported like types – not interior movements that threatened to undermine the orderly business of downsizing – and this was backed by both the metropole and international law. Second, British democracy has played a role. Secession from the mid twentieth century onward was assisted by liberal democratic norms in the metropole. Such sympathies appear to have been trumped by security concerns during the interwar period, but they were clearly present after World War II, especially with the overseas units. Perhaps more importantly, the British downsizing project was organized and systematic. It aimed to create institutionally sound democratic states – which only reinforced the consequences of administrative design – and it was responsive to demands for independence provided the groups chose nonviolent and legitimate methods. In this way, it may one day see the secession of its internal countries.

The Russian/Soviet case provided weaker evidence in some ways in support of my theory, and stronger evidence in others. Overall, the Russian pattern of expansion and contraction was driven by international forces in much the same way as the UK. It is particularly in the realm of security that the invisible hand of the international system pushed the state out and then drew it back in. Although Russian contraction lagged the end of World War II by more than forty years, many of the factors that enabled it to contract – for example, the nuclear age, bipolarity – were features of the system beginning in 1945.

It is on the subject of administrative design that the Russian case showed the strongest support for my argument. Although the highly centrist regime of the imperial period permitted little autonomy, the establishment of the Soviet government set the nations of that land on a new trajectory. In a move that foreshadowed the creation of nation-based units in the latter twentieth century, the metropole began to grant national distinction to internal groups according to a ladder in which the top units, union republics, had the theoretical right to secession. The driving purpose behind these assignments, as well as the subsequent upgrades and downgrades, was to manage the many nations of the state in an orderly and efficient manner. However, as the Circassians and others discovered, being a strong nation could be a disadvantage as the state worked to suppress its centrifugal tendencies. Whether through well-founded judgment, punishment, or simple caprice, these decisions had enormous consequences when the state began to downsize in 1991. All of the first-order units were permitted to secede and this was backed by not only the union republics, which were keen to maintain their territories, but also international law, which sought to create stable countries. Indeed, the downstream consequences of the Soviet nationalities ladder resound today in debates over the secession of Crimea, Abkhazia, South Ossetia, and others who were formerly second- or third-order units under the Soviet metropole. The Soviet architecture created clear focal categories that, over time, became sufficiently salient to both channel the tidal effects of secessionism and find a basis in international law.

The Russian case provided further context for the alternative findings regarding secessionist waves and democracy. First, the metropole faced veritable tsunamis at several points in the twentieth century, and, as with India and the UK, these waves were driven by common triggers and reinforced by ongoing demonstration effects across the realm. There was mutual empowerment and mimicry but these processes were channeled by the administrative grid during the Soviet era. Second, the effects of democracy on Russian secessionism are harder to gauge mostly because democracy has been largely absent. Yet, secessionism in Russia tended to spike during periods of change, thus undermining the more linear hypothesis that secessionism becomes increasingly likely as the state becomes more autocratic.

The chapter on India provided interesting results that extended the analysis in several important ways. Like the other case studies, India provided strong evidence for the importance of administrative design. The consequences of type were clearly demonstrated by the seemingly uncontested conceptual distinction between the protectorates and the core states, a distinction that was inherited from the British who had, somewhat whimsically, applied a lasting administrative organization to the northeast of India. The salience of that distinction effectively partitioned precedent-setting issues among the core states from similar concerns with Bhutan. Moreover, the Indian administrative blueprint channeled the waves of secessionism in ways that were similar to the British and Russian cases; there were common triggers and demonstration effects, but mutual empowerment and mimicry tended to occur along administrative and categorical lines.

India offered a harder case with which to evaluate the international systemic portion of the argument. Because the state was born in 1947, there was no earlier India to compare against. Moreover, India has faced border disputes with its neighbors and has fought related wars over them. Finally, India has only seen the release of one territory in its history, so caution is necessary when drawing conclusions. Nevertheless, India permitted and even assisted the secession of Bhutan, a clear buffer state that borders land contested by China. I submit that the post-1945 emphasis on territorial integrity made this secession possible. Delhi's concession was alleviated by a confidence in a continued close relationship with Bhutan and the belief that China would not subsequently attempt to absorb Bhutan.

The analysis of Indian democracy complemented the British and Russian studies. Many scholars on India argue that the regime has been fairly successful at dampening secessionist aspirations. The federal structure with its cross-cutting cleavages has moderated centrifugal tendencies. The government has done so by both drawing nations into the political process and by showing its resolve against those who mount formal secessionist movements. In addition, the government has created what could be called a devolution ceiling: it has enabled bargaining over autonomy that fall short of full secession. Nevertheless, secessionist conflict has not been uncommon. Although some portion of the violence occurred in response to centralization policies and a weakening of democracy, there is more to the story. Not unlike Russia, the metropole's antisecessionist stance seems to have selected out all but the most determined. Secessionist groups cannot become legitimate political parties in India as they can in many other democracies. In part, this is a consequence of the state's federal structure and the regime's dedication to holding the country together. Secessionism has been curbed, but when it has emerged it has tended to be more conflictive. Overall, the Indian case demonstrated that democracy can direct secessionist impulses into nonviolent outcomes, but it cannot always do so.

Taken together, these findings shed light on the theoretical considerations and potential objections to my theory that were raised in Chapter 2. First, there is endogeneity in my explanation with respect to the effects of administrative organization, not because such designations are simply given to already coherent nations, but because once given they tend to help generate national identity and therefore increase the likelihood that the related nation will seek independence in the future. These are the generative effects of administrative design. However, the selective effects are arguably more important where metropolitan response is concerned because metropoles are less concerned with recognizing the fittest nations than they are simply managing the process of downsizing. As a result, Uganda gained independence rather than Buganda, Tajikistan rather than Chechnya, and Bhutan instead of Assam. Importantly, administrative lines and categories create selection effects by encouraging uncertain nations that possess the right status, and discouraging desiring nations that do not.

Second, some readers will have objected to a theory that offers a unified explanation for secession via both decolonization and nondecolonization. I think this is a false dichotomy and its perpetuation ends up eliding many nations such as the Baganda, Baluchis, and Karens who were colonized by a distant European power but lacked administrative rank, or the Chechens, Uyghur, and Lakota who, by many accounts, were simply colonized by contiguous empires and therefore failed the saltwater test for decolonization. I see no objectively clear threshold that distinguishes one person's colony from another's national territory. The practices surrounding decolonization, for all their good intentions, alighted on a solution that was mindful of territorial stability. The question of who counts was answered by emphasizing administrative lines and categories, rather than the coherence or even the righteousness of existing nations. This is how states disassemble and it is a common mechanism in political life. Its use predates the historical pivot of 1945 – indeed it was the legal basis for the Latin American secessions in the early nineteenth century – but its application has become more common in an era where international systemic conditions permit state fragmentation and authorities require guidelines for sorting the fortunate nations from the rest.

Finally, some readers will object that I do not get inside the state and adequately address local factors and theorize why nationalism comes about. I confess that I do not provide the full map, as Jorge Luis Borges would say, and instead begin after these ambitions arise by focusing on state response.[3] I do not offer a comprehensive theory for why secessionism occurs – the reasons are quite varied – but I conclude that secessionism and secessionist waves are largely structured by administrative designs.

Implications

Will secession in the future resemble the past seventy years? There are many ways to answer this question so let us begin at the most general level. International conditions in the post-1945 period have led to state proliferation, but such conditions are not static. Of the systemic factors I identify, polarity is the most likely to change in the near future, if it has not already. My theory suggests two potential outcomes following a return to multipolarity. First, in a multipolar world that is occupied by nuclear-armed, economically interdependent states that honor the norm of territorial integrity, we ought to see continued state proliferation, but at a reduced rate. If ascendant powers such as China and India continue to support the territorial integrity norm – and thus far they

---

[3] Borges 1998, 325.

seem keen to do so – state death should remain rare. In such a world the security and economic benefits of holding territory would be roughly similar to the bipolar and unipolar periods. The main difference and cause of the reduced rate of secession would be the competition for control over emerging states. As Michael Doyle pointed out, weaker states in a multipolar system can play one power off another.[4] Anticipating the difficulties of maintaining informal relations over new states, the great powers ought to be more likely to deny undesired secessions at home and abroad. Indeed, they would probably appeal to the norm of territorial integrity when denying these efforts.

The second outcome is a return to a past in which conquest is frequent, secession rare, and where state aggregation is more common than fragmentation. I contend that that future is far less likely given that it would require an abandonment, at the least, of the territorial integrity norm and perhaps a closure of the global economic system. Even then, the possession of nuclear weapons might deter many states from engaging in traditional conquest. Thus, to a large extent, the general conditions permitting state fragmentation are locked in. The advent of the bipolar system helped create an environment in which the long trend toward state aggregation could be reversed, but the new trend is unlikely to be undone by a return to multipolarity.

Assuming that these current international conditions continue, how much more secession should we see? One way to answer this question is to examine the long-term trend in proto-state creation and destruction. Not unexpectedly, the number of proto-states has declined from a historical high of 301 in 1947 to a little more than 200 today. Consonant with this decline in number is a pattern whereby states are becoming less articulated, with fewer administrative categories with special status. Those fortunate nations that are unique in type – Bougainville, Flanders – or members of outer-belt categories – Puerto Rico – are likely to be given their independence should they want it. However, a number of groups from Casamance to the Thai Malays lack administrative status and are therefore more likely to be denied independence, and more likely to have a conflict. However, many secessionist movements claim core federal units within secessionist-prone countries such

---

[4] Doyle 1986. However, emerging powers such as China should increasingly influence the politics of state recognition and this would affect the rate of proliferation.

as Burma (Myanmar), India, Ethiopia, and Spain, and in these cases denial should remain the norm unless the state can find a way to permit secession without risking dissolution. If the rate of secessionism continues, it may become increasingly contested.

A closer look at modern administrative design reveals a gradual change in purpose. The majority of the current proto-states are allocated to specific internal nations. In general, they are politically internal units with direct rule, and they were often developed in an attempt to placate minority nations and hold states together. Administratively, they tend to be closer to the core of metropoles and thus more likely to constitute precedent-setting issues. The great postwar contraction has nearly unraveled the earlier period of expansion, and a recurring aim in administrative design is holding together.

These domestic architectures will continue to shape secessionist outcomes in various fascinating ways. For pure federations, the issue of dissolution is more than just a political sound bite. Unlike Russia and the UK, India lacks a core administrative unit.[5] As such, Delhi cannot permit the secession of its federal units and fall back on a viable ethnoadministrative core in the same way that London and Moscow can. Similar claims can be made regarding other ethnofederations such as Ethiopia, and nonethnic federations such as Australia and the USA. Without an administrative rump state the center has to hold together or truly risk dissolution.[6]

These administrative blueprints are, however, nonstatic, and this raises the interesting issue of decentralization (or devolution). My analysis leads me to the following conjecture: decentralization ought to remain common as long as it is symmetric. As the Indian case demonstrated, decentralization can be a useful tool for managing centrifugal pressures. Indeed, the central government may actually prefer to create new administrative units and allocate them to desiring nations as a way of centralizing power. This is the counterintuitive point made by

---

[5] Russia's core would be the forty-six federal units, or oblasts, that are not autonomous and not allocated to a specific nation.

[6] Hale sees a similar relationship between federal design and the chance of fragmentation, but he identifies a slightly different mechanism (Hale 2004). For him, ethnic cores that are administratively defined actually increase the chance of state breakup because they produce dual power structures, promote a core ethnic identity, and generate security concerns among the minority ethnic groups.

Guy Grossman and Janet Lewis, who argued that administrative pro-liferation can strengthen the center by dividing and weakening existing units.[7] After all, Mizoram's gain was Assam's loss. Such policies cre-ate precedent-setting issues, but the metropole can typically enlist the help of existing states to contain them if it wants. However, these poli-cies do not create true secessionist dangers as long as the upgrades are symmetrical and culminate at the federal level. Such barriers are all the more salient when the state repeatedly demonstrates its willingness to maintain them.

Asymmetric decentralization is another matter since the metropole is creating new status categories that can be differentiated from the core units. These units are often crafted without an existing model, and the limits of decentralization are less defined and therefore more suscepti-ble to the slippery slope of continuous bargaining. Scotland, Catalonia, and Bougainville are examples. Given time, the difference in these units can achieve a degree of cognitive salience and present the region with an improved opportunity to secede because the metropole can justify its permission by pointing to administrative difference. In relation to symmetric decentralization, this sort of devolution ought to remain rare because of the open-ended precedent-setting problems it brings and because of the downstream potential for secession. Bougainville won a special status from Papua New Guinea (PNG) in 2001, and there is a good chance that its unique distinction will enable it to become independent in the years to come. It is telling that the government of PNG insisted at the time that Bougainville's status change was a one-off event and not something that the other regions of the country could hope to obtain.

When all is considered, what sort of specific predictions can we make about future secessionism? I have argued that the best candidates for peaceful secession are proto-states that are unique in type and/or mem-bers of an outer-belt category. Moreover, the findings in this book suggest that regime type adds another dimension of difference with respect to outcomes.[8] Figure 7.1 illustrates the relationships that fol-low from these two factors: the degree to which the secession of the

---

[7] Grossman and Lewis 2014.
[8] For related work on this topic, see Hirschman 1970; Snyder 2000; Hegre et al. 2001; Lake and Hiscox 2002; Ravlo et al. 2003; Van Houton 2003; Goldsmith and He 2008; Sorens 2012; Cunningham 2013.

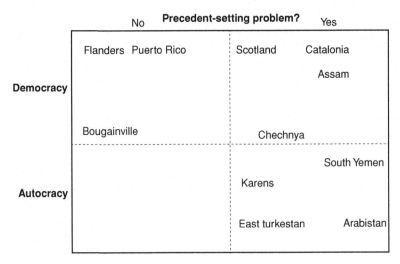

Figure 7.1 Matrix of regime type and degree of precedent setting.

region would present a precedent-setting problem; the level of democracy/autocracy. The best candidates for obtaining independence are located in the upper-left quadrant. It was the good fortune of Bhutan to be located here, along with the British overseas colonies after 1945. It is also the case currently with Puerto Rico, which is a member of the American unincorporated units. Like the Indian protectorates and the British colonies, Puerto Rico is part of an outer belt of American units that can be downsized. Flanders is currently a strong candidate because it is part of a highly democratic dyad. So too is Bougainville, a unique unit in a midlevel democracy.

Strikingly, there are no current secessionist movements in autocratic states that do not constitute a precedent-setting problem, and thus the lower-left quadrant is empty. Peaceful secession is actually quite rare in highly autocratic states. When the Soviet Union republics seceded in 1991, the state was effectively a mixed regime.[9] In only three cases have peaceful secession occurred in states that were even more autocratic. Norway seceded peacefully from semi-monarchical Sweden in 1905, Syria split from Egypt in 1961, and Equatorial Guinea seceded from Francoist Spain in 1968. Notably, in none of these cases did the seceding unit constitute a precedent-setting problem. Norway was a unique

---

[9] The polity score at this time was 10 on the 0–20 scale.

unit under Swedish rule, a lone branch in a dyad much like Syria was with Egypt in the United Arab Republic. Like the Czechoslovak velvet divorce, secession from these units was well-contained. When Equatorial Guinea seceded it was the last of Spain's overseas colonies, the sole member of a dying administrative type.[10]

The upper-right quadrant of Figure 7.1 depicts situations in which the proto-state does constitute a precedent-setting problem for a democratic regime. In recent years it is this configuration that often yields protracted processes of devolution and bargaining. There are, of course, differences in the danger of precedent setting. London can permit Scottish independence knowing that Northern Ireland or even Wales could follow because it has the English administrative core to fall back on. Neither Madrid nor Delhi has that luxury, and the placement of Catalonia and Assam to the right of Scotland represents the greater risk of permitting independence. Meanwhile, Chechnya's location indicates the weaker democracy and (relatively) milder precedent-setting problem for Moscow.

The lower-right quadrant in Figure 7.1 illustrates configurations in which secessionist violence is more likely. Secessionism among these proto-states constitutes a precedent-setting problem, but the respective metropole lacks the institutional apparatus to channel these energies into peaceful negotiation. China and Burma are somewhat similar in that regard. However, even in these cases the metropole could actually choose to downsize the secessionist units such as the Uyghur or the Karens and still retain the core of the state. Such a move may be highly unlikely, but it is available. Meanwhile, the administrative architectures of Yemen and Iran do not permit them to allow South Yemen's or Arabistan's independence with the same confidence.

One consequence of the post-1945 contraction of states is that metropoles are becoming less articulated. The remaining British and French overseas colonies along with the American unincorporated units are legacies of empire and earlier periods of expansion. As they dwindle in number so too does the number of proto-states that can secede without incurring major risks of fragmentation for their metropole, notwithstanding the occasional binary state such as Belgium or units such as Bougainville, the product of asymmetric

[10] The polity scores for these three cases were as follows: (1) Sweden in 1905 = 6; (2) Egypt in 1961 = 3; and (3) Spain in 1968 = 3.

decentralization. As long as current international conditions persist and contraction continues, the future of secessionism is best captured in the right quadrants, where decentralization and regime type will play a role. Future research should investigate the relationship between different levels of democracy and different secessionist outcomes, and determine how democracy can help build (or hinder) peaceful solutions.

Conclusion

Secession is an important topic not just in international relations and comparative politics, but also in social and political life more generally. It forces us to redraw our political maps on a regular basis. More importantly, it is one of the chief sources of violence in the world today. This book has contributed to our understanding of why governments deny secession in some cases but not others, and how those responses shape the likelihood of conflict. It has also provided a theory for the macrohistorical trend in state birth. The invisible hand of the international system has driven the expansion and contraction of states, but it is their internal structures that determine how states downsize.

Appendix A: Secessionist Movements

The unit of analysis in this study is the secessionist movement, a self-identified nation inside a sovereign state that seeks to separate and form a new sovereign state. I identify 403 secessionist movements between 1816 and 2011 using the following criteria:

1. At a minimum, the movement must last at least one week, it must involve at least 1000 people, and it must lay claim to at least 100 square kilometers.
2. The group must have a flag.
3. The group must make a claim to both a territory and a population.
4. The group must formally declare independence from its home state.

These are the criteria developed by Bridget Coggins, but my dataset constitutes an expansion on her work by including the period between 1816 and 1930 and 2001 and 2011.[1] I selected 1816 as the start date because data for prior years is currently unavailable and because 1816 is the start date for other relevant corollary datasets on sovereign state membership and conflict.

These criteria are meant to pick up formal and viable attempts at independence. The size criteria were chosen to filter small, often farcical independence efforts such as the Principality of Sealand and the Principality of Hutt River. To that end, the 1000-person threshold was a useful minimum for sorting the serious claims, which usually include significantly larger populations, from the less serious, which typically include fewer than 100 people. The second and third criteria were employed for similar reasons. In my research I found that serious secessionist efforts always chose a flag when claiming a specific territory for a specific nation. More fanciful endeavors sometimes referenced a mythical land, if they did at all.

---

[1] Coggins 2011, 2014. In her 2011 article, Coggins identifies 256 movements between 1931 and 2000.

The declaration of independence is a particularly important crite-rion, and it is often what separates formal secessionist movements from autonomous movements and other closely related endeavors. In his research on this topic, David Armitage writes that declarations of independence are "primarily assertions of sovereignty, both exter-nally, against any colonizing or occupying power, and internally, as they have defined a new state's source of legitimacy, its claim to ter-ritory, and its assertion of international legal personality."[2] Above all, these declarations are used in this study as a criterion for secessionism because they signal the intent of the group.[3] Interestingly, in a handful of instances a secessionist movement successful joined the international community without making a declaration of independence. Examples include Jamaica, Bhutan, and Tonga. In each case, the seceding unit had the apparent blessing of its metropole and independence was worked out in an amiable manner. In these instances I treat the agreed-upon moment of independence as tantamount to a declaration.[4]

Operationally, I coded the start and end of a secessionist movement in the following manner.[5] A movement begins when: (1) a declaration of independence is made, or; (2) a secessionist conflict begins and a declaration follows later, or (3) secessionists begin nonviolent politi-cal action (for example, the formation of secessionist political party) and a declaration follows later. In the latter two cases where secession-ism begins either through conflict or political activity and declaration follows later, the start date is the same as the beginning of secession-ist activity. A movement ends when: (1) the group formally renounces its independence claim, or (2) an agreement is struck granting indepen-dence or some other concession short of independence, or (3) five years pass without secessionist activity.

A number of sources were used in the construction of this dataset. Many sources were used for specific cases and I enumerate them in the Online Codebook. But my research benefited greatly from the fol-lowing general sources: *Colonial Governors from the Fifteenth Cen-tury to the Present; Dead Countries of the Nineteenth and Twentieth*

---

[2] Armitage 2007, 137.   [3] Note that Hale also uses this criterion (Hale 2008).
[4] With the exception of Liechtenstein and Bhutan, all of these cases occurred under the British metropole. It appears that a formal declaration was unnecessary since the metropoles were actively assisting in the process of secession.
[5] These start and end criteria are taken from Coggins 2011.

Centuries; Nations Without States: A Historical Dictionary of Contemporary National Movements; Ethnic Groups of South Asia and the Pacific: An Encyclopedia; Ethnic Diversity within Nations: The Former Soviet Union's Diverse Peoples; Encyclopedia of Stateless Nations; Separatist Movements: A Global Reference.[6]

Metropole	Secessionist Movement	Start	End
USA	Confederacy	1860	1865
USA	Philippines	1899	1946
USA	Dominican Republic	1916	1924
USA	Haiti	1916	1934
USA	Puerto Rico	1922	2011
USA	Marshall Islands	1979	1986
USA	Micronesia	1979	1986
USA	Hawaii	1994	2011
USA	Palau	1994	1994
USA	Lokotah	2007	2011
Canada	Quebec	1962	2011
Haiti	Dominican Republic	1838	1844
St. Kitts and Nevis	Nevis	1996	1998
Mexico	United States of Cent. America	1822	1823
Mexico	Texas	1835	1836
Mexico	Yucatan	1839	1843
Mexico	California	1846	1846
Mexico	Yucatan	1916	1916
Mexico	Yucatan	1923	1924
United States of Cent. America	Costa Rica	1826	1840
United States of Cent. America	El Salvador	1826	1840
United States of Cent. America	Guatemala	1826	1840
United States of Cent. America	Honduras	1826	1840

(cont.)

[6] In order, the authors are Henige 1970; Harding 1998; Minahan 1996, 2002, 2004, 2012; Beary 2011.

Metropole	Secessionist Movement	Start	End
United States of Cent. America	Nicaragua	1826	1840
Panama	Tule Republic	1925	1928
Gran Colombia	Ecuador	1821	1830
Gran Colombia	Venezuela	1821	1830
Colombia	Cauca	1860	1862
Gran Colombia	Panama	1899	1903
Peru-Bolivia	Bolivia	1837	1840
Brazil	Uruguay	1822	1828
Brazil	Rio Grande Do Sul	1835	1845
Brazil	Sabinadas	1837	1838
Brazil	Juliana Republic	1839	1839
Brazil	Rio Grande Do Sul	1892	1894
Brazil	Acre	1899	1903
Bolivia	Cambas	1921	1921
Bolivia	Cambas	1935	1935
UK	Ireland	1858	1922
UK	Sudan	1881	1886
UK	India	1885	1947
UK	South Africa	1885	1885
UK	Jews (Palestine/Israel)	1897	1948
UK	Transvaal	1899	1902
UK	Afghanistan	1919	1920
UK	Egypt	1919	1937
UK	Australia	1920	1920
UK	Canada	1920	1920
UK	Iraq	1920	1922
UK	New Zealand	1920	1920
UK	Sri Lanka	1926	1948
UK	Iraq	1928	1932
UK	Kuwait	1931	1961
UK	Scotland	1935	2011
UK	Burma	1938	1948
UK	Pakistan	1940	1947
UK	Shans	1942	1945
UK	Nigeria	1944	1960
UK	Sudan	1945	1956
UK	Barotseland (Lozi)	1946	1964
UK	Jordan	1946	1946

Metropole	Secessionist Movement	Start	End
UK	Karen	1946	1948
UK	Malaya (Straits Settlement)	1946	1957
UK	Baluchistan	1947	1947
UK	Nagas	1947	1947
UK	Sikhs	1947	1947
UK	Sikkim	1947	1947
UK	Travancore	1947	1947
UK	Sierra Leone	1948	1961
UK	British Somaliland	1949	1960
UK	Gold Coast (Ghana)	1949	1957
UK	Sanusis	1949	1951
UK	Mau Mau (Kenya)	1950	1962
UK	Buganda	1953	1962
UK	Uganda	1953	1962
UK	Tanganyika	1954	1961
UK	Cyprus	1955	1961
UK	Northern Rhodesia	1958	1964
UK	Basuotoland (Lesotho)	1959	1966
UK	Gambia	1960	1965
UK	Mauritius	1961	1968
UK	Brunei	1962	1984
UK	Jamaica	1962	1962
UK	Swaziland	1962	1968
UK	Trinidad and Tobago	1962	1962
UK	Fiji	1963	1970
UK	Nyasaland (Malawi)	1963	1964
UK	Rhodesia	1963	1965
UK	Zanzibar	1963	1963
UK	Bahamas	1964	1973
UK	Botswana	1964	1966
UK	Malta	1964	1964
UK	Maldives	1965	1965
UK	South Yemen	1965	1967
UK	Barbados	1966	1966
UK	Guyana	1966	1966
UK	Anguilla	1967	1971

(cont.)

Metropole	Secessionist Movement	Start	End
UK	Northern Ireland	1968	2011
UK	Tonga	1970	1970
UK	Bahrain	1971	1971
UK	Oman	1971	1971
UK	Qatar	1971	1971
UK	United Aran Republic	1971	1971
UK	Grenada	1974	1974
UK	Seychelles	1974	1976
UK	Dominica	1978	1978
UK	Solomon Islands	1978	1978
UK	Gilbert Islands/Kirbati	1979	1979
UK	St. Lucia	1979	1979
UK	St. Vincent	1979	1979
UK	Antigua	1981	1981
UK	British Honduras	1981	1981
UK	St. Kitts and Nevis	1983	1983
Netherlands	Belgium	1816	1830
Netherlands	Luxembourg	1890	1890
Netherlands	Dutch East Indies (Indonesia)	1920	1949
Netherlands	W. Papua (Irian Jaya)	1961	1962
Netherlands	Dutch Guiana (Suriname)	1973	1975
Belgium	Flanders	1917	1918
Belgium	Burundi (Bezi)	1945	1962
Belgium	Flanders	1954	2011
Belgium	Belgian Congo	1958	1960
Belgium	Rwanda	1959	1962
France	Syria	1920	1920
France	French Indochina – Vietnam	1925	1954
France	Syria	1925	1927
France	Syria	1930	1946
France	Tunisia	1934	1956
France	Hatay	1938	1939
France	Latakia	1939	1947
France	Lebanon	1941	1946
France	Mali	1942	1960

Metropole	Secessionist Movement	Start	End
France	Morocco	1944	1956
France	Dahomey	1945	1960
France	French Indochina – Cambodia	1945	1953
France	French Indochina – Laos	1945	1946
France	French Indochina – Pathet Lao	1946	1953
France	French West Africa (Ivory Coast)	1946	1960
France	Madagascar	1946	1960
France	Senegal	1946	1960
France	Casamance	1947	1960
France	Algeria	1954	1962
France	Cameroon	1955	1960
France	Mauritania	1957	1960
France	Burkina Faso	1958	1960
France	Central African Rep.	1958	1960
France	Chad	1958	1960
France	French Congo	1958	1960
France	French Eq. Africa (Gabon)	1958	1960
France	Guinea	1958	1958
France	Niger	1958	1960
France	Anyi	1960	1960
France	Togo	1960	1960
France	French Somaliland	1966	1977
France	Comoros	1968	1975
France	Brittany	1970	2011
France	Basques	1975	2011
France	Corsica	1978	2011
France	Savoy	1994	2011
Switzerland	Liechtenstein	1990	1990
Spain	Argentina	1816	1816
Spain	Bolivia	1816	1825
Spain	Chile	1816	1818
Spain	Dominican Republic	1816	1821
Spain	Gran Colombia	1816	1821

(cont.)

Metropole	Secessionist Movement	Start	End
Spain	Mexico	1816	1821
Spain	Peru	1816	1821
Spain	Dominican Republic	1863	1865
Spain	Cuba	1868	1878
Spain	Puerto Rico	1868	1898
Spain	Catalans	1873	1875
Spain	Cuba	1892	1902
Spain	Philippines	1892	1898
Spain	Spanish Morocco	1920	1926
Spain	Basques	1931	1937
Spain	Catalans	1931	1934
Spain	Asturias	1934	1934
Spain	Spanish Morocco	1944	1956
Spain	Spanish Guinea	1966	1968
Spain	Basques	1968	1998
Spain	Catalans	1974	2011
Spain	Basques	2000	2011
Portugal	Uruguay	1816	1821
Portugal	Brazil	1822	1823
Portugal	Angola	1961	1975
Portugal	Guinea Bissau	1961	1974
Portugal	Mozambique	1962	1975
Portugal	Cabinda	1963	1974
Portugal	Sao Tome and Principe	1965	1975
Portugal	Cape Verde	1974	1975
Portugal	East Timor	1974	1975
Germany	Bavaria	1918	1923
Germany	Lusatia	1918	1919
Germany	Rhineland	1918	1924
Germany	Saxony	1918	1923
Austria-Hungary	Hungary	1848	1849
Austria-Hungary	Transylvania	1918	1918
Austria-Hungary	Voralberg	1918	1918
Austria-Hungary	Western Ukraine	1918	1919
Czechoslovakia	Carpatho-Ukraine	1939	1939
Czechoslovakia	Slovakia	1992	1993
Italy	South Tyrol	1919	1919
Italy	Sanusis	1922	1931

Metropole	Secessionist Movement	Start	End
Italy	Montenegro	1941	1943
Italy	Italian Somaliland	1942	1960
Italy	Sicily	1943	1946
Italy	Giulians	1947	1954
Italy	South Tyrol	1950	1990
Italy	Sardinia	1965	1993
Italy	Padania	1996	2011
Italy	Sardinia	2002	2011
Croatia	Serbs	1991	1995
Yugoslavia	Kosovo	1981	2008
Yugoslavia	Croatia	1990	1992
Yugoslavia	Slovenia	1990	1992
Yugoslavia	Macedonia	1991	1993
Yugoslavia	Bosnia	1992	1992
Yugoslavia	Montenegro	2002	2006
Bosnia	Croats	1992	1995
Bosnia	Serbs	1992	2011
Greece	Epirus	1914	1920
Cyprus	North Cyprus	1963	2011
Moldova	Gagauz	1991	1995
Moldova	Transnistria	1991	2011
Russia	Poland	1830	1831
Russia	Gagauz	1906	1907
Russia	Crimean Tatars	1909	1919
Russia	Bashkortia	1917	1918
Russia	Chechnya	1917	1919
Russia	Dagestan	1917	1921
Russia	Finland	1917	1917
Russia	Abkhazia	1918	1921
Russia	Ajaria	1918	1922
Russia	Altai	1918	1922
Russia	Circassia	1918	1920
Russia	Don Cossacks	1918	1920
Russia	Estonia	1918	1918
Russia	Far Eastern Republic	1918	1922
Russia	Kalmykia	1918	1926
Russia	Karachais	1918	1920
Russia	Kuban Cossacks	1918	1920

(*cont.*)

Metropole	Secessionist Movement	Start	End
Russia	Latvia	1918	1918
Russia	Lithuania	1918	1918
Russia	Sakhas	1918	1920
Russia	Siberia	1918	1922
Russia	Tatarstan	1918	1920
Russia	Tereks	1918	1920
Russia	Buryatia	1919	1920
Russia	Ingria	1920	1921
Russia	Chukotka	1921	1922
Russia	Karelia	1921	1922
Russia	Western Ukraine	1941	1941
Russia	Kalmyks	1942	1944
Russia	Karachay-Balkaria	1942	1943
Russia	Lithuanians	1945	1952
Russia	Ukrainians	1945	1954
Russia	Ajars	1988	1991
Russia	Estonians	1988	1991
Russia	Abkhazia	1989	1991
Russia	Armenia	1990	1991
Russia	Azeris	1990	1991
Russia	Latvians	1990	1991
Russia	South Ossetia	1990	1991
Russia	Uzbeks	1990	1991
Russia	Belarus	1991	1991
Russia	Chechnya	1991	1996
Russia	Georgia	1991	1991
Russia	Kazakhs	1991	1991
Russia	Khyrgiz	1991	1991
Russia	Lithuanians	1991	1991
Russia	Moldova	1991	1991
Russia	Tajiks	1991	1991
Russia	Tatars	1991	2002
Russia	Turkomen	1991	1991
Russia	Ukrainians	1991	1991
Russia	Chechnya	1999	2011
Russia	Dagestan	1999	2011
Ukraine	Crimea	1992	1992
Georgia	Abkhazia	1992	2011
Georgia	South Ossetia	1992	2011

Metropole	Secessionist Movement	Start	End
Azerbaijan	Nagorno-Karabakh	1991	2011
Azerbaijan	Talysh	1993	1993
Sweden	Norway	1905	1905
Denmark	Iceland	1940	1944
Denmark	Faeroe Islands	1946	1948
Senegal	Casamance	1982	2011
Ivory Coast	Anyi	1961	1969
Cameroon	Southern Cameroons	1999	2011
Nigeria	Edos	1967	1967
Nigeria	Ibos (Igbo)	1967	1970
Dem Rep Congo	South Kasai	1960	1963
Dem Rep Congo	South Katanga	1960	1963
Dem Rep Congo	Stanleyville	1960	1962
Uganda	Bankonjo	1962	1982
Uganda	Bankonjo	1986	1988
Somalia	Somaliland	1981	2011
Ethiopia	Tigray	1943	1943
Ethiopia	Eritrea	1961	1993
Ethiopia	Somali	1963	1964
Ethiopia	Tigray	1975	1991
Ethiopia	Somali	1976	2011
Angola	Cabinda	1975	2006
South Africa	Namibia	1966	1990
South Africa	Inkatha (Kwazulu)	1993	1995
Namibia	Basters (Rehoboth)	1990	1991
Namibia	Lozi	1998	2011
Comoros	Anjouan	1997	2001
Comoros	Moheli	1997	2001
Comoros	Anjouan	2007	2008
Morocco	Saharawis	1975	2011
Sudan	South Sudan	1956	1972
Sudan	South Sudan	1983	2011
Iran	Gilan	1918	1921
Iran	Arabistanis (Ahwaz) (Khuzestan)	1923	2011
Iran	Azeris	1945	1947
Iran	Kurds	1945	1947
Iran	Kurds	1979	2011

(cont.)

Metropole	Secessionist Movement	Start	End
Turkey	Greece	1816	1828
Turkey	Egypt	1831	1833
Turkey	Montenegro	1858	1878
Turkey	Romania	1862	1878
Turkey	Bulgaria	1869	1898
Turkey	Serbia	1878	1878
Turkey	Albania	1910	1912
Turkey	Asiris	1914	1917
Turkey	Hejaz	1916	1916
Turkey	Kurds	1984	2011
Iraq	Kurds	1972	1975
Iraq	Kurds	1980	1988
Iraq	Kurds	1991	1992
Iraq	Kurds	1995	1996
United Arab Republic	Syria	1961	1961
Israel	Palestinians	1947	1949
Israel	Palestinians	1965	2011
Saudi Arabia	Asiris	1926	1934
Yemen	South Yemen	1994	1994
Yemen	South Yemen	2007	2011
China	Eastern Turkestan	1871	1874
China	Mongolia	1911	1921
China	Tannu Tuva	1911	1911
China	Tibet	1912	1913
China	Manchukuo	1926	1945
China	Northern Tai	1926	1936
China	Eastern Mongols	1928	1928
China	Uighurs	1932	1934
China	Southern Mongols	1934	1937
China	Uighurs	1944	1949
China	Eastern Mongols	1946	1947
China	Tibet	1950	1951
China	Hui	1953	1953
China	Tibet	1956	1961
China	Tibet	1979	2011
China	Uighurs (Xinjiang)	1990	2011
Japan	Ezo	1869	1869
Japan	Taiwan	1895	1895
India	Kashmir	1947	1949

Metropole	Secessionist Movement	Start	End
India	Hyderabad	1948	1948
India	Nagas	1948	2011
India	Meitei	1964	2011
India	Mizos	1966	1986
India	Bhutan	1971	1971
India	Tripuras	1978	2011
India	Assam	1979	2010
India	Sikhs	1981	1993
India	Boro/Bodo	1986	2011
India	Kashmir	1989	2011
Pakistan	Pashtuns	1947	2011
Pakistan	Baluch	1958	2011
Pakistan	E. Pakistan	1969	1972
Bangladesh	Chittagong	1975	1997
Burma	Arakanese	1948	1958
Burma	Kachin	1949	1950
Burma	Karenni	1949	2011
Burma	Karens	1949	2011
Burma	Mons	1949	1995
Burma	Shans	1958	2011
Burma	Arakanese	1960	2011
Burma	Kachin	1961	1995
Burma	Kachin	2011	2011
Sri Lanka	Tamils	1975	2009
Thailand	Malays	1959	2011
Vietnam	Chams	1964	1966
Malaysia	Singapore	1965	1965
Philippines	Mindanao	1972	2011
Philippines	Abu Sayyaf	1991	2011
Indonesia	Ambonese	1950	1950
Indonesia	Atjeh	1950	1980
Indonesia	Sulawesi	1958	2011
Indonesia	Irian Jaya	1962	2011
Indonesia	East Timor	1975	2002
Indonesia	Atjeh	1988	2005
Australia	Papua New Guinea	1972	1975
Papua New Guinea	Bougainville	1975	1976
Papua New Guinea	Bougainville	1988	2001

(*cont.*)

Metropole	Secessionist Movement	Start	End
New Zealand	Samoa (W. Samoa)	1927	1962
New Zealand	Maori	1975	2011
Solomon Islands	Guadalcanal	1999	2000
UK–France	Tafea	1974	1974
UK–France	Vemeranans	1975	1975
UK–France	Tafea	1980	1980
UK–France	Vanuatu	1980	1980
UK–France	Vemeranans	1980	1980
Spain-France	Andorra	1993	1993

Appendix B: Proto-states

Proto-states are the second type of data in this study. I define proto-states as identifiable administrative jurisdictions with the following traits:

1. They have a minimum population of 1000 people *and* a minimum size of 100 square kilometers and,
2. They *either* possess complete internal independence (indirect rule),
   a. *or* they are granted specific rights in accordance with a unit-wide ethnic group or nation,
   b. *or* they are the result of a territorial transfer,
   c. *or* they are separated from the metropole by at least 100 miles.

A proto-state is a particular type of political unit, one that is organized administratively, given some degree of autonomy, and is typically (though not always) constructed around a local ethnic group. Such units are common throughout history, particularly to larger, compound states; they have been political building blocks since the satrapies of the Persian Empire up through the republics of the Soviet Union.

My efforts to create this dataset were facilitated by Phil Roeder's work on segment states. In his 2007 book, Roeder identified 368 segment states between 1900 and 2000, defined as follows: "Segment states are not simply territorial jurisdictions within a federal state; they also contain juridically separate communities of peoples who purportedly have special claim to the jurisdiction as a homeland."[1] I began with this data and then modified it in several ways. First, I augmented the dataset by looking both further back in time to include the period from 1816 to 1900 and forward in time to include the years 2001 to 2011. Second, I coded beyond first-order units to include second-, third-, and even fourth-order units as well. This was essential given my hypotheses

[1] Roeder 2007, 12–13.

regarding levels of organization.[2] Finally, I defined proto-states in a different way. Whereas Roeder's focuses on political divisions that fall along national lines, I developed a broader set of criteria which I explain subsequently.

Scope

There are two general challenges when constructing a dataset of this type. The first has to do with scope. The organization of political systems is complex and the number of potential administrative units is vast. For example, the USA organizes its internal political units in fairly clear layers. At the top level are states; beneath states are counties (sometimes called parishes or boroughs); beneath counties are a set of potential units that include townships, towns, and municipalities. These last units could be further divided depending on local arrangements and terminology. In essence, political units are nested. To merely take the top level (that is, first-order units) in each country over the entire time period would be a massive undertaking. More importantly, a very high percentage of those units will be nonstarters (that is, cases in which secessionism is unlikely to arise).

The criteria are designed to pull out the most important units. Although it is set rather low, the size criteria is important for filtering out extremely tiny units and, perhaps more importantly, possessions of a military purpose that lack any local population (for example, Palmyra Atoll). I chose the floor of 1000 people and 100 square kilometers because that is also the minimum size for secessionist movements.

The second set of criteria aims to establish distance (politically, ethnically, or geographically) between the proto-state and its metropole. A state that possesses complete domestic sovereignty and is free to conduct its internal but not its external affairs is a prime example of a proto-state. It is a "state-in-the-making," with its own political apparatus. All it lacks is freedom over its foreign affairs. Therefore, any unit that is ruled indirectly is a proto-state. Note that this includes *de facto* indirect rule as well. What matters here are conditions on the

---

[2] In this regard, the only clear distinction Roeder makes is between internal and external units, in which the point of difference is whether the unit's territory is contiguous with that of the metropole.

ground; if the unit practices complete internal rule, then it is a proto-state, regardless of what the arrangement is in theory. However, that autonomy has to be permitted to some extent, or go largely uncontested, by the metropole. For example, I did not count the American Confederacy because its autonomy was always contested by the Union. It is when the central government permits *de facto* autonomy that it counts. There is a potential endogeneity problem I am trying to avoid here; proto-states will often give rise to secessionism and civil war, not the other way around.

This distinction between direct and indirect rule is important and deserves added attention. The difference between the two is that an indirectly ruled unit enjoys internal autonomy. Examples include Oman, Bhutan, and Khiva. In a directly ruled unit, the internal politics and administration are to some extent controlled by the metropole. However, in neither case does the unit conduct its own foreign relations. Therefore, according to the definitions used in the International System(s) Dataset (ISD), as well as by the Correlates of War (COW) project, neither type would qualify as a sovereign state and, thus, make it onto the state list.[3] An indirectly ruled unit is, of course, closer to being a sovereign state insofar as it enjoys a greater level of autonomy and its relationship with the central government is conducted on a more decentralized basis. In fact, such units typically possess what Krasner refers to as domestic sovereignty, the ability of the government to exercise effective control within its borders.[4] On the spectrum running from hierarchy to anarchy, a relationship of direct rule is closer to hierarchy.

The importance of the criterion regarding ethnic distance (or difference) is fairly obvious. Proto-states that possess a different ethnic or national group are more likely to attempt secession. This was the key criterion in Roeder's definition of segment states. It is not enough that the unit simply possesses an ethnic group that is different from that of the metropole; the group in question has to be accorded special status by the central government, one that designates the administrative unit as a homeland of a distinct population. By emphasizing juridical distinctions in this way, I hew quite closely to Roeder's criterion. There

---

[3] Griffiths and Butcher 2013; Correlates of War Project 2011. Also see Fazal 2007.

[4] Krasner 1999.

are numerous other ways in which such groups can be identified, but none of them captures the intention of the central government quite as well.[5] By publicly acknowledging a distinct nation within the larger state, and designating a territory as that nation's homeland, the central government is foregoing the policy of "one nation, one land."

Another method of identifying proto-states is to look at territorial transfers. One of the reasons the world map has changed so much over time is that countries exchange territory. They barter it and they purchase it from one another. I used the COW dataset on territorial change to code transferred units as proto-states as long as they are transformed into administrative units in the new state and meet the criteria for minimum size and population.[6] However, for these transfers I created a sunset clause; in each case, I coded the territory as a proto-state and then dropped them from the list after ten years if they failed to meet the other criteria. In general, many of these units qualified as proto-states anyway because they meet one or two of the other criteria (for example, they possess a unique ethnic group). If so, then the unit remained a proto-state beyond the ten-year limit. If, however, the unit did not meet any of these other criteria, then it seemed unreasonable to code it continuously as a proto-state. Without internal rule, ethnic difference, or geographic distance, the potential for fragmentation ought to fade over time.

In general, I did not code occupations as transfers. Although occupied territories may constitute an empirical transfer of territory, I did not count these as proto-states unless one of two conditions was met: (1) The occupation became formalized – that is, it was included in the COW dataset on territorial change; (2) The occupation lasted for at least ten years. According to these criteria, the great majority of war time occupations do not count as proto-states.

Although it is tempting to stop there, the inclusion of an alternate criterion of distance is important. Without one, many overseas colonies would not count as proto-states. The distance criterion makes sense logically given that significant distance can result in increasingly

---

[5] Certain characteristics may help demonstrate a unique group but they are neither necessary nor sufficient – for example, the ability to use the group's language for official business; the group constitutes a clear majority and is empowered; the right to local, not appointed, governance.

[6] Tir et al. 1998.

different polities.[7] Moreover, the relevant sociopolitical issues in the metropole are likely to differ from those in the peripheral unit. As such, the temptation to bring the locus of decision making closer to home – to separate – is likely to be greater in these units than in similar regions much closer to the metropole. In general, with greater distance comes increased autonomy and ethnic difference, particularly in earlier periods when communication was poorer. It is for this rationale that some metropoles chose to grant special autonomy status to units for reasons having to do with geography and not ethnicity.[8] The requirement that a unit be separated from its metropole by at least 100 miles of water or foreign territory is consistent with Coggins's distance threshold and the set of values used in the COW dataset on colonial possessions.[9]

In sum, proto-states must be above a certain size, encompass at least 100 square kilometers, and include at least 1000 inhabitants. In addition, the territory must meet at least one of the following criteria: (1) it possesses internal autonomy (that is, indirect rule); (2) it possesses "national" distinction; (3) it is separated from the metropole by more than 100 miles of water or foreign territory; (4) it qualifies as a recently transferred territory.

The total set of proto-states meet these criteria in various combinations. For example, both Quebec and Scotland are currently proto-states on account of their national distinction. Neither meets any of the other criteria, although Quebec did meet the distance criteria prior to 1840 when it was directly subordinate to the UK. Of the fifty states in the USA, only two are currently proto-states on account of their geographic distance (Alaska and Hawaii). However, states such as Texas and Florida did count during earlier periods as transferred units. Some proto-states were indirectly ruled, geographically distant, and nationally distinct. In numerous cases, this appears to be the status of the unit on the run-up to sovereign independence (for example, Australia, the Philippines). A small number managed to meet all four criteria; Annam did so from 1884 until 1897 when it became part of French Indochina. Although many proto-states will meet several of these criteria only one is necessary provided the unit is of sufficient size.

---

[7] Roeder seems to employ this criterion too. He includes both Hawaii and Alaska as segment-states, but none of the other forty-eight states.

[8] Examples include Madeira and the Azores since 1979.

[9] Coggins 2011, 2014; Correlates of War 2 Project, n.d.

Administrative Architecture

The second challenge in constructing the dataset is how to identify levels of administrative organization. I derived a system that accommodates different approaches in the literature. One common way used is to rank first-, second-, and third-order units by how they are nested relative to the metropole (the method used in the CIA ranking system). In the case of the USA, all states, territories, and possessions would be first-order because they are directly subordinate to the central government. Counties would then be proper second-order units since because are directly subordinate to states that are, in turn, subordinate to the central government.

Another method for classifying proto-states is to examine how they are perceived. Metropoles typically draw a distinction between internal and external territories. For example, the USA delineates political units by whether they are incorporated. If so, then the territory is subject to the full weight of the US Constitution and is meant to remain part of the USA. In contrast, nonincorporated states are viewed as external possessions. The first units of this type were the territories gained from the Spanish American War; none of them were subject to the Constitution and none were perceived as permanent US territory. Similarly, France draws a distinction between those regions (or departments) that are considered to be an integral part of the Republic, and those that are viewed as external.

This internal/external distinction varies by metropole and some metropoles have altered their use of the distinction over time. For example, France reclassified many of its colonies immediately following World War II and made them internal polities. Likewise, Portugal expanded its internal/external perimeter to include more of its territories in 1951. The Netherlands did the same in 1954. This expansion of the internal/external perimeter is akin to what Doyle refers to as crossing the Caracallan threshold: removing the distinction between core populations and subject populations.[10] Including this distinction in the data is important for at least two reasons. First, it seems plausible that metropoles would behave differently with respect to the potential fragmentation of a unit they deem internal (or integral) and a unit they

[10] Doyle 1986, 97–98.

consider to be a foreign possession. For instance, some historians point out that France worked much harder, and fought a prolonged conflict, to keep "internal" Algeria than it did to keep the "external" colonies of Tunisia and Morocco. Second, this distinction does not correspond perfectly with the other dimensions of classification. Internal political units are not always near (for example, Hawaii, French Guyana, Suriname). Meanwhile, politically external regions are often contiguous (for example, Khiva, Bhutan), and they can be first-, second-, and even third-order units.

Yet another method for classifying proto-states is to gauge their level of autonomy. This is important since highly autonomous units are thought to be more likely to develop secessionist tendencies. However, as before, the level of autonomy does not necessarily correspond with how the unit is nested (that is, whether it is a first-order unit), how it is perceived (internal or external), or whether it is contiguous with the metropole.

My system balances these different factors by sorting proto-states into four different levels.

- Level 0. These are proto-states that were recently transferred from another state, but lack any special autonomous or national status.
- Level 1. These are core-level proto-states. In many cases they are federal units (for example, Hawaii), but oftentimes they are departments, prefectures, and so on, that count as proto-states because of distance.
- Level 2. These are intermediate-level proto-states that possess local autonomy or national distinction. They are not politically external units.
- Level 3. There are outer-level units that that are first-order and politically external.

All of the proto-states are sorted into this system, but the coding is sensitive to the specific architecture of the metropole. For example, the states of Hawaii and Alaska are core-level proto-states because they are separated from the metropole by more than 100 miles.[11] Most Native American reservations are intermediate-level proto-states because they

[11] The remaining forty-eight states are core units but not proto-states because they do not meet any of the secondary criteria.

are nationally based.[12] The Commonwealth of Puerto Rico is an outer-level proto-state because it is geographically distant, nationally based, and regarded as an external possession (that is, an unincorporated territory).[13]

Overall, my dataset deconstructs the manner in which metropoles are organized and codes along several different dimensions. These include the order of the unit (first, second, third), its internal or external classification, and its level of autonomy (both in general and with respect to the specific metropole). As it turns out, metropoles are organized in a surprising variety of ways. Some, such as France, opted to maintain a rather centralized administrative apparatus. In fact, many of the states born in the post-1945 period have organized their administration in a concentric and centralized fashion in which the constituent units are neither autonomous nor nationally distinct. This is particularly so with the former French colonies. Many states simply do not possess any proto-states as I have defined them and are, by implication, in less danger of fragmentation. Others opted to grant quasi-autonomy to peripheral regions.[14] For example, the Soviet regime radically transformed its administrative architecture when it created a large number of units organized along national lines. In fact, this approach to organizing political space has become much more common since the mid twentieth century and is currently employed in a number of countries from Ethiopia to India. Meanwhile, the British metropole has employed a diverse set of organizing practices over the past 200 years.

Importantly, proto-states are always subordinate to a metropole, or central government, that I located geographically in the capital city. In the organizational mapping of each state I begin with an administrative core, but such cores are not always obvious. In political systems that were set up in a traditional "hub-and-spokes" format – empires are quite often designed in this manner – the core is not hard to identify.[15] In the Soviet Union, the Russian Republic would be the core. In the former British Empire, England could be thought of as the core. In federal

---

[12] Some units are too small to count.   [13] Wunnicke 1989, 22.

[14] Cooley decomposes imperial frameworks and compares them with U-Form (Unitary) and M-Form (Multidivisional) business models (Cooley 2005).

[15] "Hub and spokes" is a metaphor used by Motyl to characterize imperial systems that resemble a wheel, with the imperial core radiating out to the periphery (Motyl 2001).

systems such as the USA, however, the administrative core is less clear. It is not the District of Columbia (Washington, DC) that constitutes the core, but rather the collection of states themselves. In his application of organization theory to political hierarchy, Alexander Cooley draws an analogy between a federation and a holding company. Unlike multidivisional or unitary business organizations – which are analogous to imperial networks – holding companies (and some federations) lack a distinct core.[16] The fifty states that compose the core of the USA are all potential proto-states, should they meet the necessary criteria. Similarly, in both India and Australia the federal units collectively constitute the core. These realities are captured in the mapping of each state's administrative architecture.

Finally, one of my main hypotheses holds that metropoles are less likely to release a proto-state when issues of precedence exist. To that end I coded a dummy variable (1 = no peer) that records whether a proto-state is unique member of an administrative category. For example, Slovakia had no peer between 1949 and 1993, and its potential secession did not constitute a precedence issue for the Czech metropole because the larger state, Czechoslovakia, was a two-unit country. Importantly, many of these cases are not classic binary states such as Czechoslovakia or Norway-Sweden. For example, PNG possessed a unique status in the Australian administrative framework when it became independent in 1975. Similarly, since 2001 Bougainville has possessed a special autonomous status that is unique among all the territories in PNG. What matters is that the unit in question is the only member of a particular administrative category. From the perspective of Stockholm and Prague, there were other administrative units, they were just of a lesser order.

The identification of proto-states required a large number of sources. Many of these were specific to certain regions or countries, but some of them were more generally applicable and constituted the backbone of the effort. For general data collection, the following books were quite useful: *Colonial Governors from the Fifteenth Century to the Present*; *Dead Countries of the Nineteenth and Twentieth Centuries*; *Federal Systems of the World*; *Facts about the World's Nations*; *Types of Restricted Sovereignty and of Colonial Autonomy*; *Administrative Subdivisions of Countries: A Comprehensive World Reference*,

---

[16] Cooley 2005, 26–29.

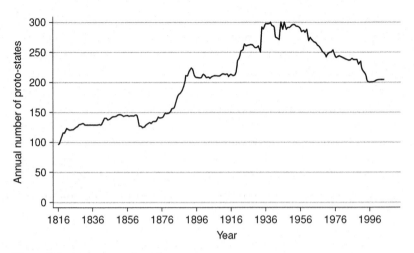

Figure B.1 Annual number of proto-states.

1900 through 1998; Latin American History, a Teaching Atlas; The Correlates of War (COW) Colonial/Dependency Contiguity Dataset (v3.0).[17]

Results

The resulting dataset identifies 638 proto-states between 1816 and 2005 and further records whether secessionist movements between 2006 and 2011 corresponded with a proto-state.[18] In the data these proto-states lasted an average of sixty years. Figure B.1 graphs the number of proto-states over time. There were ninety-seven proto-states in 1816 and 205 in 2005. There is an initial increase at the beginning of the nineteenth century, a much sharper increase in the late nineteenth century, and a third significant increase in the interwar period. After World War II, the number of proto-states drops off rather steadily and then levels off at a little more than 200 in the mid 1990s.

[17] In order, the authors are Henige 1970; Harding 1998; Elazar 1994; O'Mara 1999; Willoughby and Fenwick 1919; Law 1999; Correlates of War 2 Project, n.d.

[18] The mapping of each state's administrative architecture does not extend beyond 2005. I do record whether each secessionist movement possessed a proto-state from 2006 to 2011.

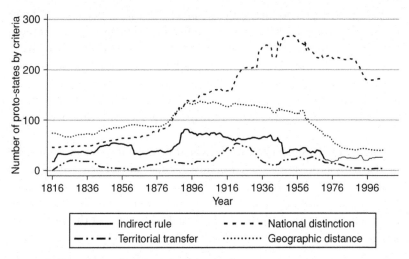

Figure B.2 Number of proto-states by criteria.

Figure B.2 illustrates the number of proto-states that were indirectly ruled, geographically distant, nationally distinct, or a territorial transfer.[19] The graph points to a few interesting patterns. The late nineteenth century increase in the number of proto-states follows from an increase in indirectly ruled, nationally distinct, and externally distant units. This is not surprising given what we know about colonialism. The so-called global enclosure that occurred during these years resulted in the imperial acquisition of numerous territories.[20] Some of these acquisitions were previously sovereign (for example, Dir, Fouta Djallon), and thus proto-state creation in this period was partly responsible for the simultaneous reduction in the number of sovereign states (see Figure 1.1).[21] Other units were simply created from territory that was regarded by the core European powers as *terra nullius* (Northeastern Rhodesia).

The second sharp increase in the number of proto-states during the interwar period is very informative. The cause is a growth in the number of nationally distinct units; the other types are all declining during this period. The explanation seems to be that a number of metropoles

---

[19] Note that these four categories are not mutually exclusive and therefore sum up to more than the total number of proto-states.
[20] Jackson 1990, 71; Abernethy 2000, 6; Scott 2009, 5.
[21] Griffiths and Butcher 2013.

including Russia and the USA adopted domestic policies of ethnic recognition and established internal units that were juridically assigned to a specific group of people. In general, such designations were given not to newly acquired territories, but rather to units that the metropole already possessed. These policies were effectively transformations of previously sovereign territory, and they compounded with the previous wave of proto-state formation to bring the total number above 300.

Finally, the post-1945 years in which proto-states are in decline is increasingly dominated by nationally distinct units. Forms of indirect and geographically distant rule, along with territorial transfers, have become less common. Where proto-states exist in the late twentieth and early twenty-first centuries, it is usually by virtue of their national distinction.

Metropole	Proto-state	Start	End
USA	Florida	1819	1838
USA	Indian Territory	1834	1907
USA	Texas	1845	1864
USA	Isleta Pueblo	1863	2011
USA	Alaska	1867	2011
USA	Navajo	1868	2011
USA	Papago	1874	2011
USA	Hawaii	1898	2011
USA	American Samoa	1900	2011
USA	Canal Zone	1903	1978
USA	Colorado River	1912	2011
USA	Haiti	1915	1934
USA	Allegheny	1922	2011
USA	Yankton	1932	2011
USA	Fort Apache	1934	2011
USA	Hopi	1934	2011
USA	Salt River	1934	2011
USA	San Carlos	1934	2011
USA	Fort Hall	1934	2011
USA	Nez Perce	1934	2011
USA	Leech Lake	1934	2011
USA	Red Lake	1934	2011
USA	White Earth	1934	2011

Metropole	Proto-state	Start	End
USA	Blackfeet	1934	2011
USA	Crow	1934	2011
USA	Flathead	1934	2011
USA	Fort Balknap	1934	2011
USA	Fort Peck	1934	2011
USA	Northern Cheyenne	1934	2011
USA	Omaha	1934	2011
USA	Acomo Pueblo	1934	2011
USA	Jemez	1934	2011
USA	Jicarilla	1934	2011
USA	Laguna Pueblo	1934	2011
USA	Mescalero	1934	2011
USA	Ramah	1934	2011
USA	Santo Domingo Pueblo	1934	2011
USA	Taos Pueblo	1934	2011
USA	Zuni Pueblo	1934	2011
USA	Cherokee	1934	2011
USA	Fort Berthold	1934	2011
USA	Fort Totten	1934	2011
USA	Turtle Mountain	1934	2011
USA	Cheyenne River	1934	2011
USA	Pine Ridge	1934	2011
USA	Rosebud	1934	2011
USA	Sisseton	1934	2011
USA	Uintah and Ouray	1934	2011
USA	Yakima	1934	2011
USA	Wind River	1934	2011
USA	Cheyenne and Arapaho	1936	2011
USA	Chickasaw	1936	2011
USA	Chocktaw	1936	2011
USA	Osage	1936	2011
USA	Seminole	1936	2011
USA	Warm Springs	1938	2011
USA	Gila River	1939	2011
USA	Comanche	1946	2011
USA	Kiowa	1946	2011
USA	Crow Creek	1949	2011
USA	Ute Mountain	1951	2011
USA	Ryuku Islands	1952	1991

(*cont.*)

Metropole	Proto-state	Start	End
USA	Rocky Boys	1957	2011
USA	San Felipe Pueblo	1962	2011
USA	Canancito	1965	2011
USA	Quinault	1969	2011
USA	Annette Island	1971	2011
USA	Hoopa Valley	1973	2011
USA	Hualapai	1976	2011
USA	Micronesia	1979	1986
USA	Kosrae	1980	2011
USA	Duck Valley	1985	2011
Canada	Nunavut	1999	2011
Mexico	Guetemala	1821	1840
Mexico	Honduras	1821	1840
Mexico	El Salvador	1821	1840
Mexico	Nicaragua	1821	1840
Mexico	Costa Rica	1821	1840
Mexico	Chiapas	1821	1840
Mexico	Yaqui	1936	2011
Columbia (Gran Columbia)	Leticia	1934	1953
Brazil	Uruguay	1816	1828
Brazil	Cacheu	1816	1852
Brazil	Bissau	1816	1878
Brazil	Cape Verde Islands	1816	1975
Brazil	Sao Tome e Principe	1816	1975
Brazil	Angola	1816	1975
Brazil	Mozambique	1816	1975
Brazil	Portuguese India	1816	1980
Brazil	Portuguese Timor	1816	1994
Brazil	Macao	1816	1998
Brazil	Azores	1816	2011
Brazil	Madiera Isles	1816	2011
Brazil	Acre	1904	1922
Chile	Tacna	1883	1948
Chile	Antofagasta	1884	1903
Chile	Easter Is.	1944	2011
UK	Demerara and Essequibo	1816	1831
UK	Berbice	1816	1831
UK	Tobago	1816	1832
UK	Leeward Islands A	1816	1833

Metropole	Proto-state	Start	End
UK	Leeward Islands B	1816	1833
UK	Ontario	1816	1841
UK	Rewa	1816	1862
UK	Travancore	1816	1862
UK	Ionian Islands	1816	1863
UK	Rupert's Land	1816	1869
UK	Red River Colony	1816	1870
UK	Prince Edward Island	1816	1873
UK	Penang	1816	1874
UK	Cape Colony	1816	1885
UK	New South Wales	1816	1901
UK	Ireland	1816	1922
UK	India	1816	1947
UK	Ceylon	1816	1948
UK	Hyderabad	1816	1956
UK	Sierra Leone	1816	1961
UK	Jamaica	1816	1962
UK	Trinidad and Tobago	1816	1962
UK	Malta	1816	1964
UK	Barbados	1816	1966
UK	Newfoundland	1816	1968
UK	Mauritius	1816	1968
UK	Bahama Islands	1816	1973
UK	Seychelles	1816	1976
UK	St. Lucia	1816	1979
UK	Jersey	1816	2011
UK	Quebec	1816	2011
UK	Scotland	1816	2011
UK	Wales	1816	2011
UK	Mysore	1816	2011
UK	Peshwa	1817	1836
UK	Udaipur	1817	1852
UK	Indore	1818	1837
UK	Nagpur	1818	1837
UK	Bikaner	1818	1862
UK	Jaipur	1818	1862
UK	Kishangarh	1818	1862
UK	Jodhpur	1818	1862
UK	Jaisalmer	1818	1862

(cont.)

Metropole	Proto-state	Start	End
UK	Kotah	1818	1862
UK	Bundi	1818	1862
UK	Loharu	1819	1835
UK	Dhar	1819	1857
UK	Bhopal	1819	1862
UK	Bilaspur	1819	1862
UK	Maler Kotla	1819	1862
UK	Sirmur	1819	1862
UK	Suket	1819	1862
UK	Singapore	1819	1965
UK	Gold Coast	1821	1957
UK	Tasmania	1825	1901
UK	Tenasserim	1826	1861
UK	Kapurthala	1826	1862
UK	Straits Settlements	1826	1945
UK	Swat	1826	1969
UK	Arakan	1826	2011
UK	Western Australia	1828	1901
UK	Man	1828	2011
UK	Gambia	1829	1965
UK	British Guiana	1831	1966
UK	Bahawalpur	1833	1862
UK	Winward Islands	1833	1960
UK	Leeward Islands	1834	1958
UK	South Australia	1836	1901
UK	Sind	1839	1858
UK	Aden Colony	1839	1963
UK	New Zealand	1840	1920
UK	British Honduras	1840	1981
UK	Canada	1841	1920
UK	Hong Kong	1841	2011
UK	Natal	1843	1929
UK	Punjab	1846	1865
UK	Kashmir	1846	2011
UK	British Kaffraria	1847	1866
UK	Turks and Caicos	1848	2011
UK	Victoria	1851	1901
UK	Lagos	1851	1906
UK	British Columbia	1858	1871

Metropole	Proto-state	Start	End
UK	Andaman and Nicobar Islands	1858	1946
UK	Vancouver	1859	1866
UK	Queensland	1859	1901
UK	Bahrain	1861	1971
UK	Basutoland	1868	1966
UK	Songei Ujong	1874	1894
UK	Perak	1874	1945
UK	Selangore	1874	1945
UK	Pahang	1874	1945
UK	Fiji	1874	1970
UK	Falkland Islands	1874	2011
UK	Las Bela	1876	1955
UK	Ulu Muar	1878	1894
UK	Jempol	1878	1894
UK	Johol	1878	1894
UK	Cyprus	1878	1961
UK	Zululand	1879	1897
UK	Afghanistan	1879	1920
UK	Transvaal	1881	1929
UK	Aden Protectorate	1882	1937
UK	North Borneo	1882	2011
UK	Kharan	1884	1947
UK	British Somaliland	1884	1960
UK	British Bechuanaland	1885	1894
UK	Oil Rivers Protectorate	1885	1900
UK	Johore	1885	1945
UK	Bechuanaland	1885	1966
UK	Rambau	1886	1894
UK	Northern Nigeria	1886	1914
UK	Kantarawadi	1886	1947
UK	Bawlake	1886	1947
UK	Kybogyi	1886	1947
UK	Jelebu	1887	1894
UK	Sudan	1887	1956
UK	Maldive Islands	1887	1965
UK	British New Guinea	1888	1945
UK	Kenya	1888	1962
UK	Brunei	1888	1984

(cont.)

Metropole	Proto-state	Start	End
UK	Sarawak	1888	2011
UK	Cook Islands	1888	2011
UK	Sri Menati	1889	1894
UK	Tampin	1889	1894
UK	Northeastern Rhodesia	1889	1911
UK	Northwestern Rhodesia	1889	1911
UK	Chitral	1889	1969
UK	Mashonaland	1890	1895
UK	Hsipaw	1890	1947
UK	Tawngpeng	1890	1947
UK	North Hsenwi	1890	1947
UK	South Hsenwi	1890	1947
UK	Manglun	1890	1947
UK	Yawnghwe	1890	1947
UK	Lawksawk	1890	1947
UK	Samka	1890	1947
UK	Mongpai	1890	1947
UK	Laikha	1890	1947
UK	Mongkung	1890	1947
UK	Mongnai	1890	1947
UK	Mawkmai	1890	1947
UK	Mongpawn	1890	1947
UK	Mongpan	1890	1947
UK	Kengtung	1890	1947
UK	Mongmit	1890	1947
UK	Nyasaland Protectorate	1891	1964
UK	Hunza	1891	1969
UK	Oman	1891	1971
UK	Zanzibar	1891	2011
UK	Nagar	1892	1969
UK	Abu Dhabi	1892	1970
UK	Dubai	1892	1970
UK	Sharjah	1892	1970
UK	Ajman	1892	1970
UK	Umm Al Qaiwan	1892	1970
UK	Gilbert and Ellice Islands	1892	1975
UK	Matabeleland	1893	1895
UK	Uganda	1893	1962
UK	Solomon Islands	1893	1978
UK	Negri Sembilan	1895	1945

Metropole	Proto-state	Start	End
UK	Southern Rhodesia	1895	1965
UK	Amb	1895	1969
UK	Dir	1896	1969
UK	Weihaiwei	1898	1929
UK	Southern Nigeria	1900	1914
UK	Tonga	1900	1970
UK	Cayman Islands	1900	2011
UK	Niue Island	1900	2011
UK	Australia	1901	1920
UK	Orange River Colony	1902	1929
UK	Kuwait	1904	1961
UK	Swaziland	1907	1968
UK	Bhutan	1910	1971
UK	Northern Rhodesia	1911	1964
UK	Iraq	1914	1932
UK	British Togoland	1914	1956
UK	Nigeria	1914	1960
UK	British Cameroons	1916	1960
UK	Tanganyika	1918	1961
UK	Palestine	1920	1948
UK	Inner Oman	1920	1959
UK	Transjordan	1921	1946
UK	Northern Ireland	1922	2011
UK	Burma	1937	1948
UK	Western Aden Protectorate	1937	1959
UK	Eastern Aden Protectorate	1937	1963
UK	Malaya	1946	1957
UK	Ras Al Khaimah	1952	1970
UK	Fujairah	1952	1970
UK	West Indies Federation	1958	1962
UK	Federation of South Arabia	1959	1967
UK	British Virgin Islands	1960	2011
UK	Grenada	1962	1974
UK	Dominica	1962	1978
UK	St. Vincent	1962	1979
UK	Antigua	1962	1981
UK	St. Kitts-Nevis	1962	1983
UK	Montserrat	1962	2011

(*cont.*)

Metropole	Proto-state	Start	End
UK	UAE	1971	1971
UK	Gilbert Islands/Kiribati	1976	1979
Netherlands	Coromandel Coast	1816	1824
Netherlands	Malacca	1816	1844
Netherlands	Curacao	1816	1848
Netherlands	Dutch Gold Coast	1816	1870
Netherlands	Netherlands East Indies	1816	1949
Netherlands	Surinam	1816	1975
Netherlands	Bencoolen	1824	1843
Netherlands	Jambi	1834	1858
Netherlands	Luxembourg	1839	1890
Netherlands	Bulelang	1841	1856
Netherlands	Badung	1841	1894
Netherlands	Klungkung	1841	1894
Netherlands	Karangaasem	1841	1894
Netherlands	Lombok	1843	1894
Netherlands	Tabanan	1843	1894
Netherlands	Netherlands Antilles	1848	2011
Netherlands	Gianyar	1849	1894
Netherlands	Mengwi	1849	1894
Netherlands	Bangli	1849	1894
Netherlands	Netherlands New Guinea	1950	1982
Netherlands	Aruba	1986	2011
Belgium	Belgian Congo	1887	1960
Belgium	Ruanda-Urundi	1916	1962
Belgium	Flanders	1970	2011
Belgium	Wallonia	1970	2011
France	Guadeloupe	1816	2011
France	Martinique	1816	2011
France	French Guiana	1816	2011
France	Reunion	1816	2011
France	French India	1816	2011
France	St. Pierre–Miquelon	1816	2011
France	Senegal	1828	1960
France	Algeria	1830	1962
France	Nosy Be	1841	1896
France	Wallis and Futuna	1842	2011
France	Grand Bassam	1843	1893
France	Assini	1843	1893
France	Mayotte	1843	2011

Metropole	Proto-state	Start	End
France	Marquesas Is.	1844	2011
France	French Polynesia	1847	2011
France	Austral Is.	1850	2011
France	New Caledonia	1853	2011
France	Cochin China	1862	1949
France	Cambodia	1863	1953
France	Tunisia	1881	1956
France	French Guinea	1882	1958
France	Annam	1884	1949
France	French Somaliland	1884	1977
France	Diego Suarez	1885	1896
France	Madagascar	1885	1960
France	Grand Comoro	1886	1912
France	Anjouan	1886	1912
France	Moheli	1886	1912
France	Gabon	1886	1960
France	Congo	1886	1960
France	Tonkin	1888	1949
France	French Sudan	1892	1960
France	Laos	1893	1953
France	Ivory Coast	1893	1960
France	Dahomey	1895	1960
France	Kwanchowan	1898	1945
France	Mauritania	1902	1960
France	Ubangi-Shari and Chad	1906	1920
France	Morocco	1911	1956
France	Togo	1914	1960
France	Cameroon	1916	1960
France	Upper Volta	1919	1960
France	Syria	1919	1961
France	Lebanon	1920	1946
France	Niger	1920	1960
France	Ubangi-Shari	1920	1960
France	Chad	1920	1960
France	Jebel Druze	1921	1942
France	Latakia	1924	1942
France	Inini	1930	1946
France	Fezzan	1943	1970
France	Saar	1945	1976

(*cont.*)

Metropole	Proto-state	Start	End
France	Comoro Archipelago	1947	1975
France	Vietnam	1950	1954
France	Nice	1960	1979
France	Corsica	1978	2011
Switzerland	Neuchatel	1816	1848
Switzerland	Liechtenstein	1919	1990
Spain	Argentina	1816	1816
Spain	Chile	1816	1818
Spain	United States of Central America	1816	1820
Spain	Mexico	1816	1821
Spain	Columbia (Gran Columbia)	1816	1821
Spain	Venezuela	1816	1830
Spain	Ecuador	1816	1830
Spain	Peru	1816	1839
Spain	Bolivia	1816	1840
Spain	Guadalajara	1816	1840
Spain	South Peru	1816	1848
Spain	Puerto Principe	1816	1897
Spain	Cuba	1816	1909
Spain	Caroline Islands	1816	1913
Spain	Dominican Republic	1816	1924
Spain	Philippines	1816	1946
Spain	Palau	1816	1994
Spain	Puerto Rico	1816	2011
Spain	Canary Islands	1816	2011
Spain	Guam	1816	2011
Spain	Spanish Guinea	1855	1968
Spain	Spanish West Africa	1903	1958
Spain	Spanish Morocco	1911	1975
Spain	Ifni	1934	1968
Spain	Spanish Sahara	1958	1995
Spain	Rio Muni	1960	1968
Spain	Catalunya	1978	2011
Spain	Euskadi	1978	2011
Spain	Galiza	1978	2011
Portugal	Brazil	1821	1822
Portugal	Angra do Heroismo	1831	1976
Portugal	Horta	1831	1976

Metropole	Proto-state	Start	End
Portugal	Ponta Delgada	1831	1976
Portugal	Portuguese Guinea	1879	1974
Germany	Hanover	1866	1885
Germany	Hesse Electoral	1866	1885
Germany	Schleswig-Holstein	1866	1885
Germany	Saxony	1867	1886
Germany	Hesse Grand Ducal	1867	1886
Germany	Mecklenburg-Schwerin	1867	1886
Germany	Bavaria	1871	1890
Germany	Baden	1871	1890
Germany	Wuerttemburg	1871	1890
Germany	Alsace-Lorraine	1871	1938
Germany	Kamerun	1884	1915
Germany	German New Guinea	1884	1945
Germany	Togo	1885	1913
Germany	German East Africa	1885	1917
Germany	German Southwest Africa	1885	1990
Germany	Kiauchau	1898	1921
Germany	Northern Marianas	1899	2011
Germany	German Samoa	1900	1962
Germany	Marshall Islands	1906	1986
Poland	Upper Silesia	1918	1939
Poland	Danzig	1920	1939
Austro-Hungary	Hungary	1867	1918
Austro-Hungary	Bosnia-Hercegovina	1878	1992
Czechoslovakia	Slovakia	1949	1993
Italy	Sardinia	1816	2011
Italy	Eritrea	1882	1993
Italy	Somaliland	1889	1960
Italy	Aegean Islands/ Dodecanese	1923	1946
Italy	Libya	1928	1942
Italy	Italian East Africa	1936	1940
Italy	Trentino–Alto Adige	1948	2011
Italy	Valle d'Aosta	1948	2011
Italy	Friuli–Venezia Giiulia	1963	2011
Two Sicilies	Sicily	1816	2011
Yugoslavia	Croatia	1945	1992
Yugoslavia	Slovenia	1945	1992

(*cont.*)

Metropole	Proto-state	Start	End
Yugoslavia	Macedonia	1945	1993
Yugoslavia	Vojvodina	1980	1992
Yugoslavia	Kosovo	1980	2011
Bosnia	Republicka Sprska	1992	2011
Bosnia	Brcko District	2000	2011
Greece	Thessaly	1881	1900
Greece	Macedonia	1913	1932
Greece	Epirus	1913	1932
Moldova	Gaguazia	1991	2011
Moldova	Transniestra	1992	2011
Romania	Southern Dobruja	1913	1959
Romania	Bessarabia	1920	1939
Romania	Transylvania	1920	1939
Russia	Poland	1816	1864
Russia	Finland	1816	1917
Russia	Armenia	1828	1991
Russia	Bukhara	1864	1924
Russia	Khiva	1873	1924
Russia	Kars	1878	1897
Russia	Port Arthur	1897	1969
Russia	Tannu Tuva	1911	2011
Russia	Volga German ASSR	1918	1941
Russia	Turkmenistan	1918	1991
Russia	Bashkir	1919	2011
Russia	Chuvash	1920	2011
Russia	Kalmyk	1920	2011
Russia	Tartarstan	1920	2011
Russia	Udmurt	1920	2011
Russia	Mari	1920	2011
Russia	Mountainous ASSR	1921	1924
Russia	Crimea	1921	1992
Russia	Dagestan	1921	2011
Russia	Abkhazia	1921	2011
Russia	Karbodina-Balkar	1921	2011
Russia	Adjaria	1921	2011
Russia	North Ossetia	1921	2011
Russia	Transcaucasia	1922	1936
Russia	Ukraine	1922	1991
Russia	Belorussia	1922	1991
Russia	South Ossetia	1922	2011

Metropole	Proto-state	Start	End
Russia	Gorno-Altai (Altai)	1922	2011
Russia	Karachay-Cherkess	1922	2011
Russia	Komi	1922	2011
Russia	Yakut	1922	2011
Russia	Adyghe	1922	2011
Russia	Chechnya	1922	2011
Russia	Nagorno-Karabakh	1923	2011
Russia	Karelia	1923	2011
Russia	Buryat	1923	2011
Russia	Karalkalpak	1924	1990
Russia	GBAO	1924	1990
Russia	Moldavia	1924	1991
Russia	Tajikistan	1924	1991
Russia	Kyrgyzstan	1924	1991
Russia	Uzbekistan	1924	1991
Russia	Kazakhstan	1924	1991
Russia	Nakhicheven	1924	1991
Russia	Ingushetia	1924	2011
Russia	Marchlewszczyzna	1926	1935
Russia	Karachay Oblast	1926	1957
Russia	Cherkess Oblast	1926	1957
Russia	Dzierzynszczyzna	1932	1935
Russia	Mordovia	1934	2011
Russia	Jewish Oblast	1934	2011
Russia	Khakas	1934	2011
Russia	Georgia	1936	1991
Russia	Azerbaijan	1936	1991
Russia	Chechen-Ingush	1936	1991
Russia	Estonia	1940	1991
Russia	Latvia	1940	1991
Russia	Lithuania	1940	1991
Russia	Kaliningrad	1991	2011
Finland	Aaland Island	1921	2011
Sweden	Norway	1816	1905
Norway	Svalbad	1992	2011
Denmark	Tranquebar	1816	1844
Denmark	Iceland	1816	1944
Denmark	Virgin Islands	1816	2011
Denmark	Greenland	1816	2011

(*cont.*)

Metropole	Proto-state	Start	End
Denmark	Faroe Islands	1816	2011
Cameroon	Southern Cameroon	1961	1972
Nigeria	Eastern Region	1960	1967
Nigeria	Northern Region	1960	1967
Nigeria	Western Region	1960	1967
Nigeria	Mid-Western Region	1963	1967
Uganda	Baganda	1962	1967
Ethiopia	Amhara	1991	2011
Ethiopia	Tigray	1991	2011
Ethiopia	Afar	1991	2011
Ethiopia	Oromia	1991	2011
Ethiopia	Somali	1991	2011
South Africa	Transkei	1963	1994
South Africa	Ovamboland	1968	1989
South Africa	Hereroland	1968	1989
South Africa	Kvangoland	1970	1989
South Africa	East Caprivi	1972	1989
South Africa	Bophuthatswana	1972	1994
South Africa	Ciskei	1972	1994
South Africa	Lebowa	1972	1994
South Africa	Venda	1973	1994
South Africa	Gazankulu	1973	1994
South Africa	Kwazulu	1973	1994
South Africa	Qwaqwa	1974	1994
South Africa	Kwandebele	1977	1994
South Africa	Tswanaland	1979	1989
South Africa	Damaraland	1980	1989
South Africa	Namaland	1980	1989
South Africa	Tswanaland	1980	1989
South Africa	KaNgware	1984	1994
Namibia	Walvis Bay	1994	2011
Morocco	Tangier	1956	1975
Sudan	Southern Region	1972	1983
Ottoman Empire	Moldavia	1816	1862
Ottoman Empire	Wallachia	1816	1862
Ottoman Empire	Hejaz	1816	1932
Ottoman Empire	Egypt	1816	1937
Ottoman Empire	Cyrenaica	1816	1970
Ottoman Empire	Tripolitania	1816	1970
Ottoman Empire	Montenegro	1816	2011

Metropole	Proto-state	Start	End
Ottoman Empire	Serbia	1817	1878
Ottoman Empire	Crete	1822	1932
Ottoman Empire	Samos	1832	1912
Ottoman Empire	Romania	1862	1878
Ottoman Empire	North Yemen	1871	1918
Ottoman Empire	Qatar	1872	1971
Ottoman Empire	Bulgaria	1878	1898
Turkey	Hatay	1939	1958
Israel	Gaza	1967	2011
Israel	West Bank	1967	2011
China	Mongolia	1842	1921
China	Easter Turkistan	1842	2011
China	Tibet	1842	2011
China	Inner Mongolia	1925	2011
China	Guangxi Zhuang AR	1959	2011
China	Ningxia Hui AR	1959	2011
Japan	Formosa	1895	1944
Japan	Karafuto	1905	1924
Japan	Chosen (Korea)	1905	1944
Japan	Pacific Islands Mandate	1914	1979
Japan	Pohnpei	1920	1979
Japan	Yap	1920	1979
Japan	Truk	1929	1979
India	Sikkim	1947	2011
India	Assam	1947	2011
India	Punjab	1947	2011
India	West Bengal	1947	2011
India	Patiala and EPSU	1948	1956
India	Madhya Bharat	1948	1956
India	Saurashtra Union	1948	1956
India	Orissa	1948	2011
India	Rajasthan	1949	1956
India	Travancore-Cochin	1949	2011
India	Andhra Pradesh	1953	2011
India	Tamil Nadu	1956	2011
India	Gujarat	1960	2011
India	Maharashtra	1960	2011
India	Nagaland	1963	2011
India	Manipur	1972	2011

(cont.)

Metropole	Proto-state	Start	End
India	Meghalaya	1972	2011
India	Tripura	1972	2011
India	Mizoram	1986	2011
India	Arunachal Pradesh	1987	2011
India	Chhattisgarh	2000	2011
India	Jharkhand	2000	2011
India	Uttarakhand	2000	2011
Pakistan	East Bengal	1947	1972
Pakistan	Baluchistan	1947	2011
Pakistan	Northwest Frontier Agencies and Tribal Areas	1947	2011
Pakistan	Northwest Frontier Province	1947	2011
Pakistan	Punjab	1947	2011
Pakistan	Sindh	1947	2011
Pakistan	Azad Kashmir	1949	2011
Myanmar	Kachin State	1949	2011
Myanmar	Karen State	1949	2011
Myanmar	Kayeh State	1949	2011
Myanmar	Shan State	1949	2011
Myanmar	Chin State	1975	2011
Myanmar	Mon State	1975	2011
Thailand	Kelantan	1827	1945
Thailand	Trengganu	1827	1945
Thailand	Perlis	1842	1945
Thailand	Kedah	1843	1945
Australia	Papua New Guinea	1946	1975
Australia	Christmas Island	1958	2011
Papua New Guinea	Bougainville	2001	2011
Solomon Islands	Temoto (Santa Cruz Is.)	1981	2011
Spain-France	Andorra	1816	1993
UK–France	New Hebrides	1887	1980

Bibliography

Abernethy, David B. 2000. *The Dynamics of Global Dominance: European Overseas Empires 1415–1980*. New Haven, CT: Yale University Press.

Alatalu, Toomas. 1992. Tuva: A State Reawakens. *Soviet Studies* 44(5): 881–895.

Alesina, Alberto, and Enrico Spolaore. 2005. War, Peace, and the Size of Countries. *Journal of Public Economics* 89: 1333–1354.

Allworth, Edward A. 1990. *The Modern Uzbeks: From the Fourteenth Century to the Present*. Stanford, CA: Hoover Institution Press.

Armitage, David. 2007. *The Declaration of Independence: A Global History*. Cambridge, MA: Harvard University Press.

2010. Secession and Civil War. In *Secession as an International Phenomenon*, edited by Don H. Doyle. Athens: University of Georgia Press.

Aspinall, Edward. 2007. The Construction of Grievance: Natural Resources and Identity in a Separatist Conflict. *Journal of Conflict Resolution* 51(6): 571–585.

Atzili, Boaz. 2012. *Good Fences, Bad Neighbors: Border Fixity and International Conflict*. Chicago: University of Chicago Press.

Ballis, William. 1941. Soviet Russia's Asiatic Frontier Technique: Tana Tuva. *Pacific Affairs* 41: 91–96.

Barbieri, Katherine, Omar Keshk, and Brian Pollins. 2008. Correlates of War Project Trade Data Set Codebook, Version 2.0. Online: http://correlatesofwar.org/.

Bartkus, Viva Ona. 1999. *The Dynamics of Secession*. Cambridge: Cambridge University Press.

Bartos, Tomas. 1997. Uti Possidetis. Quo Vadis? *Australian Year Book of International Law* 18: 37–96.

Baruah, Sanjib. 1999. *India against Itself: Assam and the Politics of Nationality*. Philadelphia: University of Pennsylvania Press.

Bates, Robert H. 2001. *Prosperity and Violence: The Political Economy of Development*. New York: W. W. Norton.

Beary, Brian. 2011. *Separatist Movements: A Global Reference*. Washington, DC: CQ Press.

Becker, Seymour. 1968. *Russia's Protectorates in Central Asia: Bukhara and Khiva, 1865–1924*. Cambridge, MA: Harvard University Press.

Beissinger, Mark R. 2002. *Nationalist Mobilization and the Collapse of the Soviet State*. Cambridge: Cambridge University Press.

Bennett, Andrew. 1999. *Condemned to Repetition? The Rise, Fall, and Reprise of Soviet-Russian Military Interventionism, 1973–1996*. Cambridge, MA: MIT Press.

Bhattacharya, Mohit. 1992. The Minds of the Founding Fathers. In *Federalism in India: Origins and Development*, edited by Nirmal Mukarji and Balveer Arora. New Delhi: Vikas.

Black, Allida M. 2000. *Courage in a Dangerous World: The Political Writings of Eleanor Roosevelt*. New York: Columbia University Press.

Blacker, Coit. 1991. Learning in the Nuclear Age: Soviet Strategic Arms Control Policy, 1969–1989. In *Learning in U.S. and Soviet Foreign Policy*, edited by George Breslauer and Philip Tetlock. Boulder, CO: Westview Press.

Boeck, Brian J. 2009. *Imperial Boundaries: Cossack Communities and Empire Building in the Age of Peter the Great*. Cambridge: Cambridge University Press.

Borges, Jorge L. 1998. On Exactitude in Science. In *Collected Fictions*, translated by Andrew Hurley. New York: Penguin Books.

Boutros-Ghali, Boutros. 1992. *An Agenda for Peace: Preventive Diplomacy, Peacemaking and Peace-keeping*. New York: United Nations.

Boyce, David G., ed. 1990. *The Crisis of British Power: The Imperial and Naval Papers of the Second Earl of Selborne, 1895–1910*. Portland, OR: Intl Specialized Book Service.

Brass, Paul R. 1991. *Ethnicity and Nationalism: Theory and Comparison*. New Delhi: Sage.

Bregel, Yuri. 2003. *An Historical Atlas of Central Asia (HACA)*. Leiden: Brill.

Breuilly, John. 1994. *Nationalism and the State*. 2nd ed. Chicago: University of Chicago Press.

Brooks, Stephen. 1999. The Globalization of Production and the Changing Benefits of Conquest. *Journal of Conflict Resolution* 43(5): 646–670.

Brown, Judith M. 1998. India. In *The Oxford History of the British Empire, Volume IV*, edited by Judith M. Brown and Roger Louis. Oxford: Oxford University Press.

Brutzkus, Boris. 1953. *The Historical Peculiarities of the Social and Economic Development of Russia*. Indianapolis, IN: Bobbs-Merrill.

Buchanan, Allen. 1997. Self-Determination, Secession, and the Rule of Law. In *The Morality of Nationalism*, edited by Robert McKim and Jeff McMahan. Oxford: Oxford University Press.

Bunce, Valerie. 1985. The Empire Strikes Back: The Evolution of the Eastern Bloc from a Russian Asset to a Soviet Liability. *International Organization* 39(1): 1–46.

1993. Domestic Reform and International Change: The Gorbachev Reforms in Historical Perspective. *International Organization* 47(1): 107–138.

1999. *Subversive Institutions: The Design and the Destruction of Socialism and the State.* Cambridge, MA: Cambridge University Press.

Butcher, Charles R., and Ryan D. Griffiths. 2015. Alternative International Systems? System Structure and Violent Conflict in 19th Century West Africa, Southeast Asia, and South Asia. *Review of International Studies* 41(4): 715–737.

Carter, David B., and H. E. Goemans. 2011. The Making of the Territorial Order: How Borders Are Drawn. *International Organization* 65(2): 275–310.

Carter, David B., and Curtis S. Signorino. 2010. Back to the Future: Modeling Time Dependence in Binary Data. *Political Analysis* 18: 271–292.

Catudal, Honore M. 1988. *Soviet Nuclear Strategy from Stalin to Gorbachev: A Revolution in Soviet Military and Political Thinking.* Atlantic Highlands, NJ: Humanities Press International.

Chamberlain, M. E. 1999. *Decolonization.* Oxford: Blackwell.

Chandra, Kanchan. 2005. Ethnic Parties and Democratic Stability. *Perspectives on Politics* 3(2): 235–252.

Chester, Lucy P. 2009. *Borders and Conflict in South Asia: The Radcliffe Boundary Commission and the Partition of Punjab.* Manchester: Manchester University Press.

Clayton, Anthony. 1998. Imperial Defense and Security, 1900–1968. In *The Oxford History of the British Empire, Volume IV,* edited by Judith M. Brown and Roger Louis. Oxford: Oxford University Press.

Clodfelter, Michael. 2002. *Warfare and Armed Conflicts: A Statistical Reference to Casualty and Other Figures, 1500–2000.* 2nd ed. Jefferson, NC: McFarland.

Coggins, Bridget L. 2011. Friends in High Places: International Politics and the Emergence of States from Secessionism. *International Organization* 65(3): 433–468.

2014. *Power Politics and State Formation in the Twentieth Century: The Dynamics of Recognition.* Cambridge: Cambridge University Press.

Cohen, Benjamin. 1973. *The Question of Imperialism.* New York: Basic Books.

Collier, Paul, and Anke Hoeffler. 2002. *The Political Economy of Secession.* Washington, DC: Development Research Group, World Bank.

Collins, Randall. 1995. Prediction in Macrosociology: The Case of the Soviet Collapse. *American Journal of Sociology* 100(6): 1552–1593.

Cooley, Alexander. 2005. *Logics of Hierarchy*. Ithaca, NY: Cornell University Press.

Cornell, Svante E. 2001. *Small Nations and Great Powers: A Study of Ethnopolitical Conflict in the Caucasus*. Surrey, UK: Curzon Press.

Correlates of War 2 Project. n.d. Colonial/Dependency Contiguity Data, 1816–2002. Version 3.0. Online: www.correlatesofwar.org/data-sets/colonial-dependency-contiguity.

Correlates of War Project. 2011. State System Membership List, v2011. Online: http://correlatesofwar.org/.

Council of the European Union. 2009. *Independent International Fact-Finding Mission on the Conflict in Georgia*. Online: http://news.bbc.co.uk/2/shared/bsp/hi/pdfs/30_09_09_iiffmgc_report.pdf.

Crawford, James. 2006. *The Creation of States in International Law*. 2nd ed. Oxford: Clarendon Press.

Crawford, Neta C. 2002. *Argument and Change in World Politics*. Cambridge: Cambridge University Press.

Creveld, Martin Van. 2003. The Fate of the State. *Parameters* 26(1): 4–17.

Cunningham, Kathleen G. 2011. Divide and Conquer or Divide and Concede: How Do States Respond to Internally Divided Separatists? *American Political Science Review* 105(2): 275–297.

  2013. Understanding Strategic Choice: The Determinants of Civil War and Nonviolent Campaign in Self-Determination Disputes. *Journal of Peace Research* 50(3): 291–304.

Curtis, Curtis E. 1996. *Russia: A Country Study*. Washington, DC: GPO for the Library of Congress.

Curzon, George N. 1892. *Persia and the Persian Question*. London: Longmans, Green.

Darwin, John. 1998. The Third British Empire? The Dominion Idea in Imperial Politics. In *The Oxford History of the British Empire, Volume IV*, edited by Judith M. Brown and Roger Louis. Oxford: Oxford University Press.

Dasgupta, Jyotirindra. 1970. *Language Conflict and National Development: Group Politics and National Language Policy in India*. Berkeley: University of California Press.

  1997. Community, Authenticity, and Autonomy: Insurgence and Institutional Development in India's Northeast. *Journal of Asian Studies* 56(2): 345–370.

Deudney, Daniel. 1995. Nuclear Weapons and the Waning of the Real-State. *Daedalus* 124 (2): 209–231.

Deudney, Daniel, and G. John Ikenberry. 1992/93. The International Sources of Soviet Change. *International Security* 16(3): 74–118.

Diamond, Jared, and James A. Robinson, eds. 2010. *Natural Experiments of History*. Cambridge, MA: Harvard University Press.

Downing, Brian M. 1992. *The Military Revolution and Political Change*. Princeton, NJ: Princeton University Press.

Doyle, Michael W. 1986. *Empires*. Ithaca, NY: Cornell University Press.

The Economist. 2007. Scotland's Eurodreams (April 21).

Elazar, Daniel J. 1994. *Federal Systems of the World*. Farmington Hills, MI: Gale Group.

1998. *Constitutionalizing Globalization*. New York: Rowman and Littlefield.

Elster, Jon. 1989. *The Cement of Society*. Cambridge: Cambridge University Press.

Engman, Max. 1989. Finland as a Successor-State. In *Finland: People, Nation, State*, edited by Max Engman and David Kirby. London: Hurst.

Fabry, Mikulas. 2010. *Recognizing States: International Society and the Establishment of New States*. Oxford: Oxford University Press.

Fazal, Tanisha M. 2007. *State Death: The Politics and Geography of Conquest, Occupation, and Annexation*. Princeton, NJ: Princeton University Press.

Fazal, Tanisha M., and Page V. Fortna. 2014. Civil War Initiation and Termination (C-WIT).

Fazal, Tanisha M., and Ryan D. Griffiths. 2014. Membership Has Its Privileges: The Changing Benefits of Statehood. *International Studies Review* 16(1): 79–106.

Fearon, James D. 2004. Separatist Wars, Partition, and World Order. *Security Studies* 13(4): 394–415.

Fearon, James, and David Laitin. 2003. Ethnicity, Insurgency, and Civil War. *American Political Science Review* 97(1): 75–90.

Fieldhouse, D. K. 1961. Imperialism: An Historiographical Revision. *Economic History Review* 14(2): 187–217.

1966. *The Colonial Empire: A Comparative Survey*. London: Weidenfeld and Nicolson.

1998. The Metropolitan Economics of Empire. In *The Oxford History of the British Empire, Volume IV*, edited by Judith M. Brown and Roger Louis. Oxford: Oxford University Press.

Finnemore, Martha. 1996. Constructing Norms of Humanitarian Intervention. In *The Culture of National Security*, edited by Peter J. Katzenstein. New York: Columbia University Press.

Forsberg, Erika. 2013. Do Ethnic Dominoes Fall? Evaluating Domino Effects of Granting Territorial Concessions to Separatist Groups. *International Studies Quarterly* 47(2): 329–340.

Frieden, Jeffry A. 1994. International Investment and Colonial Control: A New Interpretation. *International Organization* 48(4):559–593.

Fry, Michael Graham. 1997. Britain, France, and the Cold War. In *The End of Empire? The Transformation of the USSR in Comparative Perspective*, edited by Karen Dawisha and Bruce Parrott. New York: M. E. Sharpe.

Gaddis, John Lewis. 1992/93. International Relations Theory and the End of the Cold War. *International Security* 17(3): 5–58.

GADM. 2012. GADM Database of Global Administrative Areas. Online: www.gadm.org/.

Gallagher, John. 1982. *The Decline, Revival and Fall of the British Empire.* Cambridge: Cambridge University Press.

Gallagher, John, and Ronald Robinson. 1953. The Imperialism of Free Trade. *Economic History Review* 6(1): 1–15.

Ganguly, Sumit. 1996. Explaining the Kashmir Insurgency: Political Mobilization and Institutional Decay. *International Security* 21(2): 76–107.

    1997. *The Crisis in Kashmir: Portents of War, Hopes of Peace.* Cambridge: Cambridge University Press.

Garthoff, Raymond L. 1990. *Deterrence and the Revolution in Soviet Military Doctrine.* Washington, DC: Brookings Institution Press.

Gartzke, Eric, and Dominic Rohner. 2011. The Political Economy of Imperialism, Decolonization and Development. *British Journal of Political Science* 41(3): 525–556.

George, Alexander L., and Andrew Bennett. 2005. *Case Studies and Theory Development in the Social Sciences.* Cambridge, MA: MIT Press.

Gilpin, Robert. 1981. *War and Change in World Politics.* Cambridge: Cambridge University Press.

Gleditsch, Kristian S., and Michael D. Ward. 1999. A Revised List of Independent States since the Congress of Vienna. *International Interactions* 25(4): 393–413.

Goldgeier, James M., and Michael McFaul. 1992. A Tale of Two Worlds: Core and Periphery in the Post–Cold War Era. *International Organization* 46(2): 468–491.

Goldsmith, Benjamin E., and Baogang He. 2008. Letting Go without a Fight: Decolonization, Democracy, and War, 1900–94. *Journal of Peace Research* 45(5): 587–611.

Gourevitch, Peter. 1978. The Second Image Reversed. *International Organization* 32(4): 881–912.

Grant, Thomas D. 1999. *The Recognition of States: Law and Practice in Debate and Evolution*. Westport, CT: Praeger.

Greengrass, Mark, ed. 1991. *Conquest and Coalescence: The Shaping of States in Early Modern Europe*. London: Edward Arnold.

Griffiths, Ryan D. 2010. Security Threats, Linguistic Homogeneity, and the Necessary Conditions for Political Unification. *Nations and Nationalism* 16(1): 169–188.

2014. Secession and the Invisible Hand of the International System. *Review of International Studies* 40(3): 559–581.

2015. Between Dissolution and Blood: How Administrative Lines and Categories Shape Secessionist Outcomes. *International Organization* 69(3): 731–751.

Griffiths, Ryan D., and Charles R. Butcher. 2013. Introducing the International System(s) Dataset (ISD), 1816–2011. *International Interactions* 39(5): 748–768.

Griffiths, Ryan D., and Ivan Savic. 2009. Globalization and Separatism: The Influence of Internal and External Interdependence on the Strategy of Separatism. In *The Nation in the Global Era: Conflict and Transformation*, edited by Jerry Harris. Leiden: Brill.

Grossman, Guy, and Janet I. Lewis. 2014. Administrative Unit Proliferation. *American Political Science Review* 108(1): 196–217.

Hale, Henry. 2004. Divided We Stand: Institutional Sources of Ethnofederal State Survival and Collapse. *World Politics* 56(2): 165–193.

2005. The Makeup and Breakup of Ethnofederal States: Why Russia Survives Where the USSR Fell. *Perspectives on Politics* 3(1): 55–70.

2008. *The Foundations of Ethnic Politics: Separatism of States and Nations in Eurasia and the World*. Cambridge: Cambridge University Press.

Harding, Les. 1998. *Dead Countries of the Nineteenth and Twentieth Centuries: Aden to Zululand*. Lanham, MD: Scarecrow Press.

Hatton, Ragnhild Marie. 1974. Russia and the Baltic. In *Russian Imperialism from Ivan the Great to the Revolution*, edited by Taras Hunczak. New Brunswick, NJ: Rutgers University Press.

Hechter, Michael. 1992. The Dynamics of Secession. *Acta Sociologica* 35(2): 267–283.

2000. *Containing Nationalism*. Oxford: Oxford University Press.

Heckman, James J. 1976. The Common Structure of Statistical Models of Truncation, Sample Selection and Limited Dependent Variables and a Simple Estimator for Such Models. *Annals of Economic and Social Measurement* 5(4): 475–492.

Hegre, Havard, Tanja Ellingsen, Scott Gates, and Nils Petter Gleditsch. 2001. Toward a Democratic Civil Peace? Democracy, Political Change, and Civil War 1816–1992. *American Political Science Review* 95(1): 16–33.

Henige, David. 1970. *Colonial Governors from the Fifteenth Century to the Present*. Madison: University of Wisconsin Press.

2004. *Princely States of India*. Bangkok: Orchid Press.

Heraclides, Alexis. 1990. Secessionist Minorities and External Involvement. *International Organization* 44(3): 341–378.

1991. *The Self-Determination of Minorities in International Politics*. London: Frank Cass.

Herbst, Jeffrey. 2000. *States and Power in Africa*. Princeton, NJ: Princeton University Press.

Herz, John. 1976. *The Nation-State and the Crisis of World Politics*. New York: McKay.

Hironaka, Ann. 2005. *Neverending Wars: The International Community, Weak States, and the Perpetuation of Civil War*. Cambridge, MA: Harvard University Press.

Hirschman, Albert. 1970. *Exit, Voice, and Loyalty: Responses to Decline in Firms, Organizations, and States*. Cambridge, MA: Harvard University Press.

Holmes, Charles W. 1999. The Little War with Big Stakes: Russia's Conflict in Dagestan Has Major Implications for its Own Stability. *The Montreal Gazette*, August 22, 3.

Holsti, K. J. 1991. *Peace and War: Armed Conflicts and International Order, 1648–1989*. Cambridge: Cambridge University Press.

Horowitz, Donald L. 1985. *Ethnic Groups in Conflict*. Berkeley: University of California Press.

Hosking, Geoffrey. 1997. *Russia: People and Empire, 1552–1917*. Cambridge, MA: Harvard University Press.

Huntington, Samuel. 1968. *Political Order in Changing Societies*. New Haven, CT: Yale University Press.

Ikenberry, G. John. 2001. *After Victory: Institutions, Strategic Restraint, and the Rebuilding of Order after Major Wars*. Princeton, NJ: Princeton University Press.

Jackson, Robert. 1990. *Quasi-States: Sovereignty, International Relations and the Third World*. Cambridge: Cambridge University Press.

1992. Juridical Statehood in Sub-Saharan Africa. *Journal of International Affairs* 46(1): 1–16.

1993. The Weight of Ideas in Decolonization: Normative Change in International Relations. In *Ideas and Foreign Policy: Beliefs, Institutions, and Political Change*, edited by Judith Goldstein and Robert O. Keohane. Ithaca, NY: Cornell University Press.

James, Lawrence. 1994. *The Rise and Fall of the British Empire*. London: Little, Brown.

Jenne, Erin K., Stephen M. Saideman, and Will Lowe. 2007. Separatism as a Bargaining Posture: The Role of Leverage in Minority Radicalization. *Journal of Peace Research* 44(5): 539–558.

Jervis, Robert. 2002. Theories of War in an Era of Leading-Power Peace. *American Political Science Review* 96(1): 1–14.

Jusilla, Osmo. 1989. Finland from Province to State. In *Finland: People, Nation, State*, edited by Max Engman and David Kirby. London: Hurst.

Jusilla, Osmo, Seppo Hentila, and Jukka Nevakivi. 1999. *From Grand Duchy to a Modern State: A Political History of Finland since 1809*. London: Hurst.

Kahler, Miles. 1984. *Decolonization in Britain and France*. Princeton, NJ: Princeton University Press.

1997. Empires, Neo-empires, and Political Change: The British and French Experience. In *The End of Empire? The Transformation of the USSR in Comparative Perspective*, edited by Karen Dawisha and Bruce Parrott. London: M. E. Sharpe.

Kalyvas, Stathis, and Laia Balcells. 2010. International System and Technologies of Rebellion: How the Cold War Shaped Internal Conflict. *American Political Science Review* 104(3): 415–429.

Kaysen, Carl. 1990. Is War Obsolete? A Review Essay. *International Security* 14(4): 42–64.

Kennedy, Paul. 1987. *The Rise and Fall of the Great Powers*. New York: Vintage Books.

Keohane, Robert, and Joseph Nye. 1977. *Power and Interdependence*. New York: HarperCollins.

Ker-Lindsay, James. 2012. *The Foreign Policy of Counter Secession: Preventing the Recognition of Contested States*. Oxford: Oxford University Press.

Kerner, Robert J. 1942. *The Urge to the Sea*. Berkeley: University of California Press.

King, Charles. 2012. The Scottish Play. *Foreign Affairs* (September/October).

Kohli, Atul. 1997. Can Democracies Accommodate Ethnic Nationalism? Rise and Decline of Self-Determination Movements. *Journal of Asian Studies* 56(2): 325–344.

2001. *The Success of India's Democracy*. Cambridge: Cambridge University Press.

Kohli, Manorama. 1993. *From Dependency to Interdependence: A Study of Indo-Bhutan Relations*. New Delhi: Vikas.

Kohn, Hans. 1974. Introduction. In *Russian Imperialism from Ivan the Great to the Revolution*, edited by Taras Hunczak. New Brunswick, NJ: Rutgers University Press.

Kokoshin, Andrei. 1998. *Soviet Strategic Thought*. Cambridge, MA: MIT Press.

Kolsto, Pal. 2006. The Sustainability and Future of Unrecognized Quasi-States. *Journal of Peace Research* 43(6): 723–740.

Krasner, Stephen. 1999. *Sovereignty: Organized Hypocrisy*. Princeton, NJ: Princeton University Press.

Laitin, David D. 1998. *Identity in Formation*. Ithaca, NY: Cornell University Press.

Lake, David. 1997. The Rise, Fall, and Future of the Russian Empire. In *The End of Empire? The Transformatin of the USSR in Comparative Perspective*, edited by Karen Dawisha and Bruce Parrott. New York: M. E. Sharpe.

——— 1999. *Entangling Relations*. Princeton, NJ: Princeton University Press.

——— 2003. The New Sovereignty in International Relations. *International Stud ies Review* 5(3): 303–323.

Lake, David, and Michael J. Hiscox. 2002. Democracy, Federalism, and the Size of States. Working paper.

Lake, David, and Angela O'Mahony. 2004. The Incredible Shrinking State: Explaining the Territorial Size of Countries. *Journal of Conflict Resolution* 48(5): 699–722.

——— 2006. Territoriality and War: State Size and Patterns of Interstate Conflict. In *Territoriality and Conflict in an Era of Globalization*, edited by Miles Kahler and Barbara Walter. Cambridge: Cambridge University Press.

Lalonde, Suzanne N. 2002. *Determining Boundaries in a Conflicted World: The Role of Uti Possidetis*. Montreal: McGill-Queens University Press.

Lansing, Robert. 1921. *The Peace Negotiations: A Personal Narrative*. Boston: Houghton Mifflin.

Law, Gwillim. 1999. *Administrative Subdivisions of Countries: A Comprehensive World Reference, 1900 through 1998*. Jefferson, NC: McFarland.

Ledonne, John P. 2004. *The Grand Strategy of the Russian Empire, 1650–1831*. Oxford: Oxford University Press.

Lehner, B., and P. Döll. 2004. Development and Validation of a Global Database of Lakes, Reservoirs and Wetlands. *Journal of Hydrology* 296(1–4): 1–22.

Lenin, V. I. 1939. *Imperialism: The Highest Stage of Capitalism*. New York: International.

Levesque, Jacques. 1997. *The Enigma of 1989: The USSR and the Liberation of Eastern Europe*. Berkeley: University of California Press.

Liberman, Peter. 1996. *Does Conquest Pay? The Exploitation of Occupied Industrial Societies*. Princeton, NJ: Princeton University Press.

Lieberman, Evan. 2005. Nested Analysis as a Mixed-Methods Strategy for Comparative Research. *American Political Science Review* 99(3): 435–452.

Lieberman, Victor. 2003. *Strange Parallels: Southeast Asia in Global Context, 800–1830*. Cambridge: Cambridge University Press.

Lincoln, Abraham. 1953. Message to Congress in Special Session, July 4, 1861. In *The Collected Works of Abraham Lincoln, Volume 4*, edited by Roy P. Basler. New Brunswick, NJ: Rutgers University Press.

Louis, Roger. 1998. The Dissolution of the British Empire. In *The Oxford History of the British Empire, Volume IV*, edited by Judith M. Brown and Roger Louis. Oxford: Oxford University Press.

Lugard, Frederick J. D. 1893. *The Rise of Our East African Empire, Volume II*. London: Blackwood.

Lujala, Paivi. 2009. Deadly Combat over Natural Resources: Gems, Petroleum, Drugs, and the Severity of Armed Civil Conflict. *Journal of Conflict Resolution* 53(1): 50–71.

Lustick, Ian S. 1993. *Unsettled States, Disputed Lands: Britain and Ireland, France and Algeria, Israel and the West Bank-Gaza*. Ithaca, NY: Cornell University Press.

Lynch, Allen. 1989. *Gorbachev's International Outlook: Intellectual Origins and Political Consequences*. New York: Institute for East-West Security Studies.

Maddison, Angus. 2008. Historical Statistics of the World Economy: 1–2008 AD. Online: www.ggdc.net/MADDISON/oriindex.htm.

Maier, Charles. 1987. The Two Postwar Eras and the Conditions of Stability in Twentieth Century Western Europe. In *In Search of Stability: Explorations in Historical Political Economy*, edited by Charles Maier. New York: Cambridge University Press.

Mampilly, Zachariah Cherian. 2011. *Rebel Rulers: Insurgent Governance and Civilian Life during War*. Ithaca, NY: Cornell University Press.

Manela, Erez. 2007. *The Wilsonian Moment: Self-Determination and the International Origins of Anticolonial Nationalism*. Oxford: Oxford University Press.

Manor, James. 2001. Making Local Governments Work: Local Elites, Panchayati Raj and Governance in India. In *The Success of India's Democracy*, edited by Atul Kohli. Cambridge: Cambridge University Press.

Marshall, Monty G., and Keith Jaggers. 2011. *Polity IV Project: Political Regime Characteristics and Transitions, 1800–2011 – Dataset Users' Manual*. College Park: Center for Systemic Peace, University of Maryland.

Milgrom, Paul, and John Roberts. 1982. Predation, Reputation, and Entry Deterrence. *Journal of Economic Theory* 27: 280–312.

Minahan, James. 1996. *Nations without States: A Historical Dictionary of Contemporary Nationalist Movements*. Westport, CT: Greenwood Press.

2002. *Encyclopedia of the Stateless Nations: Ethnic and National Groups around the World*. Westport, CT: Greenwood Press.

2004. *The Former Soviet Union's Diverse Peoples: A Reference Sourcebook*. Santa Barbara, CA: ABC CLIO.

2012. *Ethnic Groups of South Asia and the Pacific: An Encyclopedia*. Santa Barbara, CA: ABC CLIO.

Mongush, Mergen. 1993. The Annexation of Tannu-Tuva and the Formation of the Tuvinskaya ASSR. *Nationalities Papers* 21: 47–52.

Motyl, Alexander J. 1997. Thinking about Empire. In *After Empire: Multiethnic Societies and Nation-Building*, edited by Karen Barkey and Mark Von Hagen. Boulder, CO: Westview Press.

2001. *Imperial Ends: The Decay, Collapse, and Revival of Empires*. New York: Columbia University Press.

Mueller, John. 1988. *The Retreat from Doomsday: The Obsolescence of Major War*. New York: Basic Books.

2009. War Has Almost Ceased to Exist: An Assessment. *Political Science Quarterly* 124(2): 297–321.

Nag, Sajal. 1999. *Nationalism, Separatism, and Secessionism*. New Delhi: Rawat.

Nahaylo, Bohdan, and Victor Swoboda. 1989. *Soviet Disunion: A History of the Nationalities Problem in the USSR*. New York: Macmillan.

Nath, Sunil. 2009. Assam: The Secessionist Insurgency and the Freedom of Minds. In *Faultlines: Writings on Conflict and Resolution, Volume 13*. New Delhi: South Asian Terrorism Portal.

Nation, Craig R. 1992. *Black Earth, Red Star: A History of Soviet Security Policy, 1917–1991*. Ithaca, NY: Cornell University Press.

Nevakivi, Jukka. 1989. Independent Finland between East and West. In *Finland: People, Nation, State*, edited by Max Engman and David Kirby. London: Hurst.

Nexon, Daniel H., and Thomas Wright. 2007. What's at Stake in the American Empire Debate. *American Political Science Review* 101(2): 253–271.

O'Leary, Brendan, Ian S. Lustick, and Thomas Callaghy, eds. 2001. *Right-Sizing the State: The Politics of Moving Borders*. Oxford: Oxford University Press.

O'Mara, Michael, ed. 1999. *Facts about the World's Nations*. New York: H. W. Wilson.

Osterud, Oyvind. 1997. The Narrow Gate: Entry to the Club of Sovereign States. *Review of International Studies* 23: 167–184.

Owen, Nicholas. 1998. Critics of Empire in Britain. In *The Oxford History of the British Empire, Volume IV*, edited by Judith M. Brown and Roger Louis. Oxford: Oxford University Press.

Paquin, Jonathan. 2010. *A Stability-Seeking Power: U.S. Foreign Policy and Secessionist Conflicts.* London: McGill-Queen's University Press.

Parliamentary Papers. 1886. *Final Report of the Royal Commission on the Depression of Trade and Industry.* XXIII.

Parrott, Bruce. 1997. Analyzing the Transformation of the Soviet Union in Comparative Perspective. In *The End of Empire? The Transformation of the USSR in Comparative Perspective,* edited by Karen Dawisha and Bruce Parrott. New York: M. E. Sharpe.

Pavkovic, Aleksandar. 2015. What Is Secession? The Contest of Definitions. In *Territorial Separatism in Global Politics: Causes, Outcomes and Resolution,* edited by Damien Kingsbury and Costas Laoutides. New York: Routledge.

Pavkovic, Aleksandar, and Peter Radan. 2007. *Creating New States: Theory and Practice of Secession.* Burlington, VT: Ashgate.

, eds. 2011. *The Ashgate Research Companion to Secession.* Burlington, VT: Ashgate.

Pegg, Scott. 1998. *International Society and the De Facto State.* Burlington, VT: Ashgate.

Pierson, Paul. 2004. *Politics in Time.* Princeton, NJ: Princeton University Press.

Platt, D. C. M. 1968. Economic Factors in British Policy during the "New Imperialism." *The Past and Present Society* 39(April): 120–138.

Pravda, Alex. 1992. Soviet Policy toward Eastern Europe in Transition. In *The End of the Outer Empire,* edited by Alex Pravda. London: Sage.

Radan, Peter. 2002. *The Break-up of Yugoslavia in International Law.* London: Routledge.

2008. Secession: A Word in Search of a Meaning. In *On the Way to Statehood: Secession and Globalization,* edited by Peter Radan and Aleksandar Pavkovic. Burlington, VT: Ashgate.

2012. Secessionist Referenda in International Law. *Nationalism and Ethnic Politics* 18: 8–21.

Rao, P. Raghunadha. 1978. *Sikkim: The Story of Its Integration with India.* Delhi: Cosmo.

Ratner, Steven R. 1996. Drawing a Better Line: Uti Possidetis and the Borders of New States. *American Journal of International Law* 94(4): 590–624.

Ravlo, Hilde, Nils Petter Gleditsch, and Han Doruseen. 2003. Colonial War and the Democratic Peace. *Journal of Conflict Resolution* 47(4): 520–548.

Rice, Condoleezza. 1991. The Evolution of Soviet Grand Strategy. In *Strategies in War and Peace,* edited by Paul Kennedy. New Haven, CT: Yale University Press.

Roeder, Phil. 2007. *Where Nation-States Come From*. Princeton, NJ: Princeton University Press.

Rose, Leo E. 1977. *The Politics of Bhutan*. Ithaca, NY: Cornell University Press.

Rosenau, James N. 2000. Governance in a New Global Order. In *The Global Transformations Reader*, edited by David Held and Anthony McGrew. Cambridge: Polity Press.

Roy, Mihir Kumar. 1981. *Princely States and the Paramount Power, 1858–1876*. New Delhi: Rajesh.

Ruggie, John G. 1983. International Regimes, Transactions, and Change: Embedded Liberalism and the Postwar Economic Order. In *International Regimes*, edited by Stephen D. Krasner. Ithaca, NY: Cornell University Press.

Saideman, Stephen M. 1998. Is Pandora's Box Half Empty or Half Full? The Limited Virulence of Secessionism and the Domestic Sources of Disintegration. In *The International Spread of Ethnic Conflict: Fear, Diffusion, and Escalation*, edited by David A. Lake and Donald Rothchild. Princeton, NJ: Princeton University Press.

   2001. *The Ties That Divide: Ethnic Politics, Foreign Policy and International Conflict*. New York: Columbia University Press.

   2002. Discrimination in International Relations: Analyzing External Support for Ethnic Groups. *Journal of Peace Research* 39(1): 27–50.

Sambanis, Nicholas. 2006. Globalization, Decentralization, and Secession. In *Globalization and Self-Determination*, edited by David Cameron, Gustav Ranis, and Annalisa Zin. New York: Routledge.

Sambanis, Nicholas, and Branko Milanovic. 2011. *Explaining the Demand for Sovereignty*. Washington, DC: Development Research Group, World Bank.

Sambanis, Nicholas, and Annalisa Zinn. 2005. From Protest to Violence: An Analysis of Conflict Escalation with an Application to Self-Determination. Working paper.

Sarkees, Meredith Reid, and Frank Wayman. 2010. *Resort to War: 1816–2007*. Washington, DC: CQ Press.

Sarkisyanz, Emanuel. 1974. Russian Imperialism Reconsidered. In *Russian Imperialism from Ivan the Great to the Revolution*, edited by Taras Hunczak. New Brunswick, NJ: Rutgers University Press.

Sartori, Anne E. 2003. An Estimator for Some Binary-Outcome Selection Models without Exclusion Restrictions. *Political Analysis* 11: 111–138.

Sawyer, Geoffrey. 1969. *Modern Federalism*. London: C. A. Watts.

Schelling, Thomas C. 1960. *The Strategy of Conflict*. Cambridge, MA: Harvard University Press.

Scherer, Frederick M. 1980. *Industrial Market Structure and Economic Performance*. 2nd ed. Boston: Houghton Mifflin.

Schumpeter, Joseph. 1950. *Capitalism, Socialism, and Democracy*. New York: Harper and Row.

Scott, James C. 2009. *The Art of Not Being Governed: An Anarchist History of Upland Southeast Asia*. New Haven, CT: Yale University Press.

Seeley, John Robert. 1883. *The Expansion of England*. N.p.: Little, Brown.

Selten, Reinhard. 1978. The Chain Store Paradox. *Theory and Decision* 9(2): 127–159.

Shabad, Theodore. 1945. Political-Administrative Divisions of the USSR. *Geographical Review* 36(2): 303–311.

Sharman, Jason. 2013. International Hierarchies and Contemporary Imperial Governance: A Tale of Three Kingdoms. *European Journal of International Relations* 19(2): 189–207.

Shaw, Malcom N. 1996. The Heritage of States: The Principle of Uti Possidetis Juris Today. *British Yearbook of International Law* 67: 75–154.

1997. Peoples, Territorialism, and Boundaries. *European Journal of International Law* 8(3): 478–507.

Shenfield, Stephen. 1987. *The Nuclear Predicament: Exploration in Soviet Ideology*. Chatham House Papers 37. London: Routledge and Kegan Paul.

Simon, Gerhard. 1991. *Nationalism and Policy toward the Nationalities in the Soviet Union: From Totalitarian Dictatorship to Post-Stalinist Policy*. Boulder, CO: Westview Press.

Siroky, David S. 2011. Explaining Secession. In *The Ashgate Research Companion to Secession*, edited by Aleksandar Pavkovic and Peter Radan. Burlington, VT: Ashgate.

Slezkine, Yuri. 1992. From Savages to Citizens: The Cultural Revolution in the Soviet Far North, 1828–1938. *Slavic Studies* 51(1): 52–76.

1994. The USSR as a Communist Apartment, or How a Socialist State Promoted Ethnic Particularism. *Slavic Studies* 63(2): 414–452.

Smith, Benjamin. 2013. Separatist Conflict in the Former Soviet Union and Beyond: How Different Was Communism? *World Politics* 65(2): 350–381.

Smith, Tony. 1981. *The Pattern of Imperialism: The United States, Great Britain, and the Late-Industrializing World since 1815*. New York: Cambridge University Press.

Snyder, Jack. 1991. *Myths of Empire: Domestic Politics and International Ambition*. Ithaca, NY: Cornell University Press.

2000. *From Voting to Violence: Democratization and Nationalist Conflict*. New York: W. W. Norton.

Sorens, Jason. 2011. Mineral Production, Territory, and Ethnic Rebellion: The Role of Rebel Constituencies. *Journal of Peace Research* 48(5): 571–585.

2012. *Secessionism: Identity, Interest, and Strategy*. Montreal: McGill-Queen's University Press.

Spruyt, Hendrik. 2002. The Origins, Development, and Possible Decline of the Modern State. *Annual Review of Political Science* 5: 127–149.

2005. *Ending Empire*. Ithaca, NY: Cornell University Press.

Stepan, Alfred. 2001. Toward a New Comparative Politics of Federalism, (Multi)Nationalism, and Democracy: Beyond Rikerian Federalism. In *Arguing Comparative Politics*, edited by Alfred Stepan. Oxford: Oxford University Press.

Stepan, Alfred, Juan J. Linz, and Yogendra Yadav. 2011. *Crafting New States: India and Other Multinational Democracies*. Baltimore: The Johns Hopkins University Press.

Sterio, Milena. 2012. *The Right to Self-Determination under International Law: "Selfistans," Secession, and the Rule of the Great Powers*. New York: Routledge.

Strachey, John. 1888. *India*. London: Kegan Paul.

Szporluk, Roman. 1997. The Fall of the Tsarist Empire and the USSR: The Russian Question and Imperial Overextension. In *The End of Empire? The Transformation of the USSR in Comparative Perspective*, edited by Karen Dawisha and Bruce Parrott. New York: M. E. Sharpe.

Talreja, Kanayalal. 1996. *Secessionism in India*. Mumbai: Rashtriya Chetana Prakashan.

Themnér, Lotta, and Peter Wallensteen. 2012. "Armed Conflict, 1946–2011." *Journal of Peace Research* 49(4): 565–576.

Tilly, Charles. 1975. Reflections on the History of European State-Making. In *The Formation of the Nation-States of Western Europe*, edited by Charles Tilly. Princeton, NJ: Princeton University Press.

Tir, Jaroslav, Philip Schafer, Paul Diehl, and Gary Goertz. 1998. Territorial Changes, 1816–1996: Procedures and Data. *Conflict Management and Peace Science* 16(1): 89–97.

Toft, Monica. 2002. Indivisible Territory, Geographic Concentration, and Ethnic War. *Security Studies* 12(2): 82–119.

2003. *The Geography of Ethnic Conflict: Identity, Interests, and the Indivisibility of Territory*. Princeton, NJ: Princeton University Press.

Tomz, Michael, Gary King, and Langche Zeng. 1999. *RELOGIT: Rare Events Logistic Regression, Version 1.1*. Cambridge, MA: Harvard University. Online: http://gking.harvard.edu/.

Treisman, Daniel S. 1997. Russia's "Ethnic Revival": The Separatist Activism of Regional Leaders in a Postcommunist Order. *World Politics* 49(2): 212–249.

1999. *After the Deluge: Regional Crises and Political Consolidation in Russia*. Ann Arbor: University of Michigan Press.

2007. *The Architecture of Government: Rethinking Political Decentralization*. Cambridge: Cambridge University Press.

Tummala, Krishna K. 1996. The Indian Union and Emergency Powers. *International Political Science Review* 17(4): 373–384.

Van Houten, Pieter. 2003. Globalization and Demands for Regional Autonomy in Europe. In *Governance in a Global Economy: Political Authority in Transition*, edited by Miles Kahler and David Lake. Princeton, NJ: Princeton University Press.

Verma, Ravi. 1988. *India's Role in the Emergence of Contemporary Bhutan*. Delhi: Capital.

Vyas, R. P. 1991. *British Policy towards Princely States in India*. Jodhpur: S. K. Enterprises.

Wallis, Joanne. 2014. Nation-Building, Autonomy Arrangements, and Deferred Referendums: Unresolved Questions from Bougainville, Papua New Guinea. *Nationalism and Ethnic Politics* 19(3): 310–332.

Walter, Barbara. 2006a. Information, Uncertainty, and the Decision to Secede. *International Organization* 60(1): 105–135.

2006b. Building Reputation: Why Governments Fight Some Separatists but Not Others. *American Journal of Political Science* 50(2): 313–330.

2009. *Reputation and Civil War*. Cambridge: Cambridge University Press.

Waltz, Kenneth. 1979. *Theory of International Politics*. New York: McGraw-Hill.

Walzer, Michael. 1977. *Just and Unjust Wars: A Moral Argument with Historical Illustrations*. New York: Basic Books.

Wendt, Alexander. 1999. *Social Theory of International Politics*. Cambridge: Cambridge University Press.

Weyland, Kurt. 2009. The Diffusion of Revolution: "1848" in Europe and Latin America. *International Organization* 63(3): 391–423.

Wheeler, Geoffrey. 1974. Russian Conquest and Colonization of Central Asia. In *Russian Imperialism from Ivan the Great to the Revolution*, edited by Taras Hunczak. New Brunswick, NJ: Rutgers University Press.

Willoughby, W. W., and C. G. Fenwick. 1919. *Types of Restricted Sovereignty and of Colonial Autonomy*. Washington, DC: Government Printing Office.

Wimmer, Andreas. 2013. *Waves of War: Nationalism, State Formation, and Ethnic Exclusion in the Modern World*. Cambridge: Cambridge University Press.

Wolhforth, William C. 1994/95. Realism and the End of the Cold War. *International Security* 19(3): 91–129.

Wunnicke, Pat. 1989. The Accidental Empire. *State Legislatures* (October).

Yonuo, A. 1974. *The Rising Nagas: A Historical and Political Study*. New Delhi: Vivek.

Zacher, Mark W. 2001. The Territorial Integrity Norm: International Boundaries and the Use of Force. *International Organization* 55(2): 215–250.

Ziegler, Philip. 1985. *Mountbatten*. New York: Alfred A. Knopf.

Zubok, Vladislav M. 2007. *A Failed Empire: The Soviet Union in the Cold War from Stalin to Gorbachev*. Chapel Hill: University of North Carolina Press.

Index